ODD MAN OUT:
An Autobiography

By Jeff Commings

I dedicate this book to those who know the true meaning of unconditional love, those who have never known it and those who lose that love when they make the bold risk of being true to themselves.

Prologue

"One, two, three, four, five, six, seven, eight. Big breath and go!"

Arms thrashing, legs kicking, eyes focused on the beam running the length of the ceiling. I couldn't believe it. I was in Sydney, Australia, swimming 50 meters of backstroke and feeling great. Almost 28 seconds after I started, I touched the wall and felt utter elation. I had dreamed of this moment for years.

Ten seconds after climbing out of the pool, I was greeted by four male friends, who gave me big hugs and congratulated me on a fine swim. One of them kissed me.

My first reaction to the kiss was to dart my eyes around to see who had noticed the act of two men kissing on the lips. I waited to hear the quick inhalation of air someone would take in shock over seeing this man kiss another man. Maybe another would hold a cross to my forehead and pray for my soul.

But people kept walking by.

I was at the 2002 Gay Games, and it wasn't the first time my life as a gay man and a swimmer had come together, but it was the first time I'd been kissed by a man after a race.

In the 10 years leading up to that day, I had hoped that such a scene could be possible, that it could be broadcast around the world as I or another openly gay man waved to his husband, who was crying tears of joy in the stands.

To this day, there has been no elite swimmer who has publicly come out of the closet while actively competing as a member of a United States national team. There have been a few gay Olympians, but they kept their gay lives private until retirement. Whether they wanted it that way or not is not the point.

It shouldn't be an option to stay in the closet for fear of reprimand.

I wasn't a fully open gay man until I was 25. For about a quarter of my life, I had peeked out of the closet, only to force myself back in and lock the door. Many reasons kept me from talking about my sexuality to my close friends. I will tell of many of those circumstances in this book.

One of the driving forces behind my decision to move forward with writing this book after three or four years of hemming and hawing was the fairly recent phenomenon of black men living "on the down-low," a term used to describe men who choose to live publicly as straight men while having relationships or numerous sexual encounters with men. I don't want any black man to consider this as an option. The black community unfairly categorizes gay culture as exclusively white and promote the ideal of ubermasculinity through hip-hop and rap music. And many young black men believe what their musical idols tell them, especially when it comes to objectifying women and getting them pregnant before they've graduated from high school. Gangs are also popular through this line of communication.

Finding gay male role models in the black community is not easy, which could be a reason why so many men choose to live "on the down-low," marrying women while carrying on a double life. The pressures of conforming to community and family ideals run strong and deep in the black community, but the ideals aren't restricted to the straight men. As a gay black man, I can assure you that I treasure my heritage, my race and my family more than anything in this world. I am proud to be black and gay at the same time. I hope there will come a time when the general African-American community embraces its gay men and women as openly as they embrace the celebrities who condone cop killing, teenage pregnancy, gang life and drug use.

As many friends persuaded me to write this book, I thought of Greg Louganis, Billy Bean, Rudy Gallindo. They had written books about being gay. The swimming world didn't need to have a celebrity come out in a tell-all book, but swimmers hiding in the closet need to know that they are not alone.

I was also made aware of the rising popularity of being a black swimmer. Is it really popular to be a black swimmer? Let's use Cullen Jones, one of the fastest swimmers in the world, as an example. Ever since he made the national team in 2005, he's been touted as the next great hope for black swimmers. I feel his pain. The media attention given to him is not the same attention focused on Michael Phelps or Natalie Coughlin or Ryan Lochte. When the media talk to those three, it's all about swimming. When they talk to Cullen Jones, it's all about being black.

I had the same experiences when I was an elite swimmer, and I hope you understand why I shake my head at the media when Cullen Jones steps up to the blocks. Like him, I never thought being a black swimmer was a big deal. Just like I hope that in the 21st century, a gay swimmer – or just a gay person – is not a big deal.

I did not write this book alone. I consulted with many people who filled in some gaps in my memory. I bounced ideas off friends, who were very encouraging without being pushy. And I had a wonderful soul holding my hand as I relived the painful memories.

I don't expect closeted athletes to read this book and promptly stand up in the middle of the baseball field, football huddle or swimming facility and shout out "I'm out and proud!" while kissing their boyfriends or girlfriends. That's not realistic.

I only want to inspire courage in all of you, whether you are gay, straight or questioning. To those who are gay or questioning, I hope you find the courage to be honest with yourself, then work towards being honest with those close to you. That means, in no particular order, your family, your friends, your coaches and your teammates.

To those who are straight, I ask that you find the courage to accept and understand that the gay man or woman sharing a lane in the pool with you, preparing to take the baton from you in a running race or working in the cubicle next to you is just another human being who wants to live as proudly as you do.

If I can inspire that in a small percentage of those who read this book, the four years spent reliving old memories and putting them on the page will have been worthwhile.

Waiting with about 5,000 other athletes for the start of the opening ceremonies of the 2002 Gay Games in Sydney, Australia

Chapter One

I was thrown into the pool at four years old. Literally. The man who would become my coach for the first nine years of my swimming career tossed me into the pool and watched me find my bearings. It was a normal routine in the beginning swimming classes at the Herbert Hoover Boys Club in St. Louis. Many kids were thrown in while their parents watched from the bleachers. I kicked and screamed on that first day, but I was one of the very few who returned the next day eager for more.

On a family trip to California when I was 2, I got my first feel of the water when my mother held my hand as the waves tickled my feet. If the stereotype that blacks have an instant fear of the water is true, how do you explain my affinity for swimming just as I became comfortable with walking? I could point to the small percentage of Native American heritage in my blood. But is that logical? Native Americans aren't renowned swimmers, either. I guess that even in adolescence, I was an anomaly. The photographs show me smiling as the ocean waves tickled my feet.

This experience on the ocean shore would be the first time I'd crash down preconceived notions.

I was the only person in my family who ever found happiness in a pool, so what part of my DNA clicked with the smell of chlorine and longed for the sensation of thrashing around in a cement hole? No one can possibly know. History books tell of African slaves being great swimmers as they caught fish for their masters or guided European settlers through the treacherous waters of Africa. Could that affinity for the water have survived through generations to find its way into my DNA?

My mother was certainly happy that I found a sport I liked. She would drive me to the boys' club just about every day to continue my swimming lessons. I don't think there were any aspirations of grooming me to be the swimmer I would become; it was just a way to keep me active – and the activity proved to be a decent babysitter.

At six years old, I was officially a member of the swim team. You couldn't keep me out of the pool. At the boys' club, kids my age had so many options, but I always chose to head straight for the pool and play in the water for hours. That summer I swam in my first meet, and I won my first swimming trophy: sixth place in the 25-yard butterfly. Sixth place was last place, but the concept of winning and losing wasn't spoken of then. All I wanted was one of those shiny trophies everyone seemed to be carrying. I've won hundreds more trophies in my lifetime, and most of them have been donated to companies that recycle them. But that first trophy will always remain part of my collection.

Most 6-year-olds would be enjoying their time in first grade, but I was able to skip kindergarten and enter first grade as a 5-year-old. I took a simple test in preschool that proved I didn't need to go through the experience of kindergarten. Apparently, I was already able to color inside the lines and count to 10 by the time I was five years old. I went through my entire school career a year younger than my classmates, but it didn't bother me at all. I liked telling people I got to skip kindergarten, like it was some sort of badge of honor.

When I was in fourth grade, my reading and math skills were so far advanced that I was able to leave my classroom and take reading and math classes with the fifth graders. It was a supremely fantastic experience to take my books and walk across the hall twice a day. Once I got to eighth grade, I was obviously unable to go to another class during reading and math classes. Instead, I was given the task of helping in the cafeteria for an hour each day. It was named "service learning," and it was menial work. Some days, I had to stir the large pot of stew that would be on that day's lunch menu. Or, I had to help unload the truck bringing the new cartons of milk to the school. Near the end of the eighth grade year, I got to work on a class project with another student who was able to get out of a couple of classes a day. Her name was Carmen, and we collaborated on a cookbook that would help raise money for a school field trip. Carmen was a very smart girl, and she disliked the idea of "wasting" almost five hours a week at school not doing any learning. I was happy because we got to use the school computers, which in 1987 were very clunky and could only do basic word processing tasks. But it was still better than learning pre-algebra and geometry.

*****

Most kids raised in the inner city would describe sports as an escape from their harsh home lives. Not so with me. My childhood was far from idyllic, but it was never rough. I lived in a nice two-story home on Goodfellow Avenue in St. Louis, Missouri, with my mother and older brother, Darryl. I am 10 years younger than my brother, and with an age gap that severe, we had little in common. While he was off doing teenage things, I was happy to sit in my room activating my expansive imagination. Perhaps that's a romanticized way of saying I invented imaginary people with whom to play regularly. I could have entire conversations with the thin air.

My parents divorced when I was barely a year old, so I have no memories of living with my father. Being raised by one parent didn't have a profound effect on me in my formative years. I never thought much about not having a father in my daily life.

It is said that single parents often become the mother and the father, and that's just what my mother did. It couldn't have been easy. She was trying to make a living, raise two children, keep a home and make us happy.

I knew that it was unusual for me to live in a house without a mother and a father. Most of my friends had both their parents married and living together. I suppose I had every right to lash out and be angry at my parents for not sticking together for my sake. I never resented my parents for the divorce, and I never felt like I was missing out on something by not having a father in my life. Even before I was 10 years old, I had accepted – and was happy with – the fact that I was being raised by a single parent. Not knowing what it was like to live in a two-parent household made me rarely pine for that life. It's to her credit that I never felt a need to have a father figure – or my father, for that matter – in the house. My mother's love was more than adequate.

If there was something special a father was supposed to do, I don't recall ever feeling like I missed it. When I learned to ride my bike, I had my brother there to teach me and my mother to take pictures. If there was something that the mother typically waits for the father to tell the kid, my mother just had to say it herself.

Being such a good athlete at a young age was just one of many things that made me stand out in my family. I can't say much about my father's side of my genetic makeup, because I don't know any of my family on that side. But the people on my mother's side of the family – the Remberts – they're not extraordinary. For a family based in St. Louis, I'm sad to say we had all the stereotypical relatives. My female cousin became pregnant at 15. Not unusual or scandalous, because it was happening everywhere. One of my cousins was put in jail for a lengthy period of time, leaving his daughters in the care of his mother. Again, not scandalous. The family just dealt with it.

My mother is the oldest of her siblings. She had an older brother who died before I was born, and many of my aunts say I look like him.

My mother was – still is – fiercely independent. I tried for many years to get her to remarry. I thought she was headed in that direction a couple of times in my preteen years, but she always told me, "I've lived that life. I don't want to live it again." But she never regretted having two sons. I learned a lot about sacrifice in my younger years from my mother. She always made sure we had the best things we could afford, though we were never raised to want too much. My mother's teachings of living life within your means still resonate with me today.

"Do you really need that?" my mother would ask after I pleaded with her for a certain item at the toy store. And usually after a few minutes, I figured that I didn't. If I did get something, I was never one of those children to play with it once and discard it. These days, I find myself asking that same question when pondering purchases or major life decisions.

We lived across the street from a grocery store, and my brother would play stickball with his friends in the parking lot on Sundays, when the store was closed. I'd pretend I was Evel Knievel on my bike, traversing the many obstacles in the parking lot and behind the store. One summer day, when I was probably 9 years old, I dared myself to ride my bike as fast as I could toward a parked semi-truck's trailer at one end of

4

the parking lot. From my vantage point about 50 yards away, I could easily ride under the trailer at full speed. About 10 yards away, I suddenly realized that even my bike wouldn't clear the bottom of the trailer. Unfortunately, I was pedaling too fast, and when I applied the brake and tried to turn away from the trailer, I fell off the bike, skidding underneath the trailer and stopping on the other side.

After about a minute, I began to feel the stinging pain in my right arm and left leg. I had fallen under my bike, which had given me a cut on my right elbow. The skid on the pavement produced a bloody scrape on my left thigh. I looked toward the other end of the lot, where my brother was too involved in a game of stickball to notice that his brother had just fallen off his bike. I was glad he didn't notice; he might have told my mother, who would have taken away my bike-riding privileges.

I got to my feet and did my best to walk back home without Darryl seeing me. But he saw me just before I began crossing the street, and after noticing the blood running down my leg, ran toward me. As he approached me, I finally let loose with the sobbing, mostly because I was certain he would tell Mom.

But Darryl did his best to keep my mother from knowing. He escorted me across the street and helped me wash the blood and dirt off my arms and legs. We didn't know how to hide the cuts, but at least the blood was gone.

Mothers have a special sense that tells them when something is wrong with one of their children. She must have heard the hose running on the side of the house, because she suddenly appeared with a look of horror on her face. Without a word, she grabbed me and took me inside to the bathroom, where she properly cleaned my wounds. She reached into the closet for a bottle of Witch Hazel ointment and applied it to each cut. Searing jolts of pain spread through my body and I let out several blood-curdling screams. My mother had to hold me down to keep me from running away. Once she was done, I pushed past her and ran up the stairs to my room, where I cried myself to sleep.

The scars from that fall are still on my right elbow and left hip.

Though I chose to go on an adventure on my own that day, I would sometimes play games with other kids on the block. But when you're essentially the only child in the house, the need to create the type of environment you want from your imagination seemed almost like a necessity, and I was never told that having imaginary friends was wrong. Looking back, I do remembering preferring time "alone" in my room over spending time with flesh-and-blood friends. Was this the start of my lifelong shyness and introversion?

I nurtured that shyness in those early years by hiding out in my room, but swimming also had its own effect. Staring at a black line with your face in the water, alone with your thoughts for minutes at a time, can usually drive people crazy. But I found it comforting.

For the first couple of years on the swim team, I practiced in the outside lanes, where the younger kids played more than they swam. The older kids used to taunt the younger ones that a shark was waiting in the drain at the bottom of the pool to eat us alive if we went too slow in workout. I was 8 years old; the impossibility of the situation never crossed my mind. When I was promoted to swim with the kids in the middle of pool at age 10, I was hesitant because it meant swimming directly over the drain every day. The space underneath the grate was pitch black, and some days I could sense the sharks hovering below for the perfect opportunity. On those days, I probably broke water speed records trying to swim away from the hungry fish waiting for me. I didn't go to the bottom of the pool to check it out for almost a year. No sharks bared their teeth at me.

The demographic of the Herbert Hoover Boys' Club swim team was 100 percent black. The head coach was black and the neighborhood was black. The movie "Pride," released in 2007, detailed the creation of the all-black Philadelphia Department of Recreation swim team and the racism they encountered in the late 1970s. They were laughed at, kicked in the head during a race and provoked into a fistfight. When the white team visited PDR's pool, they faked illnesses to avoid participating in the meet. Nothing like that happened to us in St. Louis. Other teams in the city gladly came to swim in meets at our pool, and we were always welcome at other meets in the city. It never occurred to us that we were an anomaly in swimming, because the topic was never discussed, and why should it have been?

When I was 10 years old, I watched the Olympic Games for the first time. I understood the concept of it taking place in my home country, but I didn't know how far Los Angeles was.

At the start of the Olympics, I saw Steve Lundquist, my first true swimming hero. He was a breaststroker, like me, and from what the people on the television were saying, he was the fastest breaststroker that ever lived. When he won the gold medal in the 100 breaststroke, I was happy. I watched him during his walk around the pool, waving to the crowd and smiling wide.

Watching the rest of the Olympics was very exciting. I never had the opportunity to see such fast swimmers before, and it really made me want to be like them, but I never turned to my mother and said, "I'm going to be an Olympian one day and win a gold medal." Everyone who makes the Olympic team and gets a feature on NBC always say they wanted to be an Olympian after watching one of their heroes win a gold medal. Was that the real reason why I never made an Olympic team?

I didn't care that I didn't see one black person in the pool in Los Angeles. That fact never registered with me. I just liked seeing these people swim so fast and inspire me to continue in the sport with the hopes of achieving something better. I never believed that I couldn't someday compete at an elite level because I didn't have the blond hair and blue eyes of the gold medalists on TV.

I went to swim workouts the week after the Olympics with a new goal. I wanted to be able to raise my arms in victory just like Steve Lundquist had done. Even though my meets were all local, they felt like the Olympics to me, and I started winning with a little more frequency.

When I was 11, the team moved to another boys club in the city. The pool was better, but it was only six lanes, like our previous pool. It meant the pool was packed with more than 30 swimmers during practice. We were very small compared to the three or four super teams in St. Louis.

As most parents tend to do, my mother got heavily involved in swimming. She refused to just sit in the bleachers and gossip with the other parents. She took a test and became a stroke-and-turn judge at meets. Later, she was promoted to referee and also was meet director for our swim team. When I swam, she'd drop everything she was doing and become the loudest cheerleader on the deck. When you're that young, you actually get excited to hear your mother cheering loudly for you, and I would always look for her on the deck before climbing on the blocks. Having her watch me swim gave me a little boost of confidence. Because I loved swimming, she loved it, too. Other parents would drop off their kids at swim meets and never stick around to see their kids swim. My mother saw every race I swam until I was 15 years old. She also kept a log of all my swimming times, which she would analyze with me after every meet.

"You didn't get a best time in that race," my mother would say as she pointed to an entry in the blue log book. "It looked like you weren't really trying very hard."

Then, she would write down a goal time for the next meet, and if I achieved it, I would get some kind of reward. Sometimes it would be a cash payment of five dollars or so. As I got older, my reward of choice was a new addition to my Transformers collection.

For the first few years, my brother was just as active on the deck. He was a turn judge for the meets held at the boys club when he wasn't involved in the football or baseball teams there.

A lot of my success in swimming can be pinpointed to those first eight years swimming for Val Taylor. Many kids call their coaches "Coach" or use their first name these days, but Val Taylor was always "Mr. Taylor" to the swimmers. Even the older ones had the same reverence for him.

Mr. Taylor had been stricken with polio as a child, and in his adult years he walked with a pronounced limp. He couldn't run, but he could definitely get around with no problem.

He ruled with an iron fist and a wooden paddle wrapped from one end to the other with masking tape. If a swimmer got out of line, he or she would get a few whacks on the behind with the paddle. If you did freestyle instead of breaststroke on a set, you got the paddle. If you were late, you got the paddle. In front of your teammates. And in front of other parents. The whacks were so loud they echoed off the pool walls. You could hear them underwater. After we got our licks, we would put our goggles on and fill them up with our tears. There was no crying on the Herbert Hoover Boys' Club Swim Team.

These days, Mr. Taylor would have been sued before the first whack could have been placed, but no one questioned it while I was on the team. It built character, and we always feared the paddle, so we always tried to do what we were told. If we wanted to play in the water, we could come to the open swim just before practice.

The paddle was so feared that one day we found it lying on Mr. Taylor's desk and hid it in the boiler room so no kid would get a beating that day. Naturally, Mr. Taylor sought out the guilty party and whipped them good.

The legend of the paddle was well-known on other swim teams. A couple of times when friends would come to our swim clubs for meets, we would show them the paddle and they would handle it as if it were the Ark of the Covenant.

But it wasn't all torture. I got an immeasureable amount of joy on the days we practiced "fundamentals." Another word for "fundamentals" would be "drills," but I'm glad we used "fundamentals." It had the word "fun" in it. It broke the boredom of swimming back and forth. We'd swim a length of the pool freestyle using only one arm. Or we'd see who could swim a length of breaststroke with the fewest strokes. Almost the entire workout would be spent working on "fundamentals," and hardly anyone got a whack with the paddle on those days.

I might not have been the prettiest swimmer in the pool in my pre-teen years, but my technique was solid. I was one of the best swimmers between the flags, which meant I had bad turns off the walls. I remember a race at our pool when I was 11 or 12 years old. I was racing Bobby Rodgers, the tallest kid you'll ever see under the age of 16. He was untouchable in backstroke, and on this day he definitely would have won on style points, but I touched the wall first in our 100 backstroke race. More than teaching me how to swim all the strokes, Mr. Taylor taught me how to race.

Mr. Taylor is responsible for teaching hundreds of black kids in St. Louis how to swim over a career spanning more than 30 years, and because he was able to plant the seed that made me the swimmer and person I am today, Mr. Taylor holds the closest place in my heart among all the coaches I've had. I saw him in February 2009 at a Hall of Fame induction for swimmers and coaches in the St. Louis area. I hadn't seen him since I left for college almost 18 years earlier, so the sight of him confined to a wheelchair was almost too hard to bear. On the bright side, he was still coaching and had the strong spirit I remembered from my youth. I felt that he would be able to give me a good workout if I asked for it, and a severe paddle whack if I did something wrong.

At 12 years old, with my brother now a college graduate and on his own, my mother figured it was time to downsize. We moved to a smaller home in Florissant, a suburb of St. Louis. The move meant I couldn't take the bus to the Catholic school I attended every day. My mother drove me 30 minutes to school every morning, and I always kissed her and told her I loved her before I ran into the school to avoid being late. After school, I would either walk to my grandparents' house a few blocks away or take the bus to the boys' club.

Gone was the expansive parking lot that nourished my fantasies every weekend. There were a lot of kids on Abington Road, but because I was terribly shy, I didn't make many friends on that street. However, I did get my first kiss on that street, with a girl whose name I have never been able to recall. I was 12, and we did it on a dare, in her driveway. It never went beyond that, and the girl moved away not too long after. Of all the kisses in my life, why does that one still linger? Do all first kisses get permanent places in our memories, no matter the circumstances surrounding them? Is it because it would be the only kiss I would ever give to a female?

When I was 12, I came to a major crossroads in my sporting life. A friend and I belonged to a city bowling league, and we were both quite good. I got trophies for having the best average score of all the kids, and my friend got trophies for high scores. Afterwards, there were always hamburgers and French fries at the little diner there.

But my swimming was improving much better than my bowling, and my mom told me I could choose only one sport. We weren't a poor family, but neither bowling nor swimming came cheap. Both sports required families to pay participation fees, and with swimming there was the added cost of buying swimsuits, goggles and other equipment. I stuck with swimming, even though I had been told of the potential of a professional life as a bowler when I got older. No one ever convinced me I could make a living as a swimmer, but that didn't matter. Though I didn't like showing up for practice every day, the pool was a more comfortable place for me to be. Putting my face in the water meant I didn't have to talk that much to people. And I liked the competition. Actually, I loved the competition, even if I lost. I had started breaking regional records, and I liked coming home with lots of blue ribbons and huge trophies. That trophy for the 25-yard butterfly never left the shelf, even as space got tighter.

Shortly after I decided to devote my life to swimming, I was invited to go to a regional meet in Indianapolis, which is one of the most highly regarded pools in the world. In the scheme of things, it was a fairly small meet, but at the time it was the biggest meet of my life. I was swimming against kids from cities I'd never heard of in a natatorium four times bigger than any I'd ever been in. I got to swim prelims and finals of the 50 and 100 breaststrokes, and the times I swam ranked me among the top 16 nationwide in the 11-12 age group. I knew that winning an Olympic gold medal meant you were the best in the world, but I never fathomed that at the age of 12 I would even be considered the best in the state of Missouri. Now, I was beating kids from other states and getting medals for it. Later that year, I saw my name in tiny print in an edition of Swimming World Magazine listing the fastest swimmers in each event by age group. It was a major thrill. I was only the fourth-fastest in the 11-12 age group for the 50 breast and 16th in the 100, but my coach quickly reminded me that there were *thousands* of kids my age swimming breaststroke, and only a handful of those kids were faster than me.

Despite this success with Mr. Taylor, it was time to move on. When I was 13, I moved to the North County Swim Club, which was much closer to home. Most swimmers tend to struggle in their first year with a new coach, but Paul Murphy was a very easygoing coach and saw a lot of potential in me long before I joined his team.

One year after joining Paul's club, I had a major breakthrough. In the course of two months, I broke the regional record in the 100 breaststroke for the 13-14 age group by three seconds.

At a long course (50-meter) meet during July 4 weekend in 1988, I was facing Jeff Rush, my biggest competitor in the breaststroke events. He swam on one of the bigger teams in St. Louis, and though he was also black, it never occurred to us that we were slowly breaking down stereotypes just by doing so well in the sport. Stuff like that never came up in conversation. The general acceptance of blacks in swimming in St. Louis might have been viewed with slack-jawed surprise in Philadelphia, but we never even thought there was reason to stand back and wonder why the ratio of whites to blacks in local swim meets was easily 100 to 1. Jeff Rush and I had been on the same team for about a year before he left, and we always enjoyed racing each other. Our race in the 100 breast at the holiday meet in 1988 at Clayton Shaw Park became one of my most unforgettable races.

Jeff and I swam the first 50 meters side by side, touching at the halfway point together. I noticed him out of the corner of my eye and thought to myself, "No way you're going to win today!" I took off with 35 meters to go and touched the wall in a 1:09.46, which was a new regional record.

I was later told that the time barely qualified me for the junior nationals. I didn't know what junior nationals was. The gap between my local swim meets and the Olympics was quickly shrinking. Junior nationals was apparently a step many swimmers took on their way to national and international greatness. No one told me this because at the time, it was never a realistic goal. Swimmers on the super teams in St. Louis had the ideal of junior nationals drilled into their minds from the first day they join, but the North County Swim Club (membership of close to 80 swimmers) was just striving for a local identity.

My mom would let me go to junior nationals if I really wanted to go. Paul and I decided we should wait until next year, since I would probably not place very high. Instead, I elected to go to a zone meet that year in Minneapolis instead of juniors, and it turned out to be a wise choice. I improved my national ranking in the 100 breast to fourth place in the 13-14 age group at that meet and swam best times in four other events. If I had gone to junior nationals, I would have swum only one event, and might have gotten last place.

Indianapolis and Minneapolis weren't my only excursions outside state lines. I had also traveled frequently to meets in Memphis, where my father lived with his new wife and three children -- my stepbrother, half-brother and half-sister. I visited once or twice a year for three years and got to know my father's new family well.

I had always hoped my mother would remarry so I could have a younger sibling, but that never happened. It's hard having 10 years between you and your only sibling. There isn't a lot the two of you do together. You want to watch cartoons; he wants to start dating. You read comic books; he's studying calculus. The things I wanted to do with my brother were forced upon my imaginary friends. And the secrets that you only tell your siblings were told to the thin air.

Now that the possibilities in swimming were growing quickly, I realized that maybe I could do as well as those guys I had watched on TV in the Olympics. Maybe I could actually be Steve Lundquist or Matt Biondi or Janet Evans.

Getting to meet them later in life was about as close as I'd get to actually being them.

Chapter Two

I have had lots of acquaintances in my life. Very few actual friends. It was a matter of choosing those who had the same interests as I did, and not many people liked the same things I did, so those friends I made were precious to me. My only downfall has been losing track of those friends. There are powerful moments of nostalgia when I remember all my friends in more than three decades of life. Probably 98 percent of them have not received a phone call, e-mail or Christmas card from me in more than a year. Losing touch with them is the biggest regret in my life. I'm very happy to have found Facebook, for it has helped me reconnect with long-lost high school classmates, college teammates and former competitors.

Unfortunately, one of my best friends in life is not on Facebook. Herman was one of those once-in-a-lifetime friends that you think about on your deathbed or expect to see emerge from behind the curtain on "This Is Your Life." For a time, Herman was the brother I always wanted. We were on the same swim team and were the same age, and his mother and mine were also close friends.

Of the five or six years we were close, there probably weren't more than three weeks that went by when we didn't spend a night or a weekend at each other's houses.

One sleepover at his house changed my life.

*****

I knew all about gay people when I was 12. I saw them on TV. I heard about them in conversation. I even read about homosexuality in an anatomy book I snatched from my brother's room. That book was how I really learned about "the birds and the bees." Because I was only 12, the talk of the sexual side of homosexuality never came up, but I knew gay men were attracted to other men, like "regular" guys were attracted to girls.

One night while sleeping at Herman's house, I found out what it meant to be attracted to another man.

Herman's dad was what the gay community would call a "bear." He had a full beard of thick black hair, with hairy arms and hairy legs. Many "bears" are chubby, but Herman's dad obviously worked out.

As we prepared to go to sleep one night at Herman's house, I went into the bathroom to brush my teeth. I heard the shower running and figured Herman's dad was in there.

Then he got out of the shower.

Hair covered almost every inch of him. His chest muscles and abs were very defined. I had never seen him fully naked, and never before had I seen muscle definition like this. Remember that I grew up without my father. And my brother was tall and scrawny. Some of the guys on my swim team were well-built, but Herman's dad was the embodiment of the male form. Statues could have been modeled on his physique.

Young boys look at their fathers (or their friends' fathers) all the time and gaze at what they could have in about 15 years. I found myself transfixed in a way that transcended that. And my brain was telling my body to do weird things. I had butterflies in my stomach and I couldn't feel my legs. I felt like I was floating.

I finished brushing my teeth as he dried off. I could see him in the mirror and I couldn't turn my eyes away. I ran out of the bathroom and jumped into bed. As I lay there, I could still picture his body. Boys don't think about their friend's father's body this much, do they?

Every time I saw Herman's dad after that, I felt like Superman with x-ray vision. I could see the hair, the skin, the muscles underneath his clothes. The tingles I felt in the bathroom came back. I knew this couldn't be normal.

This was the mid-1980s, a tough time to be gay. AIDS was being branded a "gay man's cancer," and the protections and social acceptance gays and lesbians enjoy today were not present then. I saw this movie on cable sometime around 1988 called "As Is," about a man with AIDS. I saw how he was outcast and how much the gay men in the movie were shunned in society. It scared me a little.

I didn't know any gay people at the time, not even a distant relative or friend of a friend, but I knew being gay wasn't something that people told everyone. I didn't know what to do next. Herman was a close friend -- the closest -- but what would he say if I told him I saw his father naked and liked what I saw?

I told no one about my newfound sexuality. And even if I were 100 percent sure about how to describe it, who could I tell? I viewed my brother as the ultimate Casanova – a new girlfriend almost every week. Would he really understand the concept of attraction to another male? My mother was definitely out of the question. A fiercely religious woman, my mother is one of those people who take words in the Bible literally. Had I told her about my feelings, would she call me an "abomination" and cast me away to some deserted island? Or, as the Bible instructs, have me put to death?

I didn't have a mentor to tell me how to handle this, but I knew enough to realize that a revelation of this sort would mean laughter and humiliation and name-calling by the few friends I had. And it would mean that my mother would have a breakdown. Plus, I was going to a Catholic elementary school. The nuns wouldn't take this news kindly.

Seeing Herman's dad naked was the societal trigger for my homosexuality and all I needed to do was erase the images from my mind and move on. But I'm quite certain that if I had seen Herman's mother coming out of the shower instead of his father, I'd still be a gay man.

My only question is: Where did the gay DNA in me come from? No one in my family has spoken of any of gay ancestors, and though life before 1980 was all about hiding homosexuality, certainly there had to be gay people in my family, as much as some might like to refute that claim. Being the only gay man in my family doesn't make me feel alone, but for most of my teenage years and young adulthood, I felt like I wasn't related by blood to the people who raised me and loved me. I foolishly thought that because I was the only one who liked to swim and had gay tendencies, I couldn't be born of my mother or father. It was only when

I turned 20 that I stopped thinking such nonsense.

In my 13th year, my mom was pushing my brother, Darryl, to marry, or at least give her a grandchild. I don't think she cared about the order in which it happened. The pushing didn't stop until the day my brother and sister-in-law officially became adoptive parents of two boys in 2007. As for me, I continually avoided my mother's requests/urges to date. I was going to St. Louis University High School, an all-boys school run by Jesuits. As my hormones began to take command of my body, I found myself uncontrollably attracted to a few of my classmates. Yes, it was torture at times in the locker room before and after gym class, but I learned a lot about willpower and strength of spirit in those four years. It also taught me very little about the teenage dating scene. Because girls weren't around during the day, I didn't see the things boys my age saw in public schools: the make-out sessions in the hallway, the hand-holding, the breakups.

It also protected me. Because girls and sex weren't hot topics of conversation, I was sheltered from making up stories about why I wasn't dating a girl or why I didn't go to a particular dance or why I didn't accept a blind date. It was a college preparatory school; everyone seemed to be more concerned about getting into the best universities.

The thing about hormones is, no matter what you tell them to do, they go their own way. To please my mother and to protect myself from humiliation, I tried to make myself attracted to girls, but it was impossible. I gave up after only a few months of trying to see the sexual beauty in girls. I was attracted to a few guys at school, but the only thing I wanted to do with these boys was admire their bodies. The thought of sex with them was very foreign, even after seeing them in various states of undress.

My puppy-dog crush on Herman's dad eventually subsided when I turned 14. It was almost as if a switch in me turned off and my focus turned toward TV and movie stars. I also was becoming a full-fledged swimmer and trying to figure out what being gay meant to me. What kind of normal life could I possibly lead?

I was spending the summer days at the Mathews-Dickey Boys Club, and as I played in the pool or read books in the library, I was unaware that I had a stalker.

His name was Devin Boyd, and he was a casual member of the swim team, which meant he wasn't very good and didn't show up to practice every day. He was 17 at the time, and my knowledge of him was in passing at best.

One day, as I was watching a movie in the recreation room at the boys' club, Devin came up behind me and asked if I wanted to go for a walk with him. Because the movie was boring, I quickly said yes.

A set of railroad tracks runs along the north side of the boys club, and a few kids can be found under the nearby bridge playing near the pile of rocks or running along the tracks. On this day, there wasn't a soul to be found under the bridge. As I mentioned, I knew very little about Devin, so I should have been on my guard about his motives. I'd been there many times before with friends, and though it was hidden from people playing in the park right next to it, I never felt like I was in danger.

Once we reached the rock quarry, he took me into a hidden space between a pile of rocks. Without saying a word, he started caressing my chest and staring into my eyes. The natural reaction might have been to run, smile or ... I don't know, join in. But all I could do was laugh. I laughed hard. I think it was the way he was looking at me. No one had looked at me that way before, and I didn't know what it meant. So I laughed.

Once I got the laughter under control, Devin proceeded to kiss me. His kiss was soft at first, but then it got more intense. I didn't know where to focus my mind. Should I be thinking about the kiss, or where his hands are going? Where were his hands going?

Kissing Devin was strange in so many ways. Besides the peck I'd given the girl a year ago, this was my first real kiss. The taste, the feel, the sensation of it was nice, but because there were other things happening throughout my body, I couldn't concentrate on what I should be doing.

The kissing lasted for what seemed like an hour. I didn't want it to end when it did because I was starting to enjoy it. The sensation in my pants was telling me how much I enjoyed it. Devin's hand was cradling my crotch and he was moaning. I'd seen actors have sex on TV and in the movies, so I knew moaning was part of the process. But my mind was going in a million different directions, so whatever noises were coming out of my mouth were not of my own accord.

The entire experience was confusing, scary, exhilarating, frightening, exciting. Devin and I walked back to the boys club a little while later. From that day on, he was no longer someone in my periphery. I wanted to be around him every possible minute. I wanted him to re-create the experience under the bridge. Because everything had happened too fast that day, I had never fully registered the sensations in my mind. I also consulted my anatomy book, which answered some questions but not all of them.

I always thank Devin for that day. I knew after that afternoon under the railroad tracks that I was 100 percent gay. No straight man goes back for a second helping.

No turning back now. Truth is, I didn't want to.

Chapter Three

The 1989 Speedo Junior Nationals-West championship was held at the University of Texas at Austin. The pool is highly regarded as one of the best in the country. I walked onto the deck in utter amazement. NCAA championship banners hung from the rafters. The giant record boards displayed times that seemed to have come from superhumans. I felt lucky to be able to dive into the pool for a weekend.

That meet was my official introduction to the national swimming community. In the course of a year since barely making the junior national time standard, I had dropped my time in the 100 breast by three more seconds. My time seeded me fourth in the event at junior nationals, which was such a big improvement from the year before, when I could have been seeded near the bottom.

On the meet's first day, I found myself in the final heat of prelims of the 100 breast. I was in lane five, and in lane four was Paul Nelsen, a man about six inches taller and three years older. I couldn't possibly keep up with him. But I did. I finished the race about a couple of tenths behind him, and we were the top two seeds going into the finals.

Nearly every male swimmer wanting to perform at his best from 2000 to 2009 wore a swimsuit that covered more than half the body. In 1989, the idea was to wear a suit that covered as little skin as possible. Sometimes, you'd see guys walking on deck with surprisingly little material around their waists, the cracks of their butts peeking out. The best of the best were wearing "paper suits," which weren't made of paper, but a really thin material that deflected water in the same way shaved skin deflects water. It was the fad of the time, but I had never put much thought into getting one. What was wrong with wearing a regular nylon suit? I had done pretty well with what I had, so why change? In the final of the 100 breast at junior nationals, I was the only swimmer out of eight not wearing a paper suit.

My choice of swimwear was not the only thing that made me stand out. I was the only black swimmer in the final. I was the lone swimmer for my team, whereas everyone else had large squads cheering for them. I felt like some fresh-faced newbie from a backwoods town just off the bus, ready to dance with the Rockettes.

My usual race strategy in those days was to take out the first 50 meters of the race a little slower than everyone else, then use the saved energy to basically sprint the last 50 while everyone got tired. I was in fifth place at the 50-meter mark and surfaced from the pullout with big knots of fear in my stomach. Paul Nelsen seemed like he was miles ahead of me, even though it was really just a body length. Would my strategy work in this race? It worked every time when I raced in St. Louis, but this was decidedly different. All these guys have probably raced many times at this level before and can anticipate my strategy. I may have been new to the scene, but I wasn't going to roll over and let their experience take me out of the race. My survival instincts took over a few strokes into the final length of the race, and every cell in my body was working hard to get me to the other end first. Out of the corner of my eye, I saw myself passing the guy on my right. Yes! But Paul, who was on my left, wasn't giving up easily. Those long arms were sure to get to the wall before me. As we sprinted to the finish, I couldn't see him out of the corner of my eye anymore, which meant we were neck and neck, fighting to get the meet record we almost broke in prelims.

I touched the wall and immediately looked to my left. Before I looked for my time on the scoreboard, I looked for my place. There was a "2" next to my lane. Damn. By this time, Paul knew he had won and was celebrating. I still hadn't noticed that I broken the 1:05 barrier for the first time. I couldn't get over the "2." I so much wanted to win the race and be at the top of the awards stand.

When I exited the pool, my coach was right there to greet me with a big smile on his face. I had just dropped 1.5 seconds in my best event in one day. The time had qualified me to swim in senior nationals. I was within a few tenths of qualifying to swim in the 1992 Olympic Trials. And various college coaches were already putting me on their list of swimmers to contact. I didn't know any of that, nor did I care. I wanted that win.

Next to my coach was a woman in a yellow shirt holding a clipboard. She said she was with drug control and would be escorting me to a room where I would take a drug test. She explained that the top three finishers in each event were to be tested, and I would pee into a cup and my urine would be tested for illegal drugs. She followed me to the warm down pool, to the awards area and up to the spectator area, where I got a big hug and a kiss from my mom. The escort was required to do this to make sure I didn't do anything to compromise the results of the test, like drink tainted water or confiscate someone else's urine.

When it was time to take the drug test, I was taken into the bowels of the swim center, where a few swimmers were waiting in a tiny room until it was time to pee. Fortunately, the blood was working overtime in my body to recover, and it was ready to flush out toxins. So I peed in the cup, poured it into a vial, signed my name and joined the rest of the human race. This is what every swimmer in every big race you see on television has to do after their races. It's second nature, and no matter how much of an inconvenience it is, you absolutely cannot put it off for another day. Refusing to show up for a drug test – whether you are doping or not – is the same as pumping steroids in your veins.

When I emerged onto the deck after my drug test, a man named Stu Isaacs approached me and said he was from Speedo. After congratulating me on a fine race, he said -- with a chuckle -- that he noticed I was the only swimmer in the 100 breast final not wearing a Speedo paper suit. Suddenly I was quite aware that it made me seem like a poor kid from the projects who couldn't afford a decent meal and nice clothes. He told me that I might have won the race if I had worn a Speedo paper suit. Stu is always good at stating the obvious, which is why he'd been so good as Speedo's marketing honcho. He reached into a large duffel bag and pulled out a small box.

"I want to give you this suit to wear for your next race," Stu said. I thought he was going to ask me for money, but he was offering it to me for free. No questions asked, nothing to sign. In 1989, Speedo was the only company making these newfangled suits. The fact that everyone was wearing them was a selling point for me. I didn't know that this innovative swimwear would be the first in a long line of suits that would take longer to put on than the length of my race. Because the suits were supposed to fit tightly, it took a lot of work for people to get the suits past the thighs without ripping the thin fabric. I thanked my parents for not making me a girl. I would have cried after trying to put on a women's suit. The first time I put on a bodysuit, I cursed often under my breath.

To what can I attribute a drop of five seconds in my 100-meter breast in 12 months? I had gained more muscle and had a generous growth spurt, but a lot had to be credited to Paul's workouts. As much as we sparred over swimming so much breaststroke in a workout, it actually was doing a lot of good in races. After most workouts, Paul would give us sprint sets to do from a dive, which tested our ability to race at the end of hard sets and gave us the chance to nurture our competitive fire. Technically, I wasn't the most beautiful swimmer in the pool, but my strength and willpower were getting me to the finish faster than most.

I had one day off after the 100 breast at junior nationals to recuperate and prepare for the 200 breast. Ever since I turned 13 and started doing the longer races, I knew I was always made to be a sprinter. I hated the 200 breast with a vengeance. The agony of making it through that race is indescribable, and it would turn into a hate relationship that lasts to this day.

So I went into the prelims of the 200 breast without the excitement I had in the 100. I wanted it to hurt as little as possible, so I went out as slow as possible for the first 100 without getting too far behind. This was a race strategy that I used for many years to decent effect. This time, it worked. I won the heat and qualified for the consolation final. Since it was far from my best event, I had no worries about not making the championship final, though my mom and coach were sure my fast 100 breast would translate into a breakout 200.

In the consolation final, I had a major sense of déjà vu. I got second in the heat by two-hundredths of a second by a guy that used my come-from-behind strategy! The defeat didn't hurt as much as it did after the 100 because I swam a best time: 2:26.17. Paul and my mother had expected me to swim in the 2:24 range, but they were happy that I came away from the meet with two best times.

That fall, I got a letter in the mail from United States Swimming. It was the first time something from the sport's governing body came to my mailbox:

Congratulations on being named to the 1989-90 United States Swimming National Jr. Team! This honor not only recognizes your outstanding accomplishments of the past year, but also identifies you as a member of the group of athletes that will most likely produce the future leaders for U.S. Swimming.

I was going to be a part of USA Swimming's junior national team, which was made of a group of guys under 17 and girls under 16 who had swum well that summer. I was invited to a four-day swim camp in Colorado Springs, where I'd meet the other members and learn about what it means to be a part of a national team.

A month before the camp, I got another letter inviting me to participate in an international trip with the junior team to Paris and East Berlin in February. Is this what happens when you swim fast? Free trips to Colorado Springs and Europe to swim? I knew swimmers got free travel to the Olympics, but I hadn't fully thought about other meets that must take place in non-Olympic years. I was learning more about how things worked in elite swimming, and liking what I learned.

As I traveled on the plane from St. Louis to Colorado Springs that November, I feared the worst. Would I fit in with the other swimmers at the training camp? I worried I wouldn't be able to keep up in workouts or know what other teens in other parts of the country were talking about. I was a kid who went to Catholic school and hung out alone in my room playing with my Transformers collection.

I had nothing to worry about. A few other swimmers also had trouble getting through the workouts at high altitude. And because we were all having our first national team experience, we felt an instant bond. We had a blast getting to know each other, and we cemented a few friendships after the camp by writing letters.

When we gathered in New York that January for our flight to Europe, we all acted like we'd know each other for years. This was long before e-mail and cell phone texts kept people in touch instantaneously, and all you had to rely on was a letter or phone call. All that correspondence kept up some great relationships that lasted while we progressed through our swimming careers. Some of them attended college with me. Others would be on future national teams. And I'm proud that some of those relationships are still active today.

The moment we boarded the plane for Europe, I knew I was entering new territory. And I wasn't scared about finding out what would happen when we landed on the other side of the Atlantic Ocean.

The two weeks in Europe were fantastic. Paris wasn't necessarily my favorite city, but we did get to do some things that I enjoyed, like climbing to the top of Notre Dame cathedral and looking out over the city; eating a five-course meal halfway up the Eiffel Tower; discovering that McDonald's food tastes the same in Europe; and eating croissants that tasted like they were made by angels. Yes, we swam, too.

The meets we attended were similar to the FINA World Cup that exists today. Swimmers traveled to different cities and swam for money. A win guaranteed professional swimmers a healthy paycheck. We were not pro swimmers, so we just went to the meet for the experience. Though we did not shave our bodies or rest much for the meet in Paris, a lot of us made it to the finals and swam against Olympians from other countries. Because the meet was held in short course meters, none of us knew if we were achieving best times. I got fourth place in the 100 breaststroke, just a few tenths away from winning a bronze medal. I was happy to swim against some of the best swimmers in the world, and they were very gracious when I spoke to them after the race.

The highlight of the meet was sitting in the stands and participating in cheers with Olympic gold medalists Tom Jager and Matt Biondi, who had come to the meet to swim on their own. It was great to get a pep talk from them and have them participate in some of our cheers. Our enthusiasm won us the meet's Spirit Award.

The team started to face setbacks shortly after arriving in East Berlin for a long course meet in the 1936 Olympic pool. Though we all took precautions against drinking the water, about half the team got sick and couldn't swim. While we toured the city, which felt like it was stuck in the 1960s, the sick ones were stuck in the hotel in bed. Personally, I swam very well. I swam a lifetime best in the 100 breast, and in the final I was in the lane next to Adrian Moorehouse, who had just won Olympic gold for Great Britain. I felt like an idiot after the race asking him to sign my shirt, but he did it with a smile.

None of us had any idea what it meant to truly represent the United States in Europe. On the surface, we were using the two weeks as a vacation from school. But the purpose of the junior team was to get experience, and about half the team would put that to good use in the future. Five of the people on that team -- Josh Davis, Brad Bridgewater, Ashley Tappin, Peter Wright and Joe Hudepohl -- became Olympians.

Many of us remained on the national team for years.

Before we left East Berlin, we had one more stop to make: the Berlin Wall. It was more impressive and ominous than it looked on television. We had known that communism in Germany was ending and the Wall was coming down soon, so we made it a point to grab little pieces of the Wall and put them into our pockets. We tried to see the other side, but the Wall was too high.

Two weeks after we returned, the world saw the official images of the Wall bulldozed to the ground by demolition balls and partying Germans.

I got back from that trip ready to celebrate my birthday, which was two days after my return. The day before my birthday I was stricken with the same stomach virus that attacked just about everyone else. That was one of the worst days of my life, trying to sweat out the bug, forcing myself to throw up and thinking that death might be a better option than curling up in the fetal position for an entire day. But at the end of the day, the bug was gone and I was able to turn 16 healthy and happy.

That spring was my first trip to senior nationals, and the swims in Europe gave me some confidence. I had swum lifetime best times unshaved and untapered in Europe, I had gotten a taste of elite swimming and I was approaching the recruiting season for college. My times were certain to get me noticed at some of the major universities. But when I got to Nashville for senior nationals, all I could think about was how many autographs I could get before the meet ended. I wasn't swimming until the third day of the meet, so I had time to stalk some of my idols and harass them for a quick autograph on one of my national team shirts.

There were lots of teams I'd never heard before on the pool deck, and many of them brought dozens of swimmers. I was the only one representing North County Swim Club. My entourage consisted of my mother and my coach. But I had lots of people cheering for me on the day of my 100 breast. Many of my new friends from the junior national team were there, and a few swimmers from St. Louis were yelling for me when I climbed on the blocks for the prelim race.

I was surprised I wasn't very nervous for the race. I'd had two days to watch the meet, so I think it enabled me to calm my nerves and not get caught up in the intensity of the meet. I didn't swim my best time in the prelims, but I qualified eighth, and got to come back and swim in the championship final.

Not many people in those days made it to the final of senior nationals on their first try, but I didn't think about that when I walked out with the other finalists. All I could think about was the accomplishments of many of the other swimmers and how puny my résumé was. Richard Schroeder had swum in the 1988 Olympics. Everyone else had been to nationals before. When the announcer spoke of my credentials, all he could say was I was a member of the junior team. I felt real small when he said that. But I waved to the crowd anyway and stared down the length of my lane, preparing to swim the best 100 breast I could.

It wasn't my best swim, but I moved up from eighth to seventh. It was two-tenths off my best time, which I did a couple of months earlier at the state high school meet to win my first state title.

I found out later that I was eligible for the Rookie of the Meet award, which is given to the swimmer who places highest in their first national meet. Joe Hudepohl, who was also on the junior team and would be a relay medalist in the 1992 and 1996 Olympics, got the award for his fourth place in the 200 free.

Besides the dozens of autographs, I did get another nice reward from my first senior nationals. Another letter came in the mail from United States Swimming, inviting me to compete in the U.S. Olympic Festival in Minneapolis. Sadly, the meet doesn't exist anymore, but it was once a breeding ground for future swimming superstars, in the same way the junior team now grooms young swimmers to be future champions.

In just about every sport but swimming, Olympians were allowed to compete at the Olympic Festival. Swimming limited the field of competitors to those who never had major national team experience (the junior team didn't count). The swimmers were picked to be on four teams in an NFL-style draft. I got to be on the East team with some of my friends from the junior team, so I was excited to spend a weekend with them.

The meet was timed finals, which meant we only swam our races once. The spectator area was packed, and I was surprised the residents of the Twin Cities were so excited about watching a bunch of teenagers swim. The Olympic Festival would be the first competition held at the University of Minnesota's new pool, and every swimmer was excited to swim in an eight-foot deep pool with great starting blocks and an atmosphere that would bring out some great swimming. We arrived in Minneapolis three days before the meet, and everyone on the East team bonded fairly quickly.

I won the gold medal in the 100 breast on the first day, and helped my team win the 400 medley relay. I had confidence I could win the 100 breast, but I also wanted to break the meet record of 1:04.20. Since I was putting in a slight taper for the meet, I figured I could surpass that time. I wasn't disappointed that I went four-hundredths slower than the record, since I won the race. I also got a bronze medal in the 200 breast, a big surprise given my inexperience in swimming the event at the national level, and the fact that many of the swimmers I raced had swum it at the national championships, whereas I was still a few seconds away from making the cut. That medal might have been handed to me simply because I rested for the meet and a few others that could have easily beaten me did not. The awards presentation was very similar to what you see in the Olympics, and the medals were big! The goal was to give young people a taste of the Olympic experience, and we got it.

If you won a race, you were escorted to the media room for interviews with newspaper and TV journalists. I'd done a few interviews before, but never in front of a dozen reporters. It was strange to be in control of who asked questions.

I got asked some of the general questions. Would you describe your race? How did you feel about your time? What do you think of the meet?

But a reporter asked me something that made me think: What do you think about being the first black swimmer to win a gold medal at the Olympic Festival?

I thought he had made some mistake. Surely another black swimmer has won a gold medal at this meet. It's been around for years. There were other black swimmers at this meet; previous meets had to have a black swimmer crowned champion. Even if what the guy was saying was true, I didn't think I had made any major statement with my swim, and certainly not one that warranted a question in a press conference. I'd been climbing up the ranks of the swimming elite for two years and never did I think about the fact that I was the only black swimmer in the finals of a major race. I just wanted to swim. Anthony Nesty probably did the same thing on his way to winning the gold medal in the 100 butterfly at the 1988 Olympics.

Also remember that I had grown up on teams that were made of black swimmers. We were never made to think that making a national team, or winning a gold medal at a major meet, was something "we have to prove to the white man." My coaches never made declarations that they wanted one of us to be the first black swimmer to win a national title. If it happened, it happened because I was a good swimmer.

It seemed like an eternity before I could find the answer to the reporter's question.

"I never thought about it until now, but I hope it inspires black people to take up swimming and know they can do it, too."

The next day, the story of my historic win was in newspapers across the country. Friends and relatives sent copies of it to our home from their hometowns.

I have many lasting memories of the Olympic Festival. The eight swimmers in each event's finals were paraded on the deck before each race, and as I walked out for the 100 breast, I saw the Steger family waving signs of support for me in the stands. The Steger kids – Alex and Karen – were on my swim team in St. Louis, and the family drove to Minneapolis to watch me swim.

I can also remember standing at the top of the medal podium in the 100 breast and 400 medley relay. The relay win was a surprise. The four of us didn't seem to have much of a chance to win against the three other relays that had more talented swimmers. I dove in for my leg more than a second behind the leader, but I managed to put us in the lead, and we held it to the finish to win by two seconds.

The team race on the men's side came down to the final event, the 400 freestyle relay. All we had to do was get first or second in the race – or finish ahead of the North team – we would win the meet. We got nervous a couple of times during the race when we slipped back to third or fourth and the North team held a commanding lead. Every member of the East team was on their feet cheering for Josh Davis, who was swimming our anchor leg against Ugur Taner, who won the 100 freestyle. The North team was almost assured of winning the race, so I'm sure they were focusing on cheering for Ugur to beat Josh. If Ugur's South team beat us, the North team would win the meet.

We finished second in the relay. We won the meet by five points.

That interview after the 100 breast, however, still has the most impact after all these years. Those questions posed to me opened my eyes to the state of swimming as far as minority involvement was concerned. I had never seen it as an issue, since I learned how to swim on an all-black swim team, was being coached by a black former swimmer and raced against black swimmers locally.

I admit that the sight of black swimmers at national meets was -- and still is -- a rarity. In 1990, only four or five other black swimmers were at the national level, but we never hung out together and remarked on our accomplishment of being the few black people at the meet. Again, we just swam. Does Steve Nash get asked about being a white basketball player? Was it the question to ask in a Larry Bird press conference?

This was in a time when the media hadn't latched on to a black swimming star, since no black swimmer had made the Olympic team. But my accomplishment at the 1990 Olympic Festival wasn't the biggest moment for black swimmers at that point.

Chris Silva had a rich swimming career, and he probably did so quietly. He swam in the 1984 and 1988 Olympic Trials and was the first black swimmer on the USA Swimming National Team. He died in 1990, about a month after my win at the Olympic Festival, but he was already trying to raise awareness about minorities in swimming by working with the International Swimming Hall of Fame.

I can understand why much is made of black people in swimming, now that Americans of African heritage have made it to the Olympics, own world records and have national titles. It's something the swimming community -- and the media -- had been waiting for since the early 1990s.

After the Olympic Festival, I had to less than a month to prepare for the summer nationals, which were in Austin, Texas, the site of last year's junior nationals. With the reporter's question still rattling around in my head from junior nationals, I scanned the deck in Austin for more black swimmers. Two of my friends from the junior team who claimed mixed heritage, Alison Terry and Indira Allick, were there. Danielle Strader, who was a promising butterflier, was there. And I did see one black male there: Byron Davis, who was all biceps and pectoral muscles. I didn't know him, didn't know what he was swimming or where he was from. But seeing him warm up in the pool kind of made me feel like I wasn't alone, that if there were eyes on me, they were certainly on him as well.

I put that all behind me when I got up to swim the 100 breast. I made it through prelims, posting a 1:03.23, breaking Tyler Mayfield's national age group record in the 15-16 age group. Tyler was waiting to swim in the next heat, and he congratulated me when I got out of the pool, but I wasn't sure if he knew I had broken the record. I made it to finals again and got fifth in the race with a 1:02.94. I saw the time and was happier than Eric Wunderlich, who had won the race. I was the youngest person in the United States to swim under the 1:03 barrier. A few days later, I found out that if I had gotten fourth place, I would have gone to Italy later that month for a swim meet.

My swim at nationals meant I had officially "made it." I dropped two seconds off the time I did the previous year and people were taking notice. When I got back from nationals, I began perusing dozens of letters from coaches at Division I universities. I didn't give many of the letters a second thought and tossed them, but most of them surprised me. Was I really good enough to go to school at Stanford University? Would a school like the University of Michigan, with its tradition of great breaststrokers, really want to include me in their roster? Coaches would call to gauge my interest in their school. It was overwhelming. No one on my team had gone through this before – not even my coach – so these were uncharted waters for me.

Texas, Michigan, Auburn, the University of Southern California and Stanford were some of the major schools writing letters to me every week "just to say hi," and to show me that my talents would fit in well at their schools. I got chills every time I got home and heard a message from Jon Urbanchek, Eddie Reese and Skip Kenney on my answering machine. They all wanted me to come to their schools! As the winter of 1990 approached, many of them began offering me full scholarships. The chance to attend college for free would become a huge factor in determining which school I attended. Paying tuition for college is not easy for a single-parent household. I attended St. Louis U. High on a partial scholarship and if I hadn't received any full-scholarship offers for college, it was off to St. Louis Community College.

One of the best parts of picking a college is going on official visits to the schools of your choice. The NCAA allows you to take five trips, but I only spent weekends at Texas, Michigan and USC. The trip to Texas was only a formality. I had attended the summer swim camp in Austin twice, had swum in major meets there twice and knew the swimmers quite well. The only thing I needed to learn on the trip was the academic situation there and how I might bond with the team. Everything felt natural at Texas. Because most of the swimmers knew me, I didn't feel any pressure. My trips to USC and Michigan were fun, but I think I tried to find something bad in each place to justify my early decision to go to Texas. The only problem was that Michigan's team was fighting very hard to get me to move to Ann Arbor, and they were doing a very good

30

job. I thought I could not do much better than go to Michigan and train with Mike Barrowman, Eric Wunderlich and other great swimmers. But I would get the same kind of training at Texas with Kirk Stackle and Daniel Watters, both of whom had made the 1988 Olympic team.

As the high school swimming season began in St. Louis, I took a trip to the U.S. Open in Indianapolis. The timing of the meet was terrible. Attending it would mean missing the annual relay meet held at Country Day School, always fun because each race was a relay and it was the first competition of the season. My teammates in high school understood that going to U.S. Open was more important to my future as a swimmer than a local relay meet.

I hadn't swum at the Indianapolis pool since I was 12 years old, racing in my first competition outside Missouri. This time, the pool deck was filled with Olympians, world record holders and NCAA champions. I had tapered for the meet, and wanted this to be my audition for the any college coaches in attendance. NCAA rules prohibited them from talking to me on the deck, but that wasn't true for the swimmers. Just before my prelim heat of the 100 breast, I got a "Good luck, Jeff" from Tyler Mayfield, a longtime rival who I rarely spoke to at meets. He was a freshman at Stanford, and his words of encouragement were obviously coming from a recruiting standpoint, not a fellow swimmer. But it was nice to know Stanford – through Tyler – cared so much about me.

My time in the 100 breast prelim was atrocious. I swam a 1:04.24, more than a second slower than my best time. I qualified for the finals, but I felt lucky to make it. Many of the top swimmers at the meet were not fully rested. Those going to the world championships the following month were still in hard training. Many of the college students were saving up for the NCAA championships.

Besides making the final, the only saving grace of my prelim swim was encouraging a group of black students from a local grade school who had come to watch the meet. Besides myself, I think they saw two or three other swimmers of color on the deck. I had won my prelim heat, and to them, that was a big deal. I remember seeing them cheering wildly after my race. I doubt my "victory" encouraged any of them to become swimmers, but I hope it inspired them in other ways.

I knew I had a chance to win the 100 breast final, and I had to forget my poor prelim swim and focus on the job at hand. I had never raced six of the seven other swimmers in the final, so I was unsure of what to expect. Roque Santos was in the final of the 100 at nationals just a few months earlier, and he had beaten me by four-hundredths of a second. Mike Barrowman, the world record holder in the 200 breast, was also in the final, but with his focus squarely on the world championships, I knew he wouldn't pose much of a threat in this race.

I dove into the water with the goal of being one of the first to reach the 50-meter mark. When I made the turn, I glanced to my right and saw myself even with pretty much the entire field. It was going to be a battle to the finish. My strategy at the time had always been to take my race out slower than my competitors and save a little bit for the final 25 meters. But I panicked a lot in the final meters of the race, thinking too much about where my competitors were and not focused on my swimming. I touched third in the race in a time just barely off my best, and I was happy in knowing I would get some hardware at this meet.

On the awards stand, I was introduced first as the third-place finisher. The announcer told the audience I was "only 16 years of age." Wow. Was it really a big deal for a 16-year-old to get third place at the U.S. Open? I guess so. Everyone else in the final was well into their 20s.

The winner of the event was Mark Warnecke, who would go on to make four Olympic teams for Germany (winning a bronze medal in 1996), and at age 35, won the 50 breast at the 2005 world championships.

This was the highest place I'd ever gotten at a meet outside of Missouri, and people were taking notice. When I got home after the meet, the phone calls and letters increased. This was getting serious.

The USA went to Australia for the world championships in January 1991. One day, somewhere in the middle of the meet, I got postcards from the University of Michigan swimmers who were at worlds, and another from the Texas swimmers.

Even when they are at the biggest meet of the season, these guys are working to get me to come to their school. I didn't know if I was the top recruit that year, but it sure felt that way.

Chapter Four

As 1991 began, I spent a lot of time thinking about where I wanted to spend the next four or five years of my life. Before this, the biggest decision I had to make was whether to paint my room light blue or dark blue. Choosing a college was going to be decidedly more difficult.

Besides the attention paid to me by my top three choices (Texas, Michigan, Stanford), I'd also been getting calls from other schools. One day, I picked up the phone and almost collapsed when I heard Melvin Stewart's voice. Melvin was a senior at the University of Tennessee and was the top swimmer in the 200 butterfly in the world. The following year, he would win the gold medal in the 200 fly at the Barcelona Olympics.

I didn't have to say much during the conversation. I was in shock because Melvin certainly had better things to do with his evening than talk to some kid from St. Louis. But he was quite willing to tell me everything there was to know about Tennessee. He spent a lot of time talking to me about the Timettes, a group of sorority girls who are timers at home meets and are the team's support group. They sounded just like the Bevo's Babes at Texas. The way he was building them up, he sounded like he was trying to tell me that the girls there were, well, very pretty to look at during swim meets. I really wanted to tell him he was wasting breath on this topic.

During that winter, just before the deadline for seniors to declare their college choices, coaches started visiting my home. They would come to watch me during a workout, then spend a couple more hours with me and my mom at home, talking about the benefits of their programs and why I would be a perfect fit at their schools. The fact that they were visiting me made me happy, but also made the decision harder.

Knowing that my swimming career was taking a major leap forward, my workouts with Paul intensified. I never enjoyed workout, and since I was the only swimmer on my team with any aspirations of competing at the national level, I would often do workouts alone. In other instances, I would do a certain set breaststroke while others did freestyle. My teammates would usually get more rest than I did, and I wasn't happy about it.

As the end of February approached, I needed to concentrate on my preparation for my final state championship meet. I had narrowed my college choices to Texas or Michigan, and put my thoughts aside for a few weeks. I wanted my final high school state meet to be one that would be remembered for many years. I didn't set many specific goals, other than dropping my state record in the 100 breast and most importantly, breaking the year-old state record in the 200 IM to prove my versatility to the college coaches who were eager to peg me only as a breaststroker. Missouri rules at the time did not permit me to swim with my USA Swimming team, nor was I allowed to compete in USA Swimming meets. I had to jump through many hoops and suffer through many miles of red tape to swim in the US Open held at the beginning of the high school swimming season in December 1990. In order to keep up the training I had begun to build that fall, my USA Swimming coach and I devised a workout schedule that I would do a few days a week separately from the rest of the high school team. That was fine with my high school coach, and some of my teammates volunteered to do many of the sets with me instead of participating in impromptu water polo games or early dismissals. Most of the time I felt like the square who didn't want to have fun. But my goals reached far beyond the high school swimming season, so I gritted my teeth and resisted the temptation to cut workouts short.

The state championships were held in Columbia at Hickman High School. The venue was literally a dungeon – dark and unheated and a little rundown. The pool itself had only six lanes and was about four feet deep at the turning end of the pool. There was hardly a warmdown pool; it consisted of a space of water just off the main competition pool that was about 10 yards long and five yards wide. The best way to warm up before a race was to stand in place and jump up and down or move your arms while standing in place. It was the best facility for such a meet in the state at the time, so we didn't really think much about a better place to swim. The University of Missouri, also in Columbia, didn't upgrade their pool until 2005 and the Rec-Plex outside of St. Louis, which is the current home of the state meet, didn't open until 2000.

St. Louis U. High brought six swimmers and two divers to the meet my senior year. In the course of the season, I felt we had the opportunity to place a few swimmers in the top 12, but I was the only swimmer to make the finals in an individual event. Our two divers did place in the top six, which was a major breakthrough for our school.

I broke the state record in the 200 IM in prelims with a 1:52.90, and it also qualified me to swim the event at senior nationals six weeks later. My goal was to break the state record, which had been set the year before by David Lane, but I was surprised I had swum so fast. My transition from backstroke to breaststroke wasn't very fast. I had misjudged the finish and glided a little bit into the wall. I did my best to make up for the slow turn, but I paid for it on the freestyle leg, where I visibly struggled just to finish. I was happy to swim so fast because I was showing college recruiters that I could do more than one event.

I also broke my state mark in the 100 breast in prelims with a 54.98. The race was far from perfect. When I dove in, my goggles began to fill with water. On the final 25 yards, I couldn't see much more than a blurry black line at the bottom of the pool and the "T" that marked the wall at the finish. Given the setback, I didn't expect to swim that fast. After the prelims, members of the media told me I was less than a second off the national high school record of 54.42, which was held by Nelson Diebel of Peddie High School. I had never imagined I could challenge the fastest time ever swum by a high school swimmer, so when I heard I was only six-tenths of a second off the mark, I got a little knot in my stomach. I knew I could concentrate on my race more without leaky goggles, but would it be enough to go six tenths faster?

If we were to make the top-three team finish we hoped for, our relays would have to place very high to take advantage of the doubled points relays offered. We started finals with a third place finish in the 200 medley relay. We were just a few tenths behind the team that finished in second place.

I won the 200 IM with a 1:54.14. I wanted to conserve some energy for my 100 breast later in the meet, but the competition was tough in the first half of the race, and I had to push a little bit harder than I wanted. I was able to hold back on the last half of the race and still win by about four seconds. I was happy with the win and spent the next hour or so preparing for the 100 breast final. I sat in the bleachers watching the races but starting to visualize what 54.42 looked like. It seemed impossible.

I got up a few times to walk off my nervousness. A few coaches asked me if I was going to break the national record. I sheepishly said, "We'll see." In the minutes before my race, I started to go into panic mode. I stopped concentrating on the race and began to think about the expectations put upon me by the people in the building. They all knew how close I was to the record (the heat sheet listed the state and national records in every event) so every race was building up to mine, the final individual event of the meet. Even though I was dressed warmly, I started shivering. I thought I was cold, so I went into the locker room to take a hot shower. It didn't help. My body was warm, but I was still shivering. My nerves had taken control of my body.

Fifteen minutes before the race, I did some meditation techniques and tried to calm down my nerves. By the time the final came, I had stopped shivering, but had tremendous butterflies in my stomach. Jeff Rush, who was a junior at one of the prestigious private schools in St. Louis and a longtime friend, was in the lane next to me. I knew he wasn't going to let me win easily. He had been disqualified in the prelims of the 100 breast the year before, and I'm sure he had something to prove.

When the starter called the swimmers to the blocks, the cheering in the cavernous facility stopped. No one was talking. No one was moving. I noticed the utter silence and said "Oh, shit" to myself.

When the race started, I swam on all cylinders. Since the pool depth at the turning end was less than four feet deep, I had to adjust my pullouts so my fingertips wouldn't scratch the bottom. Though it's in the rules that you can't touch the pool bottom with any part of your body to avoid getting an advantage, scraping your fingers on a breaststroke pullout can actually slow you down. The better bet is to push off shallower.

Just as I expected, Jeff Rush was within a body length at the 50. I had a slight fear that I hadn't taken the race out fast enough and shifted into a higher gear. I might have paid a big price by doing that, as I was carried through the final six or seven grueling strokes by the crowd. The cheering had reached a monstrous decibel. When I touched the wall, I was unsure if I had broken the record or if my nerves had defeated me. The meet used electronic timing but there was no scoreboard to see your times after the race, so we relied on the hand times. One of the timers came to edge of the lane and showed me her watch: 54.79. Those who had stopwatches in the crowd knew the time, too, and were most likely spreading the news around the deck. I hadn't broken the national record, but everyone still appreciated the fact that I still went faster than my prelim time, and the crowd broke into lengthy applause. I saw my family at the other end of the pool, and they were all smiling from ear to ear. Except for my mother, none of them really knew the true meaning of the swim, but they saw me win my second event of the day, and that's all that mattered to them. I waved to my family and to the crowd. I looked over to my teammates and saw that the school's president, principal and athletic director were all there. To know that they drove halfway across the state to see my race was overwhelming.

When an athlete doesn't break a record everyone thinks he can break, the first question reporters ask is: Are you disappointed? Of course I wasn't! I had just swum my best time. Because I hadn't set a goal to break the national high school record, I had no reason to be upset that I didn't reach that time.

As of this writing, my state record has survived 18 years of challenges. I attended the 2008 state championships in St. Peters, mildly curious to see if someone could come close to breaking the record. In all these years, I was the only one who had been under the 57-second mark in the 100 breast in Missouri. As I read the list of times that had won the 100 breast at the meet in the 16 years since, I got new perspective of my record swim.

In the 100 breast final in 2008, two seniors came closer to the record than anyone had before. The winning time was 56.41, less than 1.5 seconds off the mark. At the start of the race, I got a sudden knot in my stomach. With the birth of the high-tech suits – and the passage of time – would this be the year the record goes down? After the first 50 I finally took a relaxed breath. The top two swimmers had swum the first 50 too slow to approach the time, but I felt they could get pretty close. At the finish, I heartily applauded the fact that I had seen the fourth and fifth fastest swims in the event. I still own the top three times ever done in the state.

When will the record be broken? Could it make it to 20 years? Though my state record is in no way comparable to Janet Evans' 800 free world record or Mary T. Meagher's 200 fly world record, I can't help but think that both records were broken 19 years after they were set. No matter when it happens, I want to be able to congratulate the record-breaker in person.

After the meet in 2008, I saw many people who knew me and were at Hickman High when I broke the record. They gave me a lot of new perspective about the swim. I never knew that coaches talked to their swimmers about my record, or that the current swimmers at St. Louis U. High felt a sense of pride each year the announcer mentioned the record at the state meet.

I didn't have much time to rest on my laurels when the 1991 state meet was over. Senior nationals was just six weeks away, and I had to decide which college I would attend. I could have waited until mid-April to make my choice, but I wanted to prepare for nationals without nightly phone calls. I talked about my choices extensively with my mother. Through the whole process, she never tried to guide me toward one school or another. She knew I wouldn't make a bad decision either way, and said her support and love would still be with me wherever I went.

That day in mid-March when I picked up the phone to make my first rejection call was scary. How would the coach react?

I called the coach of my second choice, the University of Michigan, and told Jon Urbanchek I would not be coming to his school. He was vocally displeased. In no uncertain terms, he said I wasn't going to swim as well at Texas as I would at Michigan. It was a shocker. What if he was right? Should I change my mind before calling Eddie Reese and confirming Texas as my college choice?

Despite Jon's not-so-subtle remarks, I stuck to my decision and called Eddie Reese. Eddie was excited, but I think he already knew I was going to go there.

About a month later, just before nationals, Eddie personally flew to St. Louis to collect the national letter of intent I was to sign. We gathered in a swanky conference room at my school, where a couple of newspaper journalists took pictures and documented the event. I signed the papers and handed them to Eddie. It was more than a piece of paper signifying my college choice. It was a contract. I was being offered a full scholarship to Texas, which the contract said could not be reduced or taken away. My mother was most happy with that part. There were a whole bunch of conditions about redshirting and what to do if I decided to transfer, but I was certain I wouldn't do any of those.

Two weeks later, Texas won their fourth-straight national championship. In my mind, I was certain that the knowledge of my impending arrival motivated them so much they obliterated the competition at the meet. But they were swimming in their home pool and were virtually unstoppable anyway. I hoped I could help them win No. 5.

But first, I had to swim at nationals. This meet was very important because it chose three traveling teams that would swim in international meets that summer. The Pan-Pacific team would be picked from the top three swimmers in each event. They would get to go to Canada. The Pan-American team would travel to Cuba, and the World University Games team would swim in England. The hitch was that times done by Americans at the world championships in January would also be thrown in the mix. So, you could get second place at nationals, but technically be the fourth-fastest American and therefore be "bumped down" from the Pan-Pacific team to the Pan-American team because the two times done by Americans at worlds were faster than your time at nationals. Plus, I was ineligible for the World University Games team because I had not yet started college. Eric Wunderlich, a top breaststroker at the University of Michigan, swam a 1:02.05 at worlds, so that was the time I was thinking about when we marched out to swim in the finals. I couldn't place any lower than third, and I was seeded third in the final eight.

I remember two things about the swim. The first is the sight of the Texas swimmers cheering when my name was announced before the race. The other is turning at the 50-meter wall, and Mike Barrowman and I are looking right at each other as we pushed off underwater. We were two lanes apart, and the glance lasted for about a second, but we both knew we were going to fight to the finish. Seth van Neerden was in the lane separating us, and he was so far ahead I never gave it a thought about trying to catch him.

When I surfaced after the turn, the adrenaline pushed me to the finish. In breaststroke, you can't see your competitors, unless they are far ahead of you, as Seth was. In my mind, I gave myself a lot of self-talk: "Go, go, go! Don't give up! You're almost there! You're getting tired, but you've got to keep pushing!"

I touched the wall at the finish and quickly turned around to look at the scoreboard. Seth van Neerden had won the race and was already screaming for joy because he was two-hundredths of a second slower than the American record and was now the second-fastest American ever in the event, behind Steve Lundquist. Mike Barrowman, who was the world record holder in the 200 breast, placed second: 1:02.12. That meant Seth, Eric and Mike were the three people who would get to swim the race at Pan Pacs. But I didn't know that until later. All I cared about was that I got third place, which was my highest placing at senior nationals, and I swam my best time: 1:02.51. It was a national age group record for the 17-18 age group, which meant no one 17 or 18 years old had gone faster in the United States. I leaned on the lane rope and stared at the time for a minute. I was breathing heavily and smiling from ear to ear. I looked at my future Texas teammates and they were cheering.

After the awards ceremony, I was handed an envelope officially naming me to the Pan-American team. While I wish I had been able to swim fast enough to go to Canada, where the fastest swimmers from the Americas, Australia and Asia would swim, it was going to be a thrill to swim in Cuba. After I warmed down, I had to take a urine test, and while I waited for the urge to pee, I read the letter welcoming me to the Pan-American team about four times. Hans Dersch, who was a Texas alum, was also going to Cuba to swim the 100 breast. Since I met him numerous times at the swim camps in Austin, it was great knowing at least one person on the team.

I had just a few weeks of my senior year left to finish, and my thoughts were already focused on life in college. But I did my best to concentrate on my classes, since I wanted to leave St. Louis University High with decent grades. It was difficult fighting the urges of senioritis.

One day in late April, I was working on a paper in the school's computer lab. It was late in the afternoon, and most of the school was deserted. About a dozen other students were in the room, working on projects.

I noticed the editor of the school's yearbook, who I will call Fr. Smith, walk into the computer lab. As a member of the yearbook staff, I had worked with Fr. Smith often and had taken one of his art classes as a junior. Out of the corner of my eye, I noticed him walking directly toward me. Without hesitation, he put his hands on my shoulders and started gently massaging them. He asked me what I was doing, and I told him about the paper I needed to write. I should have asked him what *he* was doing.

Instead of responding, his hands made their way to the front of my body and were caressing my chest. The surprise took a little bit of breath out of me, and I was too startled to speak. One of his hands unbuttoned my pullover shirt and began feeling my chest and stomach.

I was frightened out of my mind. A student was sitting four feet away, and I wondered if he knew what was happening. I was too scared to turn my head to find out. I quickly pulled Fr. Smith's hand out of my shirt and worked to calm down my heart rate.

Fr. Smith leaned over and whispered "Let's go" into my ear. I got up quickly, not because of the invitation, but I was so scared of someone seeing that interaction that I wanted to leave the room and be somewhere else. Fr. Smith was waiting for me outside and I was ready to scold him for his actions in the computer lab. Without a word, he motioned for me to follow him to the yearbook office, where I often hung out after school.

As I stood outside the office waiting for Fr. Smith to unlock the door, I tried to figure out what was happening. After the events in the computer lab, I knew he wasn't asking me into his office for an academic consult. There was definitely something sexual in nature about to happen. Common sense told me to walk away, but my curiosity was taking over. What was in store for me on the other side of the door? My hormones were flowing so strong at the age of 17 that a soft touch by anyone who looked slightly attractive would have sent me into overdrive. And Fr. Smith had a soft touch, a soothing voice and attractive eyes. Of all the men who taught at the school, he was probably near the top of the list in terms of attractiveness.

Once inside, Fr. Smith didn't waste much time. He wanted to continue where he'd left off in the computer lab. He took off my shirt and began caressing my torso. While he did this, he gave me a look that said he wanted to do much, much more than touch my chest. I stood in the middle of the small office paralyzed in disbelief. Was this really happening to me? I wasn't questioning the things my body was telling me. I was fully enjoying the sensations his touch was creating. I fully allowed his hands to explore my torso. I looked into his eyes and noticed he was leaning in for a kiss. My heart began to beat stronger.

When we kissed, the only thing I was conscious of was his beard. The act of kissing wasn't new, but kissing a man with a beard was a first-time experience for me, and the tickling of his facial hair was a pleasant sensation. It made me want more, no matter how much I knew that a student making out with a teacher – who also happens to be a priest – is about as wrong as things can get. So why didn't I stop? A large part of me was curious to see how far this would go.

After the kiss, Fr. Smith took my hand and put it on his shoulder. I rubbed his shoulder and his chest over his shirt. He was dressed in regular clothes, which made me think less of him being a priest and more of him being a man who was becoming extremely attractive to me.

After a few more minutes of kissing, my hormones couldn't take it anymore. I liked what I was feeling, so I unbuttoned Fr. Smith's shirt to see the well-formed pecs I had been feeling for the past few minutes.

At that moment, the door opened and a student poked his head in. After only a couple of seconds, he said "I'm sorry" and left. That was it for me. I wanted to leave. I didn't thrive on the danger of getting caught, even though I suspect Fr. Smith wanted it to happen. If he didn't, why did he leave the door unlocked?

I didn't just want to leave the room. I wanted to leave the school and never come back. I was a well-known athlete at the school. To have a rumor floating around about me and Fr. Smith making out in the yearbook office would have been disastrous. I was sure my remaining weeks in high school would be ruined by gossip, teasing and downright gay-bashing. It was a Catholic school, after all; homosexuality is one of the biggest sins in the Catholic Church.

I began to put my shirt back on. Fr. Smith finally spoke, pleading with me not to leave. Whether or not he wanted to get caught is immaterial. I didn't expect to get caught, and the thought of having to explain myself if the student had run to get a teacher was more than I could stand.

Fr. Smith looked at me with his piercing blue eyes and made one more plea. I was torn. Making out with him was, at this point in my life, the best sexual experience I had ever had. Nothing I had done with Devin could compare to the 10 minutes I'd spent with Fr. Smith. If I left the room I would have sworn not to have any interaction with him again.

In the middle of his plea, a teacher burst into the room. He took a second to survey the situation, then pointed to Fr. Smith and said "Come with me." Without a word, Fr. Smith walked out the door like a child who had been caught with his hand in the cookie jar. The teacher then pointed at me and said "Stay here."

Oh, shit.

I waited in the office for five agonizing minutes. What was going on? What was happening to Fr. Smith? Was I going to be expelled a month before graduation? What was I going to say?

When the teacher returned, he asked me to tell him what happened. The only things I left out were that I voluntarily unbuttoned Fr. Smith's shirt and that I didn't ask Fr. Smith to stop. I asked him what was going to happen to Fr. Smith and he told me not to worry.

Ten minutes later, I was recounting the events of the afternoon to the principal. He seemed more concerned about my physical welfare than anything, and I assured him I was fine. When he recommended that we call my mother at work, the world fell out from under me. I could handle telling this story to the administration at school, but there was no way my mother would let these events slide with an assurance that I was OK.

About an hour after Fr. Smith was ushered out of the yearbook office, my mother arrived at school. She knew something had happened to me, but I wasn't physically hurt. I told her the same story in front of the principal, and her stern gaze never wavered. I assured her I was not hurt, physically or emotionally. The principal said I didn't have to come to school the next day so I could recover from this incident. I should have agreed, but I wondered if my absence would arouse suspicion. Would the student who caught us in the act notice I wasn't at school and spread rumors? On the other hand, if I went to school, what would happen if I bumped into the student in the hallway? Would he utter "faggot" or "queer" just loud enough for someone else to hear? In the end, I told the principal I would show up for school the next day.

I knew I had bent the truth severely in the principal's office. But survival instinct kicked in, and all I wanted to do was make sure no one knew I essentially consented to the act in the yearbook office. That would mean coming out to people that definitely didn't need to know, and I certainly wasn't prepared to come out to my mother.

I was also somewhat surprised that everyone bought my story. Either everyone was in denial that St. Louis University High School had a gay student, or they wanted to believe that this particular student was not gay.

My mother and I drove home in silence. But when we got home, we had a long talk. She was very concerned about me, whether I would be mentally scarred by the situation. Without hesitation, I told her I wouldn't. Then she leaned in for the kill.

"Jeff, I need to know if you're gay."

This statement didn't shock me. I knew from the moment the principal called my mother at work that she would venture into this territory. We had skirted around the issue for months, and the incident at school – as well as my handling of the aftermath – only raised more questions for her.

I could have come out to her then. It would have been the best moment. I might have gotten a modicum of support from her, given that I had just been "molested" by a priest. But I wasn't ready for whatever lecture she was prepared to give.

I didn't vehemently deny being gay, but I told her what happened between me and Fr. Smith didn't mean I was gay. I hated myself for dodging the question, but at the forefront were the stories I'd heard of kids who were thrown out of their homes for being gay. I didn't want that. My mom and I were so close and I didn't want to lose that.

The issue was seemingly closed after that day. The next day at school went by without incident. The teacher who caught Fr. Smith didn't bring it up when he saw me in the hallway. Fr. Smith, however, was never to be seen at school again. No one knew where he was or what had happened. If the student who walked in on us had spread any rumors, they didn't go far. I figured Fr. Smith had been moved to another rectory and was getting some sort of counseling. I felt bad if my recollection of the story caused Fr. Smith to be treated badly. Conversely, I emerged from the event unscathed.

Before graduation, I had to endure the prom. I told my mother I didn't want to go, but she insisted on attending. It was one of those events I would regret not participating in years later. The female friends I had were all attached to boyfriends, so I was without a suitable female to take to the prom. How I wish someone had invented the concept of the gay prom back then, even for a very conservative Jesuit all-boys high school. I don't care if I would have been the only one in attendance. It would have been better than the charade of my actual prom. As I got dressed for what would turn out to be the most excruciating night of my life, I tried to create a plan of action. My date and I would get to the prom in time for dinner, dance a little bit and maybe leave a couple of hours later. I walked to the car hoping my mother wouldn't make a scene and cry as she watched her youngest son take off for the prom. I tried my best to smile, but I couldn't stop thinking that I was headed toward a nightmare. My mother obviously didn't see the seething anger in my eyes. She was the proudest mother on that day. The only thing that would have made her happier would have been an engagement announcement on our return from the prom.

I was going with the daughter of my mother's hairdresser. I had never met her, and to this day, I cannot recall her name. I remember her answering the door in a flowing white dress with something in her hair. I remember being crestfallen when she looked so beautiful and smiling from ear to ear. This was obviously a big deal for her. I tried so hard that evening to make it fun for her, but with the total lack of emotional and physical attraction, the evening was a severe bust. What do two people who have never met say to each other at the prom? It's even worse when one of them is gay and would rather be on the arm of a classmate, posing for the official photo with one of the football players. If it had been a simple blind date to a movie or restaurant, I might have been better prepared. But the underlying theme at the prom is romance, and there was no sign of it from me or my date.

I sat at a table with friends who were there with their girlfriends. They all danced often to romantic songs and were obviously in love – or at least what passes for love for teenagers. I danced with my date a couple of times, placing my hand ever so gingerly on her waist. I tried very hard to express interest in the conversations we had.

I drove her home and never saw her again.

*****

Graduation from St. Louis University High School is a long-winded affair. There is a graduation mass and a ceremony that requires all students to dress in white tuxedos. I didn't mind putting on a tuxedo for the second time in two months. This was a big deal.

The day was a major family affair. My mother, brother, grandmother, aunts and uncle all came to the ceremony.

By early June, I was ready to turn my focus to only swimming. Preparing for my trip to Cuba meant some seriously hard work in the pool. I swam twice a day four days a week and did nothing else but think about swimming fast at the end of the summer. It was great to do nothing but sleep, eat and swim for two months, and even better that I was never pressured to get a job. Since I had a college scholarship waiting for me, I didn't have to worry much about money for college.

45

My mother would provide me with spending money.

My performance at the 1990 senior nationals earned me the privilege of being named to my second junior national team. When I got the letter welcoming me to the team, I had not yet broken the 100 breast high school state record, nor had I been named to the Pan American team. Our competition trip was to the Canada Cup in Vancouver, a meet now called the Mel Zajac International. The meet was a perfect opportunity to get some international racing in before the Pan American Games, and I got the chance to race Robert Fox, a Canadian who would also be going to Cuba. Robert was also a black swimmer, and it made me feel good to see him doing so well. The awards were the best thing about the meet. The top three finishers in each race won dolphins made of pewter. I brought back two of them from Canada by virtue of winning the 100 breast and being part of the winning 400 medley relay. This junior team didn't have the same future potential as the one that traveled through Europe, but many of them had good college careers. Though we all swam well at the meet, we weren't a very close team. This team didn't have as much time to know each other, mostly because we didn't have a training camp in Colorado Springs.

That same year, the National Interscholastic Swimming Coaches Association invited me and nearly 100 other swimmers from around the country to participate in the first national high school championship, which was to be held in mid-June at New Trier High School in a suburb of Chicago. Up to that point, no meet existed to pit the fastest high school swimmers against each other. This meet was an attempt to do that. Only graduating seniors were invited to the meet, and I knew almost all of the swimmers in attendance. To my surprise, Jenny Thompson had come to the meet, despite her superstar status. Jenny was easily the biggest name at the meet, though three or four others – including myself – would be representing the United States in international competition that year.

The pool itself wasn't remarkable. It had eight lanes, but the start end was only about four feet deep. Everyone had come to the meet with no expectations on swimming very fast, and no one cared about their times or placing first or second in a meet that had very little impact on our swimming careers. No one except for me.

Despite signing a contract that I would be at my peak form for the Pan American Games, I broke my training in early June to taper for this meet. Since coming so close in February, I was ecstatic to learn I could have another chance to break Nelson Deibel's national record in the 100 breast.

On the day of the meet, all I had to swim was the medley relay at the start of the meet and the 100 breast at the end. I wasn't allowed to swim the 200 IM because I wasn't in the top eight among the senior class in the event. The time between events was spent catching up with old friends and cheering for them in the pool. Jenny Thompson put up some fast in-season times and others were quite impressive as well. I was surprised that ESPN was covering the meet and a few newspaper reporters were in attendance. Besides me, all the other swimmers were using the weekend as a free trip to Chicago and not much more.

Several of my former high school teammates made a surprise appearance at the meet, ready to cheer me on. That made me more nervous than happy.

Word began to spread on the deck that I was making a run for the national record, and when it came time for the race, the noise in the building ground to a halt. It was eerily similar to the situation at the state meet almost four months earlier. Though I was mentally prepared to swim fast, I don't think I had done everything I could physically to chase the record. I only decided to taper for the meet two weeks earlier, which didn't give me time to change my focus from Havana in August to Chicago in June.

I knew I wasn't on pace to break the record when I turned at the 50-yard mark. The swimmer in the lane next to me, Steve West, was about a body length behind me. I knew I should have been faster in the first half of the race. I fought hard to the end, but I only managed a 55.72. That was a second slower than my best time. What a waste of a taper. I feared that my stupid decision would affect my performance in Cuba.

After the meet, I returned home and began training again in earnest. I was able to divert some attention away from swimming as I filled out forms to apply for college. My transcripts basically assured me I had earned enough credits in high school to be an academic sophomore when I walked onto campus in Austin. So that was one less thing to worry about.

Devin and I had a talk about me going to college. Since we hadn't made any kind of heavy bond, and never believed our relationship was based on anything more than sex, it wasn't difficult to sever the ties around the end of July, just as I was starting to taper and pack for a two-week trip in Cuba. We had only seen each other a couple of times in 1991 anyway.

*****

A few swimmers on the Pan Am team were also on my first junior team, so it was nice to know people when I arrived in Miami a week before the meet for meetings and training. One of them was Brad Bridgewater, who was also going to be a teammate at Texas. A few others were current or former Texas swimmers, so we had a nice contingent of Longhorns at the meet.

Our first order of business was to appoint team captains. It was virtually assured that Dan Veatch, who was the most experienced guy on the team, would be the men's captain. He'd gone to the 1988 Olympics in the 200 back and was a natural leader. He looked confident in the role of team captain, and I was happy knowing I could look up to him.

Before we took off for Havana, we were also told we would be the first Americans allowed in the country since the Cuban Missile Crisis. A lot of us joked that Cuba might not be ready for us, and we might not be ready for Cuba.

Cuba was ready for us. In the days leading up to the meet, we toured Havana and found that the citizens loved us. They wanted to touch our clothes and ask for money. Everything in Havana looked like it was in a time capsule. It seemed like technological and social progress stopped in the 1960s. None of the cars looked modern. Many homes were in need of repair. A local movie theater was showing "The Terminator," which had opened in the United States seven years earlier.

Still, it was great to soak up the culture. I had taken four years of Spanish, so I was able to lead a small group of us through town and into some shops. In hindsight, it might not have been a great idea to spend an entire day walking around town just before a major competition. When you are preparing for a big meet, it's always best to allow your body as much time as possible to recover and rebuild for optimum performance. Walking around town in the Cuban heat probably negated a lot of my preparation.

I suspect a lot of swimmers on the American team weren't taking the meet too seriously. The team sent to the Pan-American Games used to consist of the best swimmers in the country. People like Shirley

Babashoff, Steve Lundquist and Debbie Meyer used the meet as a warmup to the Olympics. Now, the "B" team is sent to Pan Ams while the best swimmers attend the Pan-Pacific championships. A lot of the other swimmers also didn't seem to have that mental aggressiveness seen at major championships. Case in point: After the third day of competition, the swim meet took a break for a day, and the team swam at a pool right on the ocean. After a quick swim, most of the people who still had events left played in the ocean. Having never been to a major international competition before, I thought nothing of the horseplay and shenanigans. If these guys could still swim fast and frolic in the ocean, who was I to care?

We lived in an "athlete's village," which consisted of egg-crate apartment buildings. The guys lived in one wing; the girls in the adjacent wing. Many of the guys' suites had balconies that looked right into the girls' rooms, and many of the guys took advantage of that.

I lived in a suite of three bedrooms with five other guys. Brad Bridgewater was my roommate. Dan Veatch was also in the suite, as was butterflyer Mark Dean, freestyler Adam Schmitt and freestyler Bob Utley. We all got along great.

My focus was easily distracted from swimming fast in Cuba. It's easy to allow your mind to wander to things other than swimming when you're in a new country and part of a historic moment.

In the prelims of the 100 breast, which was the first day, I swam horribly. I will admit that when I woke up that morning, my body didn't get the nervous chills that happen in the hours before a big swim. I hadn't thought much about the fact that my taper might have been ruined by my excursions around Havana, and that I hadn't done much mental preparation for the meet. I was one of the fastest swimmers in the world (in the top 20 at least), and I didn't see much of a reason to worry about my performance. I wouldn't have much trouble winning a medal of some kind. But my time in prelims would not have made finals at any other meet, and the swim was a major wake-up call. I needed to swim much faster to leave Havana with any dignity. How could I go back to my family, my coach and my future teammates at Texas and say I went all the way to Cuba to swim two seconds slower than my best time? I wanted to scratch from finals because I was so embarrassed by my swim. But the fact that I was seeded third in finals helped. Plus, I figured if I could re-energize and change my focus, I could win the race. All I needed to do, I thought, was get within a tenth of a second from my best time.

I got third in the final, which made me happy and sad. I was happy because I had won a bronze medal. I was sad because my best time would have won the race. Did my decision to taper for that national high school meet have some effect on the way I swam?

Hans Dersch won the gold medal, and Puerto Rico's Todd Torres, who trained at Louisiana State University, won the silver. I stood on the awards platform with my bronze medal around my neck, watching the two American flags and the Puerto Rican flag rise as "The Star-Spangled Banner" played. Though the anthem technically wasn't playing for me, I felt a major sense of pride and overwhelming emotion. So this is what they feel like at the Olympics. But no wave of determination swept over me. Most people would have sworn to do anything to have the anthem playing for them next summer at the Barcelona Olympics. I just lived in the moment.

I had no other swims until the final day, so I spent the next four days watching my teammates and cheering loudly. The USA won almost every event on the schedule, with a few major exceptions. Given his pedigree, Dan Veatch was almost assured a win in the 200 back, but he struggled and finished second. I knew he had a lot of confidence for his race, and to have a virtual unknown from Brazil beat him was shocking. Plus, as team captain, I thought of him as utterly invincible and unbeatable. If Dan had superpowers, it wouldn't have surprised me.

On the meet's fifth day, a Cuban named Mario Gonzalez beat two Americans to win the 200 breast. Naturally, the crowd was in bedlam. It was the only Cuban gold medal in swimming at the meet. The crowd wouldn't stop cheering for 20 minutes. Mario was carried around the pool. As an American, I was crushed that Nelson Diebel and Tyler Mayfield were beaten by an upstart swimmer, but I had to admit Mario's swim was gutsy. I got swept up in the emotion.

Just before the awards ceremony for the 200 breast, the crowd was still buzzing. And moments before the medals were handed out, Fidel Castro appeared in the stands. The crowd went nuts. Swimmers and coaches on deck scrambled for their cameras. I had forgotten mine in my room. But it was still a thrill to see Castro walk onto the deck and give Mario, Nelson and Tyler their medals. The crowd sang the national anthem as if they were attempting to make it heard 90 miles away in the United States. I can only imagine how Mario was treated in the days and weeks following the meet.

I was close to a lot of the swimmers on the team, though it was hard to get to know 40 people in only two weeks. Many of the guys were in college or about to start their freshman year, so I learned about college swimming and the excitement of dual meets. I also really felt the significance of being part of a USA Swimming national team. It's a feeling that words can't fully describe when the anthem plays.

My final event of the meet was the 400 medley relay. In the preliminaries, the second-ranked swimmers in the 100 distances of each stroke compete. That meant Bobby Brewer would swim backstroke, I handle breaststroke duties, Jim Harvey would take over on the butterfly leg and John Miranda would finish with freestyle. Our goal was simply to put the USA team in a lane for the finals. It was a fairly easy task, but I wanted to prove to myself that I was better than a 1:03.02. I swam my hardest on my leg, but only went three-tenths faster than my time from the 100 breast final, and with a relay start, it essentially meant I swam the same time. I was happy with that. It meant that I couldn't have swum faster in the final.

I returned home to find my family waiting at the airport with signs and balloons. You'd think I'd won a medal at the Olympics. My aunts were there. My uncle was there. My brother, mother and grandmother were proudly holding up signs of congratulations. One of the signs said "BRONZE '91, GOLD '92." I took my medal out of my bag and passed it around. They treated it like it was made of a rare metal.

There wasn't much time to rest on my laurels. Less than a week after my return, I packed up my mother's car and a U-Haul trailer for a long trip to Austin, Texas. I was ready to become a Longhorn.

My suitemates at the 1991 Pan American Games (from left): Mark Dean, Bob Utley, Dan Veatch, Brad Bridgewater and Adam Schmitt

Posing with my bronze medal from the Pan American Games with my brother's first wife, Karen; my brother, Darryl; and my uncle Bobby.

Chapter Five

Being away from home was both liberating and debilitating. I was glad to be out in the world on my own. I didn't have a car, so I saw the sights of Austin through the windows of city buses in the week before classes started.

As a 17-year-old plopped into the real world for the first time, I felt a little bit of fear about the responsibilities awaiting me. Luckily, I had a major university ready to wait on me hand and foot, securing the solution to just about any problem I had. Need a tutor? There were dozens ready to help me understand the week's lectures in my psychology class. Need food? I couldn't possibly starve in the athletes' dining hall, where we could go for seconds and thirds and have as much dessert as we wanted – for free! Need academic advice on which classes to take each semester? All student-athletes had access to counselors who helped us decide our majors. Life in college was somewhat similar to life in high school, only I didn't go home to my mother every night.

I missed my mom. There were some tears when she left me in Austin. Mostly from her. I tried to be the typical teenager who assured her I would be just fine in college and I would be too busy to miss her. Plus, I said goodbye to her in front of friends, and I wasn't going to have them make fun of me for crying.

But in private, I wrote at least one letter a week to my mom, filled with exclamation marks and declarations of love. I wasn't like many of the kids who only say they'll write to their parents; I enjoyed doing it. When I wasn't writing her a letter, I would call her to tell her about all the things I was doing. As much as I valued my independence, it was hard to leave the nest, and I didn't realize how much I relied on my mother, if only for emotional balance.

The eight other people in the freshman class had the same problems with homesickness, but they quickly found alcohol to be a suitable remedy. I had never had a drink outside of New Year's celebrations, and unlike my teammates, I hadn't made plans to use my new independence to discover the effects of alcohol. All I had to do was see and hear my teammates after the first week in Austin, stumbling into their dorm rooms around 1 a.m. when the beer kegs ran dry and I knew being drunk was not for me. I was glad to be the designated driver, and I never judged my friends for their behavior.

After my first three weeks in Austin, I began to feel like an outsider. Not only was I extremely shy and very soft-spoken, I was the only freshman not going to a party nearly every night. Many nights I had no reasonable excuses to stay in my dorm room and watch movies, so I would tag along to a party filled with mostly strangers and just sit there. It's not that I didn't want to talk to people; my alcohol-free brain didn't have the desire to hold conversations with people whose transition from sober to buzzed to drunk lasted less than 30 minutes.

As much as I wanted to fit in, I knew drinking wasn't the way to do it. The only thing I really had in common with my teammates was swimming, and who wants to talk about that away from the pool? I never dwelled much on being the outsider. It was simply the way things were.

I realize I am making this sound like I hated being at Texas, or that I suddenly didn't fit in with the swimmers, but that's absolutely not true. I never regretted my decision to attend college there. I did a lot of things outside the pool with my teammates, and the freshman class connected right away. It was only during the weekends that our paths diverged. While some spent the weekend looking for beer, I spent it looking for a good movie.

The first workout with the full swim team started in late August, on the same day classes started. It's a gross understatement to say I struggled in the first few months with the Texas swim team. If we were just devoting our training to 12 hours in the pool every week, I could have kept up and adjusted with no problem. But for the first time, a serious dryland program and morning workouts became a part of my training regiment, and my body had trouble adapting to doing three times the work.

I had never run more than a mile at any time in my life. Running never suited me, and trying to run three times a week in the Austin summer heat took its toll. Our dryland routine was essentially an obstacle course. We started at the practice football field, where we would run around the track and do push-ups and other exercises at various stops along the way. Once we were done there, we ran across the street to the football stadium, where the real meat of the routine was waiting. Without taking a break, we had to either climb a 20-foot rope or place our knees on a two-by-four wooden plank with wheels and use our arms to walk up the stadium's ramps. Then, we'd run up and down the stadium steps. Texas Memorial Stadium holds nearly 100,000 people. I recall somewhere between 150 and 200 steps in each aisle. The smell of pigeon and bat poop simmering in the humid air was so overwhelming it nearly suffocated me. One never gets used to it.

As the season wore on, the dryland circuit would get longer. We would have to climb the rope two or three times without touching the ground, and we'd have to "walk" up four stadium ramps on the planks. Some of the guys would run up and down almost all the stadium steps.

For the first few weeks, even though we weren't doing the full range of the routine, I never was able to finish the circuit before 3 p.m., when the pool workout started. I was always breathing too heavy to do the circuit nonstop, and I'd have to walk a little or take a drink of water. The other freshmen were performing well on the dryland circuit because they had been doing something similar to this in high school. Some of them were even keeping up with the upperclassmen. I felt like the kid who gets picked last for kickball on the school playground because he's too fat, too skinny or too asthmatic. I tried hard on the obstacle course, but my genetic oddities were showing. If blacks were supposedly born runners and averse to swimming, was I the proverbial – and literal – black sheep?

My teammates offered encouragement, but it was disheartening to see them finishing the run when I was just barely halfway through. Some days, I wanted to cry. I felt like they were laughing at me behind my back. I felt bad for the student managers who had to stay out in the heat to watch me finish.

I never made it to the pool by 3:00 on the days we did the dryland circuit. When I walked onto the pool deck, it was usually 3:15, and warmup was about over, or a team meeting had started without me. I was never yelled at, but I felt like I was letting people down. I was one of the top recruits in the freshmen class. I got a full scholarship. I was a national finalist, dammit! Why the hell can't I run a simple obstacle course?

I never really improved on the dryland course. After a few weeks, I was asked to start about 20 minutes earlier than everyone else so I could make it to the pool in time for the start of workout. That didn't make the predicament any better, though it made me work hard to keep as few people as possible from finishing ahead of me.

A month or so into the swimming season, I was tested again.

Every swimmer on the team had to climb the ladder to the three-meter springboard in the diving well and do a back dive. It seemed very easy: Close your eyes, hold your arms above your head and fall backwards. Most of the team was able to enter the water pretty close to vertical. Very few of them landed on their backs.

The freshmen are usually the first to dive. I didn't go first, because I wanted to see if I was the only one afraid of hurting myself if the dive didn't go correctly. My freshman teammates didn't have much of a problem with the dive, which gave me confidence I could do it, too. That is, until I actually found myself standing at the end of the board.

With my eyes closed and my arms clasped over my head, I was ready to go. On the deck below, my teammates were waiting in silence to see how I would land. I kept visualizing the dive and how it should be done. But I had a huge fear of the pain of hitting the water on my back or stomach, because I felt in my gut that couldn't pull off the dive correctly. I also feared that my teammates would laugh at me. I'd be the butt of jokes for weeks. I hadn't done anything yet to prove my worth to the team, and I desperately wanted this to be the thing that showed I belonged with them.

After a minute of trying to force my body to do the dive, I lowered my arms and walked away from the edge of the board. My teammates groaned. After a deep breath, I tried again, but I couldn't make myself fall backwards. The thought of a painful aftermath – physical and psychological – was weighing heavily on me.

After about 10 false starts, I gave up my spot on the diving board. I watched the upperclassmen do their dives with little problem. Why the hell couldn't I do a simple back dive?

When everyone was done, I walked to the front of the board and attempted to dive again. I was holding up the start of workout, but no one really noticed. I was quite surprised. I thought everyone would have started workout and left me there to finish the dive. But they stayed there. Even the women's team was offering up some cheers from their side of the main pool.

Thirty minutes after my first failed attempt, I fell backward. Before my feet left the board, I got scared. The way to complete the dive successfully was to not throw your head back to look for the water. You had to trust that it was there. But I threw my head back, which meant my back arched and my body over-rotated. I landed on my stomach.

I was in pain, but I didn't feel the need for oxygen right away. I felt my tear ducts filling up. I wanted to stay underwater and cry. I had failed. If I needed proof that I didn't belong on a national-champion college swim team, this was it. I stayed underwater for a while, to avoid the jeers waiting for me. When I finally surfaced, my teammates weren't laughing. Well, at least not all of them. For the most part, they were applauding and cheering. I suppose it was an achievement to simply do the dive. I gave a little wave and swam to the edge to inspect my stomach. The pain stung, but I didn't feel it very much.

At the beginning of every new season, I always dreaded the day we did the back dive. This became a familiar sight for the next four years: I would go to the edge of the board, certain I had conquered my fear. But instead of laughter, I expected people to yell at me if I didn't complete the dive. If I didn't learn from my mistake my freshman year, something had to be wrong with me. Each year, it took at least 20 minutes for me to complete the dive, and for four more years I landed on my stomach.

Despite my fears of being cast as an unhip teetotaler, despite not showing much promise on land or in the pool in my first months at Texas, I was well-liked on the team. You know you're liked when you get a nickname.

Shaun Jordan, who had won two NCAA titles in 1991, was a postgrad training for the Olympic Trials. I'd met him when I came to the school for swimming camps, and he was one of my hosts on my recruiting trip. I liked him because he was a natural leader and extremely outspoken, pretty much the opposite of me. When I went on my recruiting trip, he was one of the few people who told me what to expect at Texas, and I liked being told the unglossed truth. He was the major reason I decided on Texas.

Just before one of the workouts early in my freshman year, Shaun came up to me and told me I looked like one of those bears on the jars of honey. I had a little bit of a gut, which made the comparison more akin to Buddha, but I knew better than to argue the point. From that point on, I was called Honey Bear. As much as I wanted people to call me Jeff, I was officially Honey Bear. I was the only freshman to get a nickname that really stuck and didn't involve some manipulation of their last name. When I stood up on the blocks to race, I always heard "Go Bear!" instead of "Go Jeff!" Sometimes it made me laugh.

I began to feel better about myself when the competition part of the season rolled around in late October. I always lived to compete, and though I didn't always swim fast, I usually did the job required of me, which was to place high and score points so we could win meets. Plus, the concept of traveling to different cities about twice a month took the monotony out of the routine of training.

Though I enjoyed the competition, I never liked the dual meet format. The typical meet did not include a 100 breast race, so my usual events were swimming the breaststroke leg on the 400 medley relay and following it up with a 200 breast. I was never a great relay swimmer, and I couldn't understand why I never performed well in relay races. I wasn't more nervous in relays and I was never so pumped up for the event that I was swimming on too much adrenaline. Most would peg me as not being a team player, but that wasn't true.

I was preparing for three meets at the end of the season: the conference championship, Olympic Trials and the NCAA championship. They were all within six weeks of each other, and I was going to shave and rest for each of them. About half the team was preparing for the same three meets.

Before 1991, very few college swimmers had to worry about tapering for the conference meet. The NCAA qualifying times were fairly easy to make. But in my freshman year, the NCAA started to limit the number of swimmers that could attend the NCAA championships. Only 270 men could attend the NCAA meet, and to make sure they didn't go over the cap, the NCAA created faster qualifying times to cut down on the number of swimmers who would automatically qualify for the meet. It meant many coaches had to adjust their training for most swimmers who could not achieve the "A" cut without shaving and tapering. My best time in the 100 breast was just a hair faster than the qualifying time, and we didn't want to risk being "on the bubble." I didn't want to shave and taper for the conference meet, fearing that I would get out of shape by the time the NCAA championships arrived, and confident I could get close to the automatic standard in the 100 breast to be picked to swim in the meet.

I won my first conference championship in the 100 breast on the meet's second day, and came real close to swimming a best time. But I was happier that I had swum faster than the "A" time. It meant I would be able to swim at the NCAA championships. Out of my freshman class, only two others qualified to go to the meet.

In less than 55 seconds, the doubts I had about my abilities at Texas had been erased. At that point, it didn't matter that I couldn't finish the dryland as quickly as everyone else, or that it took me 20 minutes to do a back dive, or that I rarely was able to go first in the lane during workout. My teammates were cheering wildly when I finished, and it was great to stand at the top of the awards podium. Very few freshmen were lucky enough to do that in the Southwestern Conference, which was a much more difficult meet than Texas faces in the Big 12, where only three teams compete.

Winning the 100 breast was one of the happiest moments of my college life, made even better that my mother was there cheering me on. She hadn't seen me race in about nine months, and she was always the most enthusiastic parent in the stands. Even among a crowd of hundreds, you could easily spot her.

One of the reporters at the meet told me I was the second African-American to win a Southwest Conference swimming race. The first was Manuel Twillie, who won the 100 butterfly for Southern Methodist University about 30 minutes before my race. How did I feel about this milestone?

I remembered what I said at the Olympic Festival, when I was pelted with the surprise statistic. I said it was a great honor and hoped there would be plenty more in the future. But I was still shocked. In the 70-plus years of the storied Southwest Conference, a black swimmer hadn't won a race until 1992? Maybe it was just a case of black swimmers not attending SWC schools in high numbers. Not many black swimmers had come to Texas. I was one of two blacks on the Texas team. The other was a breaststroker from Florida named Tico Clark. Add Manuel Twillie, and there were three black swimmers in the conference. The fact that many viewed this as progress was lost on us, though the media was making us out to be the ushers of a new wave of black swimmers.

A week before Trials, I did an interview with an Associated Press reporter and another from the St. Louis Post-Dispatch. Again, I was pelted with a statistic: I could become the first black swimmer to make the Olympic swimming team. This was a fact that I subconsciously had always known. I had remembered how weird it was seeing Anthony Nesty's dark skin in the 1988 Olympics, and briefly wondered when an African-American man or woman would step up to race at the Olympics. There would be a few other black swimmers at Trials, and I am sure their hometown papers were priming their communities for possible history in the making. I felt like I was carrying the weight of an entire race, and it all hinged on one event. I did my best to block out the thoughts.

But no one made it easy to do so. Why was the public so interested in learning our thoughts about being the potentially first black swimmer on the Olympic team? I've read stories of Arthur Ashe, Tiger Woods and other black professional athletes who became barrier breakers. They wanted to go about the process of breaking through barriers quietly. When you're in the minority, as an outsider, you want to be a part of the normal crowd, to blend in. How can you blend in and just be normal when everyone points out that you're not like them?

The Olympic Trials is already a harrowing experience without the onslaught of the media added on. The meet is the culmination of years of sacrifice and training for every swimmer there. Most people have spent their lives thinking of nothing but this meet. I was preparing to compete in my first Trials, and I walked into the natatorium at Indianapolis a little unprepared for what was to come.

I was ranked fifth in the 100 breast going into the meet, and had a very good chance of making the team. Only two people get to represent the United States in the 100 breaststroke. My coach and I believed I only needed to swim five-tenths faster than my best time to grab one of those spots. Dropping five-tenths is like kicking a little bit harder on each stroke or having a fantastic start. But nothing is guaranteed at the Olympic Trials.

About one-tenth of one percent of the competitive swimming community ever makes it to Olympic Trials, so best of the best was gathered in one place for a week. I was warming up in the same water as Janet Evans, Matt Biondi and Pablo Morales. Yes, I had rubbed shoulders with the swimming elite at previous meets, but this had a different aura from the instant I walked on the deck.

I didn't have any time to adjust to the atmosphere. The 100 breast was the first men's event, and I was swimming in the fourth heat of the preliminaries. Fifteen minutes before my race, I stood on the deck trying to focus on what needed to be done while simultaneously watching the heats of the women's 100 free.

Then Jenny Thompson broke a world record in the final preliminary heat. I was as stunned as Thompson was when the time flashed on the scoreboard and was knocked out of my present state of being. They're breaking world records in prelims! As I heard the crowd cheer for Thompson, my body started to feel heavy. The weight of the Olympic Trials had officially hit me.

I shut my eyes and tried to block out the meet for a minute. I tried to think of something soothing, but nothing was coming to mind. The crowd was so noisy it was hard to block out the cheers.

It was time to swim, but I wasn't ready. My body felt like stone as I stood behind my lane. Kirk Stackle, a Texas postgrad who I trained with for the past nine months, was in the lane next to me. I checked out other swimmers in my heat, and they looked so relaxed and calm. I was shaking so badly I thought my organs would come loose.

The referee blew the whistle, commanding us to get on the starting blocks. I was shaking so hard I thought I was going to fall off.

The starter began the race and it was over before I realized it was even happening. To say the race was a blur is an understatement. In one moment I'm standing on the starting block trying to calm my nerves. In the next instant, I'm looking at the scoreboard, wondering how it is possible that I got fourth in the heat with a time that would surely not get me the chance to swim in the final.

As I climbed out of the pool, I scanned the spectator area for my mom. She also knew I hadn't swum fast enough to make the finals, but she still gave me a smile that, for just a few moments, made me realize that the bad swim didn't signal the end of the world.

The warm-down pool at the Olympic Trials is a well of sorrows. The defeated sit on the edge of the pool, trying to find an explanation for it all. Teammates often console each other with hugs and comforting words. Some find themselves sitting alone staring blankly into space. I'd had poor swims before in my life, but this one had come so far out of left field that I couldn't fully process it. I listened as the announcer named the finalists in my event. I had placed 12th overall in the preliminaries, four places shy of a lane in the finals. In 1992, there was no semifinal race. If you didn't make the top eight after prelims in 1992, you stood on the deck watching finals with everyone else.

I sat on the edge of the warm-down pool trying to find a reason why I swam more than a second slower than my best time. Was it wrong to shave and taper for the conference meet a month earlier? I knew there was nothing I had done wrong physically or mentally. To this day, I blame Jenny Thompson. It's better than blaming myself.

Many years later, I wonder if it would have been a wise choice to postpone my first year of college, stay at home and train for Trials without the distractions of college. Matt Hooper was supposed to start at Texas the same time as me, but chose to stay in San Antonio to train for Trials. He didn't make the team. Neither did Eric Wunderlich, who redshirted his senior year at Michigan to concentrate solely on making the Olympic team. He got third twice at the 1992 Trials.

Staying home to train with Paul Murphy instead of going to Texas held no guarantee of an Olympic berth. But I wonder what I would have done if the option had been presented to me. Would I have stayed in St. Louis? I had consistently improved under Paul, and I had only one bad taper meet as his swimmer. But I chose to swim for Eddie because I knew I would still be in good hands, and I believed the 1992 Texas team could win a national championship. More than 15 years later, there is no clear cut answer why it didn't happen for me. It just wasn't my day.

That evening at Olympic Trials, I watched Nelson Diebel and Hans Dersch make the Olympic team in the 100 breast. Nelson broke the American record. Hans' time was four-tenths faster than my best time. That Olympic slot would have been well within my reach if I had only been given the chance.

I didn't have time to ponder the what-ifs after Olympic Trials. The NCAA championships were two weeks away, and that was a bigger meet to everyone. Texas had a chance to win five straight titles, even though Stanford had the meet wrapped up long before the first swim.

One of the team bonding experiences that year was to have everyone shave their heads for the meet. I was utterly against shaving my head entirely, because I had never done it before and didn't see the point of going through the ritual. But after much prodding, I agreed to have my head shaved. Before I went to bed the night before the start of the meet, I looked in the mirror and instantly regretted the decision. Other swimmers looked great with shaved heads. I looked like an alien. I was certain my mother would not approve.

To make matters worse, the meet was in Indianapolis. I was in this fog that no amount of team camaraderie was able to fix. I put a large part of the blame on myself for Texas not earning its fifth-straight win and Stanford running away with the national title. I was part of the 400 medley relay that was unable to make the finals, and that cost the team serious points. I should have easily made the final in the 100 breast, but I only made it to the consolation final, finishing 11th. By the final day, I couldn't find the strength to get a decent time in the 200 breast, and I was the second-slowest swimmer in the event. Given the overwhelming 276-point margin between Texas and Stanford, it was irrational to think better swims from me would have been the catalyst for a team national championship. But I couldn't quiet the internal voices that kept telling me the outcome was partially my fault. I knew I had a lot of promise in my college career, but I couldn't pinpoint why everything was going wrong in March 1992.

I spent the summer disillusioned with the way my swimming was going after my first year at Texas. In my three championship meets, I had swum best times at the conference meet, then struggled miserably at the two more important meets. I wanted to rebound and swim well at summer nationals, but no teams would be picked at the meet, so I arrived in Mission Viejo, Calif., with little motivation. I almost didn't make the final of the 100 breast. I placed eighth in the prelims, getting an outside lane for the final. I knew I had the talent to place higher than eighth, and it was by sheer will that I earned my fourth place finish. The time wasn't very fast, but getting fourth place gave me a little more of a boost heading into the fall season.

Things improved my sophomore year. The dryland exercises didn't get much easier, but I was adjusting. I won the 100 breast at the conference meet, qualifying automatically for the NCAA championships despite not shaving or tapering. I got third in the 100 breast at the NCAA meet and swam my best time. It was one of the toughest races of my life. I swam on pure adrenaline. My major competition in the field was Tyler Mayfield of Stanford and Eric Wunderlich of Michigan. Qualifying third in the final gave me the motivation to try to get the second-place points, which weren't going to get us any closer to catching Stanford, which had another lock on the team championship. Not to say I am not a team player, but I stepped on the blocks for the 100 breast determined to swim for me. The points I gave the team were secondary.

I looked at that scoreboard at the finish and saw "53.76" next to my name, and all the cheering and screaming and applause was blocked out as I leaned on the lane line and stared at the time, as if I was burning the numbers into my brain. In the span of one day, I had dropped a full second off my best time. I hadn't had a drop like that in my pet event for two years, and I wanted to relish the fact that I had officially purged my poor 10th place finish my freshman year, my embarrassing swim at Olympic Trials and the subpar swim at summer nationals. I could see my teammates raising their arms, flashing the "Hook 'Em" sign.

Walking over to Eddie Reese, I was grinning from ear to ear. Eddie was happy for me, but only had one question: "Why couldn't you do that on the relay?" I had swum a poor split on the 400 medley relay the night before, taking us out of contention for the win and putting us in fourth place behind Stanford, Michigan and UCLA.

Just as they did the year before, Stanford walked away with the national team championship. But with the return of Eric Wunderlich to the team after taking off the 1992 meet, Michigan was able to take second in the team race. We were third, 70 points behind.

Just a week after NCAAs, I went to Nashville for spring long course nationals. I had an extra chance to redeem myself, and after the preliminaries, I wasn't exactly sure it was going to happen. I had a poor swim even though it qualified me third. I came back in the finals determined to race Seth van Neerden and Eric Wunderlich, and I did well, placing third. It was the first time I had swum under 1:03 in two years and it gave me some sense of redemption. Having swum a tough three days at NCAAs the week before, I didn't expect to swim close to a best time.

I went back to Austin prepared for a big show at summer nationals, which were to be held in my home pool. My great swim at NCAAs gave me some confidence that I could be among the top three finishers in the 100 breast and earn a trip to Japan as part of the Pan Pacific championships team. I felt like I was hitting my stride, and swimming in my home pool gave me confidence. I had three people to contend with in Austin. Tyler Mayfield and Eric Wunderlich had beaten me at NCAAs and were still on their game. Seth van Neerden was also on fire after missing the Olympic team the year before.

Somehow, I qualified first for finals with a fairly strong but controlled swim. I was only three-tenths off my best time. My competition swam remarkably slow, which made me excited and nervous. I was certain they had held back a lot in prelims and would be tough challengers in the final.

I stepped onto the blocks for the finals feeling like I was going to pass out from hyperventilating. I dove in the water with a determination I had never felt. I rarely take out a race with the goal of getting to the 50-meter mark first, but the adrenaline in my blood was taking over. I turned at the 50 and saw Seth in the lane next to me. Seth is renowned for taking races out faster than anyone, so to see myself pushing off the same time as him scared me. What if I went out too fast? I allowed myself to think that for only a split second. I had another 50 meters to swim. I felt good pushing off for the last 50, so I told myself to not back off. I sneaked a peek to my left and noticed that Tyler Mayfield, the man who was the rabbit last spring in the NCAA final, was far back. Knowing he was so far behind me made me happy.

My arms felt like rubber in the last 15 meters, but I knew I had a chance to win, and fought through every stroke to the wall. What was getting me to the wall? Not the fact that I could become the first black national champion. Not the fact that this was my home pool. It was pure instinct. Fight or flight. I chose to fight through the pain. The final three strokes to the wall were agonizing, but I didn't want to give in.

I touched the wall. I looked at the scoreboard. My heart fell into my feet. Fourth place.

How could I get fourth? Who beat me? Just above my lane on the scoreboard was lane three, and it had a "1" next to it. That was Tyler's lane. How did he make up a body length to beat me? Tyler saw the result and was celebrating. I perused the scoreboard again. Seth placed second. Eric was third. Those three guys would go to Japan and swim the 100 breast. Unlike the Olympics and World Championships, the Pan-Pacific meet allows countries to enter three swimmers in each event, though only two can swim in the finals. I was crestfallen. I had missed out on a free trip to Japan – and my first chance to race the fastest Asian, Canadian and Australian swimmers.

Then I saw the time. I improved on my best time by five-hundredths of a second, swimming a 1:02.46. Usually, I feel great when I swim a best time, but getting fourth in a race where I strongly believed I could place in the top three erased any feelings of joy. The difference between first and fourth was less than two-tenths of a second. What did I do wrong?

My coach walked over to my lane and gave me a little shrug as I to say:

"These things happen. You just move on." It didn't make it feel better. I got out of the pool and couldn't look anyone in the eye. I stood on the awards platform and meekly waved to the crowd when my name was announced.

Talking to friends that night, I found out that I essentially led the race for 99 meters. Somehow, Tyler, Seth and Eric had taken the right final stroke and gotten their hands on the wall slightly ahead of me. If I had known the race was lost at 90 meters or 75 meters, I might have felt better about the swim. But knowing I lost the race on the final stroke deflated my mood for the rest of the weekend.

About a week later the race was broadcast on TBS, and what I saw shocked me. Underwater footage of the finish showed me raising my head slightly before my hands touched, which slowed me down. But what was more shocking was the sight of Eric and Seth performing a dolphin kick as they took their final stroke into the wall. That is illegal, and all I wanted to do was take the tape and show it to every official in USA Swimming. But by then the results were official, the Pan Pacific team was already in Japan and video footage was not grounds for disqualification, no matter how obvious things are. It took many years for me to be able to watch that underwater shot without screaming in agony. If the judges had detected those dolphin kicks, I would have been enjoying the sights and sounds of Japan instead of sitting at home in the dark.

The team had a two-week break after nationals, and I couldn't get the image of getting fourth place out of my mind. If I had done just one tiny thing differently (kept my head down), I might have been on a plane to Japan instead of sitting in my house alone. I kept thinking about the words of consolation teammates offered. I felt a little bit of jealousy towards the teammates who had been able to place high enough to go to Japan. I even hated them a little bit. Eddie Reese told me I would have definitely swum faster in Japan. I couldn't get that out of my head.

Eddie had noticed that I wasn't improving as rapidly as expected, and knew something had to change in my junior year. Instead of changing the way I train or the amount of rest I get before a meet, Eddie suggested that I change my stroke. Apparently the way I swam breaststroke was getting antiquated and was a big reason why I got fourth that summer and had reached a plateau. This was the first time a coach had suggested a major change to my stroke technique. I had put so much trust in Eddie that I wasn't going to argue about it. I agreed that something needed to change, but what did I know about swimming that Eddie didn't? I spoke up a few times about wanting to go back to my old stroke, but Eddie told me to give it time. Even though I got used to the stroke, I never liked it.

Many times in my life, I chose to stay silent when I felt something was going wrong, especially when the person who suggested the change had seniority over me. Teachers, coaches, relatives – everyone was more right than I was. They knew the best course for my life than I did.

The new stroke involved lifting my head up a few degrees higher during the breath, and holding it there longer than I normally did. This was to help balance my body better and put it in a better angle to have a stroke that emphasized both the stroke and kick. What this new stroke did was slow down my stroke rate, and I lost a lot of power and it affected my sprinting. On the upside, my 200 breast started improving again.

Every once in a while, Eddie liked to surprise us with a 400 fly swim for time. We never knew it was coming until the set just before it, which was a series of 25-yard butterfly swims to warm up the proper muscles. Most of the team looked forward to the swim; sprinters like me did not. Most of my teammates could swim 400 yards of butterfly in less than four-and-a-half minutes. I could never break the five-minute mark. I was probably the worst butterflyer on the team, and as a sprinter, doing 400 yards of it was torture. The 400 fly was more of a mental exercise than a physical one, and my mind just told me to get through it and not expend too much energy.

The entire team was having a rough time with a workout in early 1994, just after Christmas training, when our bodies are put to the test. Eddie walked over to the sprinters' group and gave us the once-over. He could tell we were worn out. Eddie Reese rarely allows get-out swims, but when he does, the stakes are high. The swimmer or swimmers chosen for the get-out swim do not have an easy task. If the swimmer completes the swim as required, the entire team gets to go home early. When Eddie asked us who should do a get-out swim, the first option was like a punch in the gut.

"Honey Bear should do a 400 fly under five minutes!" The group cheered their approval. I wanted to sink to the bottom, breathe in a big gulp of water and die. That would have been less painful than a 400 fly.

My best time was about 5:15. I would have to drop 16 seconds in order to be successful. There was no way. I tried to make another suggestion, but no one would hear it. I could have said no. That would have probably meant we would continue with the workout, and I would probably get an "accidental" kick in the head or "accidentally" scratched by a passing swimmer. The alternative – doing the 400 fly – was the only viable option.

I climbed out of my lane and by then, word spread to the rest of the team that I would try this feat. I was so nervous. If I failed, the fallout would be worse than if I didn't do that back dive my freshman year. I'd be the most hated man on the team.

The men's team had gathered on the edge of the pool and was cheering loudly as I stood in front of the lane. I felt adrenaline coursing through me, but most of that was keeping me from vomiting all over the tile and into the water. The women's team had also heard of the get-out swim and had stopped their workout at the other end to cheer as well. Even the divers had stopped bouncing on trampolines. All eyes in the Lee and Joe Jamail Texas Swimming Center were on me.

Eddie Reese, in his trademark dry wit, told me there was absolutely no pressure. Everyone laughed but me. I had no plan for swimming the 400 fly. I just wanted to make it.

I dove in with a determination I hadn't felt in a long time. I swam the first 100 yards so fast I believed I was breaking records. At the 200-yard mark, pain crept in. It always did at this point. But disappointing my teammates was not an option. I felt a little boost of energy that lasted for 25 yards, then the pain was too powerful for endorphins. In the last 150 yards, I could feel nothing. The cheering from my teammates was my fuel for the remaining 90 seconds or so. Their voices were originating about two feet from my ears, and it was deafening. Even the most exciting race at Olympic Trials or NCAAs didn't seem this loud.

For the last 25, I did my best to ignore the pain and concentrate on the wall ahead of me. Only five strokes to the finish. Four. Three. Two. One!

The cheering began the instant I touched the wall. My time was 4:49. I felt like Daniel "Rudy" Ruettiger after he made the game-winning play. Except I wasn't carried out of the swim center on my teammates' shoulders.

We got the rest of the workout off.

We swam many more 400 flys after that day, and I swam under the five-minute barrier just one more time.

The rest of my junior year was borderline disappointing. My best meet of the season was the conference meet, where I won the 100 breast again and finally dipped under two minutes in the 200 breast. But at the NCAAs I got seventh in the 100 breast. My best time would have placed me second. Pure talent got me into the final of the 100 breast my junior year, and sheer will helped me to that seventh place finish. I didn't feel like a sprinter for the entire season. Changing the stroke was a big factor, as was the focus on my 200 breaststroke. I resented Eddie's demands to change my stroke, even though I never made any improvement. I should have gotten mad and taken control of my final year of swimming at Texas. But I sulked after the meet and allowed things to happen naturally. If I were meant to not go faster in my events, so be it. Maybe I was one of those swimmers that hits a peak at a very young age and can never salvage a decent swimming career. It rarely happens for males, but it does happen.

As my senior year started, things I had taken for granted started slipping away. Marty Hubbell had taken over my spot on the 200 medley relay at NCAAs my junior year, and in my senior year, he began swimming the breaststroke on the "A" medley relays more frequently. It made me angry, but I never spoke up to Eddie about giving me a chance to prove myself. I relegated myself instead to the "B" relays. At our dual meet against Stanford, I had desperately wanted to compete on the "A" relay, because there was a chance we could win. Just minutes before the meet started, Eddie announced that Marty would be the breaststroker on the "A" relay, and I would be on the "B" relay, which still had a big responsibility in getting crucial third-place points. But I wanted that spot on the top relay, and I decided I would still swim my heart out and prove to Eddie that he made a mistake.

After checking the splits, I noticed that Marty and I swam the exact same time. I'm sure it did little to convince Eddie that I had the ability to perform well on the "A" relay.

The dual meet season finished with meets against Texas A&M and Arizona State the same weekend. At both meets, I swam the 200 backstroke, an event I had never swum in a meet at Texas. But I was happy to do it, because I had always wanted to be a better backstroker. My lack of ankle flexibility hampered that goal because backstroke had become a kicker's stroke, and I didn't have the ability to do an effective underwater dolphin kick. But I swam well in both backstrokes, and to my surprise, I won the 200 back at the meet against Arizona State. I also won the 200 IM, and that achievement was noted in the Austin newspaper in its recap of the meet.

My reward for swimming well at the ASU meet was a white V-neck shirt handed out often to the swimmer who did something noteworthy. I don't know if that tradition still exists at Texas, but it was a tradition that had everyone clamoring for that V-neck (value: $1) every week. I only won it once.

My greatest achievement as a swimmer at the University of Texas was winning my fourth-straight conference title in the 100 breast my senior year. It had been a long time since someone had achieved that distinction. People told me Steve Lundquist was the last person to win four in a row, back in the 1980s. I got a standing ovation for that fourth swim, and as I waved to the crowd, I felt tears welling up. If my life was about finding some acceptance and recognition, I had finally gotten it after four years in Austin.

But the elation didn't last. My final NCAA meet followed two weeks later, and I swam poorly. In the 100 breast, I placed fifth, swimming the same time I did at the conference meet. As a team, we finished fourth, the lowest place for Texas in about 10 years.

Though Marty had been regularly taking my spot on the medley relays during the dual meet season, I fully expected to be a part of both relays at the NCAAs. I was a senior and Marty's times were not that much faster than mine. So it was with major surprise and disappointment that I learned I would not swim breaststroke on either the 200 medley or 400 medley relays in Indianapolis. Marty got those duties. It hurt a lot to watch Marty swim on those relays. I didn't think I could have swum very much faster than Marty, but as a senior I was possibly a little too presumptuous to assume the spot was automatically mine.

I got to swim the 200 IM and 200 breast in addition to the 100 breast at my final NCAA meet, but I didn't get a second swim in either event. So, I was only able to contribute 14 points for Texas. In the past, even when I placed seventh in the 100 breast my junior year, I had scored more than 20 points, taking relay points into account. Holding that fourth-place team trophy on the awards platform with the other seniors from Texas didn't feel very good.

Every swimmer hits a plateau in their career. For some people, it happens right before something remarkable happens. For me, it signaled the beginning of the end of my career in the elite ranks. I never placed higher than fifth at the NCAA meet in my last two years, and I never made a US Swimming nationals final after 1993. I couldn't get within two seconds of my best time after 1993. None of my events improved. I was sure my emergence from this funk was right around the corner.

It was a no-brainer to stay at Texas after my eligibility ended. I had another semester of school to finish, and I was fairly certain Eddie and I could work together to get a positive result at the 1996 Olympic Trials. But I spent those nine months in a fog. I think I just wanted Trials to arrive and be a part of my past. I was no longer in the top five in the 100 breast in the United States, and I had watched younger swimmers pass by me. The wind in my sails felt more like a soft breeze that was getting me nowhere. I knew I was feeling this way as I prepared for Trials, but felt powerless to do anything about it.

Possibly accounting for my poor performances in the pool was the fact that I had been having trouble in workout starting in my junior year. Sets that were normally simple were more difficult. I always found myself breathing heavily after aerobic sets, which are designed to keep your heart rate at a comfortable level. It was difficult for me to recover after hard workouts, but I brushed it off as a sign that I was training hard and would recover from it at the end of the season. But by the end of the season, my body never felt like it was ready to race. I was never 100 percent after the 1993 nationals.

That day at my second Trials in 1996 came and went as fast as it did in 1992. My only memory is back at the warm-down pool, the well of sorrows, silently announcing my retirement with a simple nod of my head. I put on my clothes after finals in the locker room without looking at a single soul. I couldn't bear the sight of anyone looking at me with any kind of empathy.

"Poor guy, he was so good three years ago. What happened? He could have done great things."

This time, the newspapers weren't that interested in me being their hope for the first black swimmer on the Olympic team. Byron Davis was the poster child. He qualified first for the finals of the 100 butterfly, and ended up fourth in the final. I remember watching that race and crying in the stands. I'd first seen Byron on the deck at the 1990 senior nationals, and had felt his career was going to end with a major victory. In all the stories I read after that race, Byron was very dignified and courteous when asked about being this year's hope for black swimmers.

When I got back to Austin after Trials, I had to think of what I was going to do with my life now that swimming wasn't going to take up a large chunk of it. I had been working part-time at Blockbuster, and after

Trials, I was promoted quickly to a full-time employee and soon got to manage my own store. I was part of the working world, and I didn't miss getting up early to swim anymore. I tasted the life of a normal person, and it was pretty good.

As the Atlanta Olympics began, I realized I didn't want to leave the sport. There was more to be done. What that was, I didn't know. I watched the United States rack up most of the gold medals in the Olympics and knew I had the potential to win one myself. I was certain there was still a great swim or two left in me.

I wanted to see if I could find that passion I lost sometime during my life in Austin. I wasn't fast enough to warrant a place on the postgraduate Texas team, so I hunted for options, and that's when I was offered a place on the United States Swimming Resident Team.

It meant moving to Colorado Springs, living in a dormitory and doing nothing but swimming. At the time, the Resident Team was just getting started, but it was successful. Three of the six swimmers on the team made the Olympics, and they ended up doing very well, especially Amy van Dyken. She had won four gold medals in Atlanta. Obviously coach Jonty Skinner had a knack for getting the full potential out of his swimmers.

The idea of making swimming a full-time job was slowly catching on in the United States, and the Resident Team was a guinea pig. All I had to do was put 100 percent into every workout and see no other goal than making the 2000 Olympic team. I signed a deal with Speedo to get a small monthly training stipend that would be supplemented by a check from USA Swimming. I would eat and live for free in the Olympic Training Center with other athletes who had similar goals. Life was sweet.

I was excited about the opportunity, and drove 13 hours though West Texas and Colorado to my new home.

The drive was fairly uneventful – at least until I arrived in Pueblo, Colorado, about an hour south of my final destination. In the middle of August, I suddenly found myself in a major snowstorm. Parts of it were so heavy I could only see a few feet in front of me. Having learned how to drive in the St. Louis winters, I was confident that I could handle the weather.

When I entered the city limits of Colorado Springs, I noticed the sign for my exit about a mile away, and proceeded to work my way from the far left lane to the exit lane on the right. Before I knew what happened, the front of my car did a sudden lurch to the left and hit the concrete median. In the next instant, the car fishtailed, with the rear bumper this time getting its taste of the concrete median. The impact pushed my car out of the left lane and into the other lanes of traffic. Miraculously, I avoided oncoming traffic as my car slipped and slid into the ditch of the road's shoulder. The car dipped violently into the ditch, then careened further into the grassy area, stopping only because a fence stopped its momentum.

I did not black out, but I was so dazed from the incident that I could not move for about a minute. I looked around my car. The large television in the back seat had been thrown against my seat, and I could feel the immense weight of the 30-inch screen pressing on my back. Nothing was damaged, but the forces put on the car rearranged everything, and nothing was in its proper place. As I began to move, I was glad to notice that all my extremities were intact, except for a minor cut on my right knee. Apparently, the impact of the car had driven my knee into several keys on my keychain.

I could see people running to my car from the road, and I got out of the car to assure everyone I was physically fine. Someone had a cellphone, and they used it to call a tow truck. As I watched the crumpled remains of my car loaded onto the truck, I could only laugh. I had worried about car failure while stuck in the desolate plains of Texas. Now, I was less than a mile from the Olympic Training Center, and unable to get there without calling someone with enough storage capacity for everything I had been hauling in my car. I had to say my goodbyes to the Honda Accord my mother had given me as a Christmas present my sophomore year of college. It was a total loss.

Posing with the rest of the freshman class of the UT swim team in 1991 (from left): Jeremy Szymanowski, Chad Kime, Murray Easton, Brad Bridgewater, C.J. Robie, Brett Weatherbie, Colin Beerline and Geoff Cronin.

Chapter Six

I sat in the car, shaking visibly. It was a warm spring day in Austin, Texas, in 1993, yet I looked like I was at the North Pole. I also had the feeling that I might throw up. It wasn't supposed to be like this.

Five minutes earlier, I was certain this would be the happiest day of my 19 years on Earth. I thought the man sitting in the driver's seat, a teammate of mine at the University of Texas, was ready to express his attraction to me after reading a letter in which I poured out my feelings to him. I wasn't expecting a wedding ring, nor did I expect a tearing-off of clothes in a mad sexual fury. But when I saw his car turn the corner to meet me at the designated place, I was certain things were finally going my way, and that memories of this day would always bring smiles and warm fuzzies.

It turned out to be another series of unfortunate events as I searched for my gay identity in college. It started in April 1992, a month or so after my dismal experience my freshman year at the NCAA championships.

During our brief break after NCAAs in 1992, I decided to try out one of those gay bars I'd seen downtown. I picked a night when just about everyone in the dorm, including my roommate, had gone to a party. No need to make up some lame excuse if no one would see me leave.

Since I didn't have a car, I rode my bike three miles down Congress Avenue to a bar called Charlie's. As I approached the building and locked my bike on a light pole, I realized I had no idea what to do. How do people act in gay bars? Is it a sexual orgy? Do I have to check my inhibitions at the door?

I wouldn't find out that night. The bar only let in those 21 and older, and though I was 18 years old, I doubt that I looked 21. I stood near the entrance, watching all the older guys with buff bodies go inside. I could feel the bump-bump-bump of the dance music coming from the other side of the wall. Most of the guys who were on their way in would stare me down, and I would stare back. Then they'd go inside and leave me there to shiver in my tight T-shirt. Thirty minutes later, Arthur arrived.

Arthur was tall and lanky and definitely Texas-bred. He was trying to look like a college student by wearing a baseball cap, but I could tell immediately he was at least 35 years old. His rush to leave the bar slowed when he saw me. He stopped in his tracks, and as we introduced ourselves, I felt very helpless. I had spent 30 minutes in my dorm room figuring out what to wear, how to act, what to do if someone picked me up in the bar. And I spent another half hour outside Charlie's rehearsing my lame pickup lines. But I couldn't remember anything I rehearsed when I talked to Arthur. It was obvious he was attracted to me, and that threw me off-balance. When I told him I wasn't old enough to go into the bar, I thought he'd run in the other direction. After I told him I came here on my bike, I expected him to laugh. But he offered to put my bike in his truck and we went to a bar that did not check for IDs. Arthur and I had sex that first night, and he was the first person with whom I'd had sex in college, and the second person in my life after Devin. I knew what I was doing this time.

After that night, I was like a bee to Arthur's honey. I had found my entry into the gay culture. Arthur willingly became my mentor. He helped me get into bars, which meant more Saturday nights out. I saw all sorts of gay people. I saw my first drag queen. I saw my first pierced nipple, on the first go-go dancer I'd seen. I saw femmes and butch men, leather bears and trolls. It was intoxicating. On some nights, I was sad when 2 a.m. came and the bars closed.

My shyness got in the way too many times of finding "tricks," or one-night-stands. I noticed a lot of cliques in bars, and it was tough for me to break into a group of people who apparently didn't want new members. Or, if I noticed a good-looking guy in the bar, I could only find the courage to flirt using eye language, which involved undressing each other with our eyes before one of us walked over and introduced himself. Arthur taught me the art of "the look," and I think I had it down to an art form. The problem was that I couldn't bring myself to take the next step.

By the time I was sitting in the car with my teammate in 1993, my comfort level with being gay had increased dramatically, but I had never considered the possibility of coming out to my teammates. Over the course of that year, my attraction to Doug Dickinson had intensified to the point that I found myself having erotic dreams about him and often staring at him in the shower a little too long. He didn't really fit into the type of guy I fall for. My type, if there ever has been such a thing, was taller and blonder. I discovered that during my many nights surveying gay men in Austin. But there was something, that intangible something that pulled me toward Doug. I knew my attraction wouldn't just go away; I had to purge it somehow. I knew if it went unchecked, it would become difficult for me to see Doug every day without losing all bodily function. That meant telling him somehow. If it resulted in sex, so be it. I knew I was taking a chance here, certain I was coming on to a certified heterosexual.

I wrote Doug a letter, one that was a couple of notches above those love letters you pass along in grade school. I didn't mince words; I let him know it was another man that was attracted to him.

If Doug had decided to come to the meeting place I mentioned in the letter, I knew his intent could have been solely to beat the crap out of me, no matter that I was a teammate. But my instinct told me he wasn't going to do that.

I thought it safer to hide behind some bushes while looking out for his car. Once Doug drove into the parking lot, I felt a deep twinge in the pit of my stomach. He had decided to meet me, which could only mean he was interested in me, right? When I got into his car, it would have been idiotic to try to engage in small talk. We both knew why we were there on this Sunday afternoon. I got up the courage to tell Doug how I felt. There was no violence, but I felt I'd been punched in the gut when he said he wasn't interested. He seemed so calm when he said it. I think he rehearsed it. Or maybe he'd been in this situation before. I was so nervous that I began to tremble.

Doug didn't probe into my sex life or try to find out if I was attracted to anyone else on the team. (I was.) There were plenty of agonizing stretches of silence.

After the sting wore off, fear set in. What would happen at workout the next day? He said what happened there was between the two of us, and I felt good hearing that, but would he make every effort to alienate me? We often swam in the same lane or adjacent lanes, so workout could be very awkward.

After that day, life continued as usual, as if to say our 10 minutes in the car never happened. Doug still wanted to be my friend, my teammate.

Doug stayed at Texas for another year or two, then left to pursue a coaching career. He once asked me to come to Wisconsin, where he was running an age group team, because he needed a breaststroke coach. I declined, but not because of our history. I just didn't want to be a coach then. But I did feel good knowing that he asked me because it was apparent that there were no hard feelings and he was comfortable working with a gay man.

I saw Doug again in 2003, when the UT alumni met in Austin at the NCAA championships. Physically, he hadn't changed much, and memories of that spring day in 1993 came rushing back. He told me he had been married for two years. It gave me closure.

Two years after coming out to my teammate, I found myself in the same situation.

The recipient of this next letter was also a teammate, and one of four others in the first house I lived in after leaving the dorms.

Surely, all four of my roommates had some idea about me. Not once did I bring a girl to the house. On very regular occasions, I could hear one or all three of my roommates having sex with girls. I turned up the TV in my room louder, or just covered my ears until it was over. Knowing that my situation was becoming more and more transparent, I felt compelled many times to get the obvious out in the open. But at the time, it seemed easier to lie than to tell the truth. They didn't really push me on my sex life, so why upset the balance?

This was during my junior year at Texas. Arthur had become my best friend – and occasional sex partner. I never asked him to come to my house, because I didn't want to skate around having to introduce him. We'd always meet at his house and go from there.

Arthur was in a rocky relationship, and we often talked about his options. In some respect, I learned a lot about relationships from him. I learned that even the worst relationship isn't worth staying in just because it's comfortable. Arthur's relationship was comfortable. It was also open. Arthur and I were "friends with benefits" for about two years, and it was nice. Since I wasn't sure what it would mean to have a gay relationship while a swimmer at Texas, having occasional casual sex with someone I knew was the only viable option. At times, I thought I could carry on a great relationship behind the scenes, but I knew it wouldn't be fair for my partner to be in the shadows. If some of the guys on my team could date in public, why couldn't I? Some of my teammates were dating girls that were held in constant scrutiny, and I feared that even if I was dating a gay supermodel with killer eyes who held the secret to curing the common cold, our relationship would be a bigger issue, and the scandal would tear apart the team.

I always got along with my roommates. We hardly argued about anything going on in the house. But one of my roommates often went out of his way to make me feel like I belonged.

Chad Kime had a girlfriend, and he hung out often with an obviously gay man, bringing him over to the house regularly. I often wondered how they met and what the gay man thought he was going to get out of this relationship. The other roommates seemed to welcome Chad's gay friend openly, which often made me think Arthur's presence would be no big deal. Or maybe my coming out wasn't going to be a problem.

One night, Chad asked me if I wanted to go to a fashion show. I asked him where it would be. He mentioned the name of one of the gay bars in town, going out of his way to mention that it was indeed a gay bar, in case I was completely unaware.

Trying to control all the sudden emotions coming over me, I nonchalantly said yes. I asked myself a hundred questions in a minute: Was Chad testing me? Would he profess his love for me at the bar? Was he trying to tell me that he might be gay? Did he ask anyone else in the house to go with him? Should I wear something sexy or very casual?

I was very attracted to Chad, and this invitation only increased my attraction to him. A lot of it went well beyond physical attraction. Most of the crushes I had on guys on the team didn't go beyond the basic sexual desires.

I spent the entire evening at the fashion show studying Chad more than I studied the models on the runway, showing off their abs and new lines of underwear. At one point, Chad shed his shirt on the dance floor and began dancing with no regard for his surroundings. Either he was totally comfortable with his heterosexuality or he was just caught up in the moment, when half the dance floor was full of young shirtless dancers. I couldn't get a read on him, but certainly this excursion meant there'd be no harm in suggesting something more.

Less than a week later, I made up my mind to get my feelings out in the open. Again, I wrote a letter because I knew I wouldn't be able to speak halfway through, most likely vomiting from nerves. Chad sat on my bed and read it quietly in front of me -- all of it -- and again I heard those words.

"I don't like you that way, but thank you for telling me."

No punch in the gut this time. More like a slowly deflating balloon. Because he was at least gay-friendly, I wasn't worried about sharing my sexuality with Chad.

I was let down easy. Chad said he asked me to the bar because he didn't want me to be sitting in the house doing nothing, which is what I usually do. He said he didn't know I was gay at all.

I wasn't worried about continuing to live in the same house or swim in the same pool. Everything went on as if nothing ever happened, but I always held out hope that he'd change his mind.

Having Chad know I was gay was kind of like Lois Lane finding out Clark Kent is Superman. You can just be yourself. We didn't go out to a gay bar again, but I knew he wouldn't be one of the few people who would give me the third degree when I snuck out of a party to dance at a gay club for an hour. In fact, I told him I was going to a gay bar one night, and he didn't bat an eye.

Chad left Texas to swim at another university during my senior year. Years later, he would move back to his hometown and become a husband and father. He sent me a picture of him holding his firstborn, and he looked very happy. Again, I got much-needed closure.

Through my five years at Texas, I found myself attracted to more swimmers than just Doug and Chad, but no one else was publicly informed of it. I never actively tried to seek out a relationship with someone not associated with the swim team, simply because I didn't have the time and energy to do so. The reasons I was attracted to some of the guys on my swim team had very little to do with their well-sculpted bodies. It had a lot to do with seeing them every day and reading a lot into the friendships I created. It's the same concept as people having relationships in the workplace. In a span of five years, I convinced myself I was misreading a lot of mixed signals.

I can't blame anyone at Texas for preventing me from coming out. I had nearly a hundred opportunities to do so. I can't fault the coaches. Eddie Reese and Kris Kubik always gave me the impression that I could talk to them about anything. College coaches are often like fathers, especially on men's teams. If I really felt compelled to let them know about my homosexuality, I had no reason to feel scared to do so.

And my teammates undoubtedly knew I was gay. Straight men don't include "Aladdin" and "Beauty and the Beast" in their movie-watching parties. I can't thank them enough for not confronting me about it. Maybe it was their way of saying they were totally fine with it, but I could never bring myself to stand in front of them and announce my homosexuality. Partly, I didn't want to upset the apple cart. But a bigger reason was my fear of just one disapproval of my lifestyle, and in a group of 30, there's bound to be dissent.

The team held regular meetings in which the coaches were not present. In those sessions, we were encouraged to speak openly. I sat in my usual spot during those meetings, on a bench in the team locker room at the top of the "U" shape we sat in, trying to find the courage to come out to my teammates. Every time I chickened out, I felt defeated.

I also felt my revelation would be something completely out of left field. Plus, what protection did I have if the majority of the team rallied against me? Without the coaches in the room, anything could have happened. At least in my mind, I could have been asked to leave the team, or someone could have suggested that I be prohibited from the locker room when people are dressing or undressing.

I wasn't the most popular person on the team, but because of my status as one of the fastest breaststrokers on the team, it was hard for me to hide in the shadows, as many could have done with ease. Had I been one of those who wasn't regularly depended on to help the team score at meets, especially NCAAs, it might have been easy to crouch into the background and just let the sneers pass until my college career ended. I was on a full scholarship, and that could not be taken away. I had no reference point for this state of paranoia, but being a fatalist, I made myself believe the only option was the worst-case scenario.

I liked being liked by my teammates. There wasn't anyone who I felt had a reason to dislike me, and I didn't want that to go away. Coming out would definitely create an enemy or two, because the odds are high that someone will not like the fact that a gay man is in the room while you are naked. Or someone will have staunch religious or moral beliefs against homosexuality. Out of the 30 or so guys on the team, I figured I might alienate four or five people outright. What if one of them swam in my lane every day? Would he find a way to kick me in the head during a set or spit in my water bottle when I'm not looking? You may think scenarios like these are preposterous, but I've read about them happening to professional and collegiate athletes. Many gay teens choose suicide over any physical or verbal abuse they might receive from those around them. Dealing with being secretly gay never caused me to fall into depression or consider suicide. I enjoyed my life in every way, but I hated lying or otherwise concealing a major part of who I was from people I trusted and liked.

No one encouraged me to come out while I was in college. God knows Arthur had every right to plead with me to come out, but he didn't. In my junior year, I convinced myself that coming out to my team was the best thing to do. Though Arthur had taught me a lot about the gay world, and I'd read coming-out stories of people in other places, I had no role model to guide me on the coming-out process. I rehearsed speeches many times, even while I sat in the locker room during our team meetings. I told myself over and over that the people who would be my friends would help me get through whatever my new enemies would dish at me.

But I couldn't face the realization that I would have to spend six days a week with even one person who didn't like me because I was gay. It was better to keep the secret than live with the evil stares in the locker room or on the pool deck. And what if this homophobe and I were matched as roommates in a hotel during an out-of-town meet? World War III, that's what. I wish my conscience wasn't so damned negative.

*****

In diving, it's normal to be gay. In 1996, the two American divers in the Olympics – Patrick Jeffrey and David Pichler -- were openly gay. They had endured some taunts and jeers, but this was post-Greg Louganis, so the negative comments were most likely very few.

I can count on one hand the number of gay American Olympic swimmers, and none of them came out publicly until well after they had retired. One of them was Bruce Hayes.

I'd read a story about the 1994 Gay Games that were happening in New York City. Some of Arthur's friends were going, and they made it out to be the Gay Olympics, which is what it's called by everyone except the people who run the event because it's copyright infringement. After the Gay Games, one of Arthur's friends told me Bruce Hayes was at the opening ceremonies and was one of the stars of the swim meet. I knew the name well. Bruce Hayes anchored the Americans to the gold medal in the 800 free relay in the 1984 Olympics. And 10 years after his historic swim, he was telling the world he was gay.

I never met Bruce, but I did wonder as I heard of his swims at Gay Games if he was a gay man while swimming in the actual Olympics. And was there anyone on the team who knew he was gay? If so, it obviously didn't affect his status on the Olympic team, nor did his eventual coming out have an impact on his legendary status. People still show video of his swim against West Germany's Michael Gross, and of course they don't preface it with "gay swimmer Bruce Hayes."

I knew about Bruce Hayes' swim at Gay Games because I traveled in those circles. But I don't think it was known in the general swimming community. If the Internet had the reach that it does today, every blogger and journalist covering swimming might have picked up on it. At the time, Greg Louganis made being a gay athlete cool. But we all knew about Greg long before he made it public. What if Bruce Hayes had done his coming out on a broader scope? Would it have opened the floodgates? It certainly did in diving, where being gay seemed to be more commonplace than not being gay. Maybe all the closeted gay people in the swimming community were waiting for someone to make the first move. As long as it wasn't them. I know I was looking for a Greg Louganis in the swimming world to make some statement. It certainly would have taken the sting out of my announcement to the guys at Texas.

Until then, I told myself it didn't matter that no one knew I was gay. When we all dove into the pool each day for workout, the fastest guy in the pool wasn't dictated by who he had sex with. So for at least two hours every day, I was just the same as everyone else. But I wasn't the same as everyone else, and that simple fact weighed on my mind all the time. Staying firmly in the closet was becoming a slow death sentence for my swimming career. I thought more about pushing down my feelings and emotions than I did about being a great swimmer. Because of that, the years 1992 through 1996 went by in a blur, and I could barely comprehend the situation as I blazed through college in a semiconscious haze.

On Labor Day weekend in 1994, I participated in the great Splash weekend in Austin, which included a frolic at the lake at Hippie Hollow, the famed nude hangout on Lake Travis. Just about every gay man in Texas makes their way to Austin for a nonstop three-day party. You could get lost in the crowd quite easily, but I feared being discovered by someone. My fear was irrational. If someone recognized me there, they were most likely gay or gay-friendly. But that was the dilemma I faced. The great legacy Texas had built over 25 years would be tarnished by the outing of a gay swimmer frolicking among other gay men.

I struggled greatly my last two years. I carried a lot on my shoulders, and I don't recall ever feeling like I did when I arrived in Austin: that life was never going to be this good and everything was going well for me. I just wanted to finish my senior year, remove that connection to the university and not care if a team member saw me out on a date or with a gay friend.

After my retirement from swimming at the 1996 Olympic Trials, I sat in my bedroom in Austin and tried to figure out what to do then. I had a job working at Blockbuster, so the financial aspect of my life was handled. I graduated from college with a degree in journalism, so I made it through college. But the biggest question was how to live my life without 30 other people instantly knowing and caring what I do?

The first thing I did was celebrate my retirement by going to a bar. With my inhibitions lowered significantly, I managed to pick up my first trick. After four years of trying, I threw every rule out the door and just forced myself on a guy who looked cute in the dark cavern of the bar.

I knew I was acting completely out of character, but it was working. I managed to bring the guy to my apartment. The sex wasn't great, and I knew it, but it felt good to be someone else for a little while. This other person I had become that night was wild and carefree. He managed to pick up a guy at a bar. He didn't listen to the negative thoughts in his head. He saw what he wanted and got it.

This part of me ruled the bars for all of May and June. I wasn't having sex often, but making out with guys in the bar was fun enough. I couldn't explain my behavior, except to say there might have been a lot of hormones stored away after almost a decade of serious swimming. I liked staying up all hours and living like a normal person, at least until the Olympics started in July.

*****

I watched some of my Texas teammates and others I knew from my many years on the national team on the television. And the itch hit me to make a return to the sport.

Shortly before I moved from Austin to Colorado Springs, I got a call from my brother. He told me my father had suffered his second stroke in two years, this one more severe than the first. The signs were clear that he might not come out of his coma. I didn't have much of a connection with my father, but the thought of him leaving this world was hard for me to grasp. I always felt that once I got a handle on my life I would attempt to rekindle communication with my father. There were many things he missed in my life – from my swimming accomplishments to graduating from college – and I always wished he could be a part of my adult life in a more present fashion.

Not less than a week after hearing the news about my father's stroke, my brother called me to utter four words: "John Commings is dead."

I had prepared myself to hear those words but I couldn't fully comprehend them. I prepared to travel to Memphis for the funeral, not sure what my father's family would be like or how I would react to seeing my father in a coffin.

I walked into the church feeling very queasy. This was the first funeral of a close relative, and I was starting to feel the gravity of losing my father. At the end of the service, the family members walked to the coffin to pay their last respects. I wanted to say goodbye to my father alone, but I couldn't get out of the pew. My brother walked to the coffin with me and held my arm as I looked at the lifeless corpse in front of me. In a split second, all the emotions I had expected days ago finally came forth. I sobbed heavily as it officially hit me that my father was dead. The last time we had talked was at my high school graduation in 1991. I instantly regretted going five years without conversation with my father.

Life had to go on when I returned to Austin. I spent a month working on a way to say goodbye to Arthur and all the friends I'd made in Austin's gay scene. Truth be told, that meant saying goodbye to maybe four people, but they were wonderful friends who made my closeted existence more bearable.

And as I packed up my U-Haul and headed to Colorado Springs, I prepared myself for the reality that I might have to remain in the closet for a few more years.

Me and the rest of the 1997 USA Swimming Resident Team (from left):
Dan Phillips, B.J. Bedford and Amy van Dyken

Chapter Seven

The United States Swimming Resident Team was created in the mid-1990s as a way to give postgrads a place to train without worrying about getting a job to pay for living expenses. The only goal was to make the Olympic Team, and many of the swimmers on the Resident Team were favored to go to Atlanta. Of the 10 or so swimmers on the Resident Team, three of them made the Olympic team, including four-time gold medalist Amy van Dyken.

After the Atlanta Olympics, all the members of the Resident Team retired or began a long sabbatical from the pool, so when I arrived in Colorado Springs in September 1996, the team was starting fresh with two new members: myself and B.J. Bedford, who was also a Texas swimmer and had just missed out on making the past two Olympic teams.

It was equally fun and challenging to be on the Resident Team. Having all of USA Swimming's facilities at our disposal was thrilling, but our lives were being paid for by membership dues of thousands of swimmers around the country, so we were under a microscope. Though Amy had done well in the Olympics, it felt like we were always first on the cutting block if the program showed any signs of failure. Because it was just me and B.J., cutting the team could have happened with very little fanfare.

But because the program was less than five years old, many of the top officials were willing to let it grow and continue to prove itself. I knew the success of the previous Resident Team was hard to follow.

I felt like an animal in a cage. We swam in a 10-lane pool that had a large window at one end. Visitors to the Olympic Training Center often crowded around the window to watch us go back and forth and back and forth. Many of them probably came hoping to see Amy, but she was taking time off to take care of shoulder problems. But when she came back to swim in 1997, the crowds hung around longer. I wonder if they expected to see us breaking records or doing something interesting, but most of the time it had to be quite boring to watch us.

The best thing about living at the Olympic Training Center – besides the free room and board, free food and monthly stipend – was using the technology available there. I had never been filmed underwater before, so it was interesting to see my stroke underwater. The camera was mounted on a track that ran down the length of the pool, and it was run from a room full of television monitors. We also got to use the Flume, which was a swimming treadmill that could move water while you swim in place. It was fun to try and swim breaststroke in the Flume at world record pace, which I could do for about 20 strokes before the current took over.

We also got poked and prodded a lot. The goals of many of our sets were to work on our aerobic capacity and how well our body handled the stress of the more difficult workloads. To fully analyze this, our blood was taken at least three times a week by pricking our finger or earlobe and drawing a few drops of blood. It would tell us how much lactate was in our body and judge if we were being overtrained.

It was difficult for me. The ideal aerobic heart rate is 150 beats per minute, and my swimming pace to keep my heartbeat at that level was pretty slow. In a set of 100-meter freestyles done 10 times on a 1:40 interval, my pace was 1:20. Amy and B.J. were often swimming faster than me in workout. I'm not sexist, but it was always disheartening to know that I could not keep up with female swimmers. My breaststroke aerobic pace was equally disheartening. I had no concrete idea why I couldn't hold a decent aerobic pace. I attributed it to the effects of swimming at altitude, where your body is robbed of much of the red blood cells that carry oxygen to muscles. I tried to ignore the fact that I wasn't training as well as Amy and B.J.

The hardest times were during testing week, which consisted of sets that helped determine our physical progress. We did the same sets about every six weeks, and while I did improve, it wasn't at the rate I had hoped. The hardest set was a 2,000-meter breaststroke for time. After the 1,000-meter mark, my body always went numb and I was on autopilot. It took me about 32 minutes, or 96 seconds per 100 meters, to complete the swim in the fall of 1996. About two years later, I managed to cut that down to 28 minutes, which was 84 seconds per 100 meters. But I knew my competitors could cover the distance in less than 26 minutes.

Our team grew by one in the summer of 1997 when Dan Phillips joined the Resident Team and became my roommate in the dormitories. Because we were such a small group of people who saw each other every day, it was very easy to become a family. Everyone knew just about everything about you, and it wasn't easy to keep secrets. I never felt closer to a group of people, but at the same time I couldn't bring myself to come out. As I mentioned, the Resident Team was constantly being watched, so I surmised that outing myself on this team would turn out to be more disastrous for everyone involved than coming out at Texas.

I didn't know any other gay athletes in Colorado Springs, which made it more difficult and uncomfortable for me. Among the 50 other athletes who lived and trained in the Olympic Training Center, wasn't there someone who shared this trait with me? Surely someone else was gay, but maybe it was common to hide it, especially in right-wing Colorado Springs. That's why I drove to Denver often to visit the gay bars there. Anything I saw in Denver was an improvement over the one gay bar in Colorado Springs, a literal hole in the wall in the outskirts of town, and if you didn't know where it was, you could easily drive by it. I suspect the bar's lack of flash had something to do with Focus on the Family, the right-wing Christian group that has headquarters in the same city. With their message of extremely conservative family values, I was surprised they allowed a gay bar to continue to exist within 20 miles of them.

I wasn't going to Denver looking for sex. My motives were simply to get away from a city where even being in the gay bar was deemed risky. On one of my trips to Denver in the spring of 1997, I noticed a man following me around one of the larger clubs. After an hour of noticing him around every corner, I finally got the courage to talk to him. The tall and lanky man's name was David, and though the lighting of the bar wasn't flattering, I thought he looked cute. And the fact that he had been stalking me all night added a degree of attraction and intrigue.

Amid the cacophony of the music in the bar, we managed to find out a lot about each other. He was a journalism student, and our common career interest gave us something to talk about beyond the superficial chitchat.

David was the first person I became friends with outside swimming since moving to Colorado Springs, and I often drove up on Saturdays after workout to hang out with him during the daytime. We both liked movies and generally disliked going to bars, so we hit it off quickly. Unfortunately, the timing of our meeting was terrible. About two weeks after we met, I was scheduled to go with B.J. and Jonty to San Jose, Calif., to train for six weeks before a meet in nearby Santa Clara.

I'll admit that while I was in San Jose, I didn't make a strong effort to continue to know David during our phone conversations. I used the time to try to stifle the attraction he was feeling for me, and to talk myself into keeping my relationship with David on a friendship level. Though I had longed dreamed of the chance to start an intimate relationship, I realized I wasn't ready for the challenges that would present themselves when I returned to Colorado.

First, there was the distance. We would only see each other on the weekends, and I wasn't sure I wanted to drive up to Denver all the time. After a long week of training, I didn't think I could commit to weekly drives to spend less than 48 hours with David.

More importantly, there was the issue of me being on the Resident Team. B.J. had found herself in a few brief relationships with male athletes at the training center, and the community is so small that everyone knew everyone else's business. If David and I officially began dating, it wouldn't be fair to him to keep it quiet. I wasn't ready for the positive or negative consequences of dating a man in this microcosm. Having known B.J. at Texas, I knew if the time came, I could talk to her about anything and she would welcome me with open arms. But if B.J. knew about me (and I always suspected she did), I was never pressured to say anything. Was this the swimming world's version of "don't ask, don't tell"?

When I returned to Colorado, David and I had a long talk. He had sensed that I was being chilly in our phone conversations, and it upset him. I told him I was not ready to date, but I would be willing to be friends. David's romantic life was similar to mine in that he was often so busy he didn't have time to date, and he was very introverted. Had things been different, I'm sure we could have actively pursued our friendship and tried to make it evolve into something else. Instead, David and I grew distant, and we hardly talked after that.

Though I was devastated by the loss of David's friendship, I didn't lose my desire to find friends, and it was certain Denver should not be my only option. Even in a town as small and as closeted as Colorado Springs has gay people, and in the fall of 1997, I found a new place to find them.

I bought my first computer and promptly signed up for AOL. Besides the e-mail, I found the chat room feature to be the coolest aspect of being in the AOL community. You could go into a virtual room and talk to anyone around the world! I got hooked on the chat rooms, especially the gay ones, and once in a while used them to talk to complete strangers. Being shielded by the anonymity of the Internet, I felt more emboldened to ask risqué questions and give more provocative answers than I would in a public setting. It had many similarities to phone sex, and I found that to be a worthy substitute, provided I was chatting with a moderately attractive person.

Most of the time, though, I'd be brave enough to ask for a face-to-face meeting. That always turned out to be disastrous, because the actual guy turned out to be much different than he described. After three or four attempts at public meetings, I only went into chat rooms to, well, chat.

One day in January 1998, I found Aaron. We started to chat around 10 p.m. one night, and we finished the chat around 2 a.m. He was great. Our conversation was honest and hardly passed into the realm of sex talk. We just talked about our lives and our values and our goals for the future. It was great to be honest and open to someone without it evolving – or sometimes, devolving – into sex talk. We didn't have a whole lot in common, but it felt easy to talk -- or type, rather -- with him. We agreed to meet for a drink later that week.

For once, the picture he sent online matched the real person. He wasn't an underwear model, but I didn't care. He made me laugh. I needed to laugh. Workouts sometimes drove us mad, and we craved social interaction with people other than athletes. Amy was married, so she had someone waiting at home for her. B.J. befriended most of the other athletes on the campus, and Dan spent much of his time watching football on TV.

After our first meeting, Aaron and I agreed to go on an actual date. I had already seen "Titanic," but I told him I'd see it again. I was more excited about going on an actual date than the actual events of the date. I was 24 years old, and I had never truly been on a date, so I was looking forward to the experience.

Aaron was a banker, but he could have had a good life as a comedian. He made me laugh a lot and was generally interested in me. He was a big sports fan and drank beer, and I was attracted to his macho personality. I talked a lot about my swimming experiences, and he seemed genuinely interested.

The differences between David and Aaron were intangible, but I wasn't attracted to Aaron just because he wasn't David, who was neat and orderly and more refined. I was attracted to Aaron because I felt I could honestly enjoy hanging out with him as a friend if we didn't become romantically involved. We never felt like we had to impress each other. We were always ourselves, and we liked that. I wanted to get romantically involved with Aaron, though I could see the same warning signs that I encountered when I met David. It had been six months since David and I parted ways. Was I ready now for a serious relationship? Because Aaron lived in Colorado Springs, the concept of a long-distance relationship was not an issue.

And before I knew it, I was dating! For the first time in my life, I had a boyfriend! The stakes were suddenly raised. I was no longer just a gay man trying to figure out how and when to come out to his teammates. Now, another person was added into the equation, and while it was a wonderful feeling, the logistics of dating him were difficult. I certainly wasn't going to introduce him simply as my friend. I had to come out to the Resident Team first, and I never found the courage to do so.

Just a couple of months after we started dating, I was falling in love with Aaron. I was being selfish, though, and I chose to protect my place on the team over being with him openly and honestly. Just as I did in college, I feared any backlash. If two of my teammates were offended, that meant more than half the team was going to be keeping their distance from me. Those were worse odds, and I couldn't stand to deal with that scenario, even if I knew it was far-fetched if not impossible.

So instead of being open and honest, I began deceiving people, and didn't think I was doing anything wrong. I would tell a half-truth every time I did something with Aaron. Yes, I was going to the movies, but I didn't say who was going with me. I knew karma would rear its ugly head during my deception. Every time Aaron and I went out, my eyes would dart around to make sure no one saw us together. What could I say if someone saw the two of us in the movie theater lobby? Unfortunately, I thought a lie was safer than the truth.

Aaron never confronted me about not coming out. I wanted him to be a part of my swimming life. Even though we did not have any swim meets in Colorado Springs, I wanted him to be able to come to the training center as my boyfriend. But until then, I did worry about my teammates seeing us if we went out to dinner or to a movie, so my eyes scanned everyone in the restaurants or movie theaters. Sometimes I convinced him to stay in.

I spent many nights at Aaron's condominium. In order to make it to 7 a.m. workout -- and not let Dan know I spent the night away from the dorm -- I would have to be back in my room by 6:30. I rarely made it. Sometimes he would have already left for the pool when I got back to the dorm. Other times, he'd already be awake. Every time I feared he would ask me where I was, but he never said a word about it. He had to know something was happening. If I were in his shoes, I would have given him the third degree every time. To this day, I wonder why my teammates never confronted me. I always knew the people Dan and B.J. were dating; to leave out my boyfriend reeked of embarrassment or fear.

It troubled me greatly to continue to tell half-truths to my teammates. It didn't create a dynamic that fostered team bonding or fun times in the pool, at least from my point of view. With my constant lies and deceit, I could feel the distance growing between me and my teammates. At the time, I was so happy to be with Aaron that I didn't think much about the welfare of others around me. Because nothing was said, I assumed everything was fine and didn't question anything.

I continued to sneak out to spend time with Aaron in the first seven months of dating, and the guilt only increased. Many mornings when I would arrive at the pool after spending the night with Aaron, I couldn't look anyone in the eye. If I made eye contact, I risked unavoidable questions, many of which I wasn't afraid to answer. I was approaching the 1998 summer nationals in Clovis, and I already had enough weighing on my mind to deal with the pressure of coming out. I tried to push all of it aside. In doing so, I was unconsciously pushing Aaron away.

*****

In July 1998, Jonty and I had a talk about my future on the Resident Team. Besides a few in-season meets, I hadn't swum very well since I got there two years earlier. One of the stipulations of being on the Resident Team and getting monthly stipends from USA Swimming was that I be ranked in the top 20 in the world. I hadn't been ranked that high since 1994, and Jonty said he was unable to keep me on the team if I didn't have a good swim at summer nationals. While it was disheartening to know that once again my swimming career hinged on one race, it didn't demoralize me. I had known for a year that my place on the team was delicate, and even if I came out to my teammates and gotten a positive response, I might not be there long enough to appreciate it.

In the early summer, we got word that Iian Mull wanted to become the newest member of the Resident Team. I was a little shocked to know that the administrators of USA Swimming were thinking about letting someone like Iian onto the team. B.J. was very much in the middle of the swimming gossip circles, and she told me Iian wanted to join the team in 1997, but wasn't ready to agree to one stipulation. I thought it was that Iian be closeted as a gay man while living in Colorado Springs, but B.J. said the only requirement was that Iian lose the body piercings. I didn't judge Iian based on his nipple and navel rings, but I understood why USA Swimming wanted him to conform to their standards. Many companies require employees to hide tattoos or piercings that aren't on the ear, and this seemed to follow those same guidelines.

It didn't make sense to me. Surely people knew Iian was gay, but no one in the administrative offices, including Jonty, seemed to care that he was a gay swimmer. He just couldn't be a gay swimmer with nipple rings.

That meant a lot to me. That meant USA Swimming wouldn't have much of a problem if I publicly came out and brought Aaron to a swim meet and held hands with him in the bleachers. Or at least their handling of Iian Mull seemed to project that understanding. It also gave me a little more encouragement to come out to the team, but I thought it would be best to wait until after nationals. The stress of trying to keep my place on the team was mounting, and I was dealing with a deteriorating relationship with Aaron.

I told Aaron about my career-altering swim that was coming up in a month. It was a career-altering time for him as well. He had been interviewing at banks in Denver, and had been spending a few nights there with friends. I never suspected he was cheating on me, and I never felt I had cause to ask him about it. But I knew he wasn't looking for work just because his career was stalling. He was looking for work in Denver because his career was stalling and his relationship was stagnating. He was sensing that a better future awaited him elsewhere, and it was an ideal time for him to make a clean getaway.

I got scared thinking about Aaron wanting to break up with me. Of all the things about to happen to me, losing Aaron was one aspect of the future I couldn't handle. I spent most of July in a mental funk, certainly not the state one needs to be in a few weeks before a major competition. On one hand, I could swim very well at nationals, but I'd be without a boyfriend who could share in my success. On the other hand, I could swim terribly at nationals and come back without a boyfriend to help console me. I could deal with the loss of my swimming career, since I had done that before. But I didn't want to lose Aaron.

But I didn't fight hard enough for him. Any mental and physical energy I wanted to use was to be saved for nationals and to create contingency plans. Mostly, I created contingency plans. I only had a month after Jonty's ultimatum to get into gear for nationals, and I already knew that my mind and body weren't fully invested in the meet. Yes, I had been training hard, but I never put any ownership in my career, at least enough to want to swim fast, make national teams and hopefully make the Olympic team.

If I didn't swim fast enough to stay on the team, what would I do? I had a journalism degree, so maybe it would be time to officially start using the knowledge I obtained in college. People who had graduated with me were probably already three rungs up the ladder. I began to create my résumé, realizing that my work experience was limited to two years at Blockbuster Video in Austin and some freelance work for USA Swimming's publication. I made my time in Colorado Springs more important than it was, and tried to make it appear that I was still actively employed in a full-time job, albeit one that had me in the pool five hours a day.

When I left for nationals, Aaron showed little enthusiasm and encouragement. I sensed something terrible would await me when I returned from nationals, no matter how I swam. I sensed Aaron was planning a quick getaway. But I needed to get through the week, and I put my thoughts about Aaron way in the back of my mind.

When I stepped onto the blocks to swim the preliminary race of the 100 breast at the summer nationals in Clovis, Calif., I didn't feel butterflies. I didn't feel like this was an all-or-nothing swim. It just felt like another meet. After swimming horrifically slow in my prelim heat, I showed no emotion. I just walked to the warmdown pool. I sat on the edge for about five minutes and watched everyone else swimming. I looked at the times on the scoreboard of the remaining heats and calculated that I had swum fast enough to be able to swim in the "C" heat of the finals, which were for the swimmers who placed 17th through 24th. The C final! I had gone from being centimeters away from winning a national championship to being just another swimmer at nationals in the span of five years. I think I had prepared for the worst, and the worst had just happened. What if I had prepared for the best? Would I instead be sitting in the warmdown pool preparing for the biggest swim of my life? As it was, I took comfort that I would at least get to swim again that evening.

Jonty and my teammates tried to get me pumped up enough to have a great swim in the finals, but I went through the afternoon like a robot. I had been swimming for 20 years, and my body knew what to do at nationals. My mind didn't shift out of autopilot mode when I stepped up for my second swim. My time was a second slower than what I swam in prelims.

As I sat in the warmdown pool again, it was as if I had traveled back to March 1996 in Indianapolis. Just as I did after my dismal swim at Olympic Trials, I sat in the pool in Clovis and nodded my head while saying to myself "I guess I'm retired." Looking back on my two years in Colorado Springs, I wonder if there was an aspect of my training that was sorely missing. I had come to Colorado Springs to regain my love for the sport, and two years later I had never really found it. It was the one thing that had motivated me when I was a teenager. It was what helped my times to drop so quickly. Every time I got up to race someone, I wanted to beat them, and that desire drove me to fast times. Somewhere in my 20s, I lost that drive. How did that happen?

At the time, I couldn't answer that question, but after more than 10 years of reflection, I realize that going to Colorado Springs to find my passion for the sport involved more than just a new coach, new environment and new training partners. It involved a mental aspect that I never fully tapped. I never made any goals. Given my history in the sport, it was always assumed that I would go to nationals every year, so there was no pressure in that. And as I grew older, I began to make assumptions that everything would continue to work out as it had in high school. I would just dive in the pool, look at the scoreboard and celebrate a best time. But that hadn't happened since 1993, and five years later I was finally snapping out of my haze.

Goals are an essential part of every athlete's progress. In Colorado Springs, Jonty and I talked about goals, and I nonchalantly figured that since we talked about goals, his workouts would get me to those goals. What else did I need to do? As I sat in the pool in Clovis, I knew I didn't do enough, but wasn't ready to grasp what I had neglected. Coaches do their best to put their swimmers on the right path to achieve their goals, but it is always up to the swimmer to make it happen.

I look back often on the 1992 Olympic Trials. Did I make a more specific goal than just making the team? If I had more mental motivation back then and invested more stock in my swimming future instead of believing wholeheartedly in my coaches, God only knows what would have happened. If I had made a goal of breaking the 1:02 barrier in the 100 breast, I might have won the national championship in 1993, and might have made the final every year thereafter.

I don't look back on my swimming career with regret. I never have. Swimming gave me so many wonderful opportunities. When I am at USA Swimming meets or college meets these days, I am remembered by coaches who were around when I swam. As befuddled as I am that people recognize me after all these years, it does make me feel like I made some sort of impact on the sport. Was it because I was one of the few black swimmers at the time and was therefore difficult to miss? Possibly. But maybe there was more to it.

To bring an even more conclusive end to my elite swimming career, my two national age group records were broken in the finals of the 100 breast at that meet, and I watched it happen. One of the new record holders was a 16-year-old kid named Brendan Hansen. Two years later, he would become a freshman at the University of Texas. Four years after that, he would win three medals at the Athens Olympics. I feel good that the guy who broke one of my age-group records went on to achieve immortality in the sport.

Before I left Clovis, I took my swimsuit and hung it on the bathroom doorknob of the hotel. The expression "to hang up your suit" is a figurative way to say you've retired from swimming. I needed to do it literally.

My return to Colorado Springs was met with emptiness. I called Aaron many times to let him know of my unemployed status, but I never got a return phone call. After two days of trying, I gave up. Not only was I homeless and unemployed, but I was single. Nowhere to go but up.

Since my teammates had gone out of town for their break, I was able to pack up my belongings and leave the Olympic Training Center without much notice. I had decided to drive north to Denver instead of trying to make it back to Austin. I always had fun when I visited Denver, and I figured it would be fun to officially start my new life in a new city.

Chapter Eight

The 70 miles from Colorado Springs to Denver on Interstate 25 takes you through wooded hills, grassy plains and majestic mountaintops. When I used to make the drive to visit Denver's gay bars, I would always marvel at the different terrains this small stretch of Colorado would offer. It certainly made the hour-long drive a little less tedious.

But in August 1998, my eyes were fixed on the road, eager to get past the horse ranches and small towns. Though I was very sad to leave behind my swimming life and my friends, I couldn't wait to see what awaited me in the real world.

I was driving to Denver without a safety net. I didn't have family there, and knew no one. I sensed Aaron had found a job in Denver, but it was clear he didn't care much about my life. I could have called David, but we hadn't talked since my return from training in California the previous year, and I wasn't sure if he was ready to talk to me after I sabotaged our relationship before it had a chance to begin.

I was able to find an apartment in Aurora, a suburb in the northeastern part of Denver. Because my financial situation didn't allow me to wait for the Denver newspapers to respond to my letters seeking a job, I decided to apply at a Blockbuster Video store. Since I knew the intricacies of running a store, I accepted the job as assistant store manager, which paid enough to cover bills. It also would allow me to replenish the savings I had to use to pay for the U-Haul trailer, write a check for the deposit on my apartment and buy furniture. Besides my stereo, VCR and TV, I didn't own anything of value. Not having anyone to help me understand the value of appearance and decor, I bought the bare minimum: full-size bed, futon for the living room, dishes and cookware for the kitchen, towels for the bathroom. I decorated the walls with swimming posters. It was definitely a bachelor pad.

The end of a long day at a normal job is somewhat similar to the end of a long day of workouts and dryland training. I wasn't feeling the usual physical exhaustion from exercise, but the mental exhaustion from the daily grind of social interaction and doing my job took its toll. I thought I would have so much energy at the end of a workday to explore Denver and find ways to meet people outside of work, but the only thing I wanted to do was sink into my futon and watch three hours of television before bed. So basically, my life in Denver wasn't much different from my life in Colorado Springs or Austin: Sleep, eat, work.

It took me four months to decide to join a gym and do some sort of exercise. I realized I was losing some of the muscles I'd worked so hard to have, and I could feel myself slowly getting out of shape. When I went to the bars, I knew the guy with the most ripples in his abs or the biggest biceps got the attention. I had very little else to offer a potential mate in the ways of financial or career status, so my vanity got the best of me, and I hit the gym twice a week. On my way in and out of the gym, I would walk by the swimming pool. It had only four lanes and was occupied by recreational swimmers doing sidestroke and very elementary backstroke. I never had an impulse to jump in and splash around for a few laps. I was never the type of swimmer who enjoyed working out for the sheer pleasure. I always worked out because I had to keep in shape for upcoming meets. Since I was no longer competing, I didn't see the need to train in the water.

But in January 1999, five months after my retirement, I felt an urge to jump into the pool and swim a 30-minute workout. I knew I was risking condemnation because I was by far the fastest swimmer in the gym pool, and it didn't seem like the swimmers wanted anyone to create big waves. Some people commented positively on my strokes, and I would smile a little and keep swimming.

The endorphin rush after that first swim was addictive. I continued to swim once a week for the next six months, just enjoying myself in the pool and not overexerting myself. I took long breaks when I felt like it and did whatever I felt like doing that day. Because I got bored easily swimming back and forth alone, my workouts rarely exceeded 30 minutes.

Even after six months I didn't know anyone in the Denver area, and I was often too scared to go to events by myself. I wanted to know more about living in Denver, and particularly, about the gay scene beyond the bars. I found a couple of gay publications, but they offered little more than advertisements about drag queen performances and drink specials at the bars.

In June 1999 I saw ads plastered all over the gay bars advertising Denver's Gay Pride Parade. What??!!!?? Gay people have a parade? I was blown away by it. I had never heard of such a thing happening. This was yet another indication of the sheltered life I led before moving to Denver. I knew that Austin had its Splash Weekend during Labor Day, but I don't recall gay people ever taking to the streets to show off their pride. If it did happen in a city I lived in, I must have been so focused on my swimming to notice. The Denver parade was going to take place in the heart of the city and run right up to City Hall. This was not to be missed.

On a warm Sunday in late June, I made my way from City Park in downtown Denver to Colfax Avenue just a few streets away to watch the Gay Pride Parade. What I saw on the way to the parade route was more than enough to satisfy my curiosity for the day.

There were drag queens, in broad daylight! Men holding hands with other men, and women holding hands with other women! Some of them were even kissing in public. I couldn't believe what I was seeing. The streets around the park and the parade route were so packed it was difficult to walk, and I think I encountered every variety of gay man and woman in a 100-yard radius.

As I waited for the parade to start, I played a little game with myself. I watched the spectators and wondered what they did for a living. The short and stocky man wearing a leather vest, leather collar and shiny boots was probably a necktie-wearing accountant during the week. The feminine-acting 20-something was probably a shoe salesman. The mullet-wearing woman looked like a truck driver, but could have easily been a schoolteacher. It wasn't surprising that there were so many gay people gathered for the event, but that there was a day that they could all come together and celebrate the joys of being gay. The journalist in me was curious about the genesis of the Gay Pride Parade, so I asked a few people. Gay Pride Month is held every June and commemorates the Stonewall riots in New York, in which gay people finally rebelled against police harassment during a raid at the Stonewall Inn in June 1969. It was a watershed moment for gay rights, and it sparked a lot of protests and marches across the country. I now understood why gay people had to have a parade. They had been pushed down to second-class citizens in the 1960s and 1970s, and the events of Gay Pride Month showed how strongly gay men and women felt about being treated equally. The fight for gay marriage is just one of the issues gays have marched for in the four decades hence.

When the parade started, I was instantly hooked. It was like Mardi Gras. Shirtless men in thongs passed by on floats, dancing to the beat of pulsing music. Many who walked the parade route handed out beaded necklaces – and unsolicited kisses – to the spectators. The cheering was deafening. The parade lasted for almost an hour and I saw so many organizations that supported gay rights. Some were nonprofits helping to raise money for AIDS research; others were trying to spread the word of tolerance. One of those groups was PFLAG, or Parents and Friends of Lesbians and Gays. On the PFLAG float stood a number of mothers and sons who waved to the crowd. This float seemed to get the largest amount of cheers from the crowd. I wondered if my mom would willingly become a member of PFLAG. That is, if she knew I was gay.

At the end of the parade, everyone hustled over to City Park, which became Party Central. Many of the parade participants had set up booths for people to learn more about their efforts. In the small amphitheater, musical acts were playing and lots of people were dancing to the music or singing along. I didn't know who the artists were, but everyone seemed to enjoy them.

I sat on the grass in the park and watched the people. I always enjoy watching strangers and contemplating on their lives. I watched the couples walk by and thought of Aaron. It was the first time since I'd moved to Denver that I had seriously entertained a thought about him. I wondered if he had found a job in Denver and was happy. Did he find someone who could make him happy? And was he here at the park? I sat there for a few more minutes wondering if he would walk by. But he didn't.

Many gay or gay-friendly organizations had booths in the park. There was a gay choir and a gay church. There were gay Realtors and gay-friendly politicians.

After a couple of hours at the park, I decided I'd had enough and wandered through the park to my car. At the edge of the park was a booth advertising a swim club called SQUID, or Swimming Queers United in Denver.

Curiosity stopped me cold in my tracks.

Sitting in the booth were four men talking to a group of people. I picked up a brochure that gave information about the swim team. It was an organized group of gay men and women that swam together three times a week and competed in Masters meets. Wait a minute. There were competitions? And there were organized teams where adults could work out regularly?

One of the guys in the booth noticed me reading the brochure and told me more about the team. He asked about my swimming experience, particularly if I could swim a length of the pool. All I said was yes without giving more away. He asked if I could swim all four strokes. Again, I was very vague and only said yes. He said there are swimmers of all levels and the team encourages competition, though no one is forced to do so. He said there are Masters meets in Denver about three or four times a year and there are national and international meets the team travels to as well.

I was in disbelief. I had never heard of any kind of organization that holds competitions for adult swimmers. I always thought that competitive swimming was not an option after a swimmer ended his participation with USA Swimming. In Austin, there were always adults that swam after our workouts, but I never fathomed they could be part of an organized team.

I learned a lot about Masters swimming that day, and the best thing I heard was that the meets have shorter distances than are normally done in competition. Not only do they do 50 yards or meters of all the strokes, but there is a 100 individual medley! The last time I did one of those in competition was at our annual college relay meet my senior year. I didn't need to know anymore about Masters. The fact that they had 50s and a 100 IM was enough for me. I got the location of the pool and promised to come to a workout after the July 4 holiday.

In the 10 days before I showed up to my first Masters swim practice, I wondered what it was like to be on a swim team full of gay people. I'd spent about a decade fully hiding my sexuality from anyone associated with swimming, and now here was a chance to truly be myself. But what did "being myself" truly mean? During all those years I agonized over coming out to my teammates, I never thought about the meaning of coming out to them. I just wanted to say the words and deal with whatever happened. I certainly didn't want to use the declaration to have an explanation for my lingering stares. I just wanted my life to be out there. That still held true as I prepared for my visit to the SQUID workouts. I figured being out among other swimmers just meant I didn't have to lie if the topic ever arose in conversation. And on a gay team, the topic was already present, and I was happy to be honest about anything.

The team swam at a run-down pool in downtown Denver on Tuesdays, Thursdays and Saturdays. Because the weekday workouts were in the evening, it was no problem going straight from work to the pool. When I got there on the first day, I walked out in my Speedo training suit. I wasn't sure what to expect from the swimmers, especially since most of them were of average build, which was about 10 levels lower than I was used to seeing on the pool deck.

I recognized two of the guys from the pride parade and said hello to them. I learned they were a couple. Patt Chaiyaroj was born and raised in Thailand and was one of the team captains. He told me about the different levels of the swimmers on the team and asked how fast I could do 100 yards of freestyle. No sense in lying to him. I told him the last time I swam a 100 free in a race was in high school, and I swam it in 47 seconds. But I could hold a 1:15 interval in workout these days, I told him, and he looked shocked for a minute. Apparently, that was a fast interval for this team. In the elite swimming world, I'd be in the slow lane. But I hadn't done a formal workout in about a year, so my goal was just to find my swimming form again.

David Gauthier was Patt's partner and the team's treasurer. He didn't swim. He made a passing reference to my semi-chiseled physique and I blushed. Everyone was extremely welcoming to me and was curious to know about my swimming background. After the workout was over and I made it through 90 minutes of various speeds of swimming, I officially gave my swimming history during the formal introduction done for every new member. For the final question, Keith, the other team captain, asked me if I was married or single. I mumbled "single," and the crowd went haywire at the response. A few of them came up to me and asked more about my swimming background. I was careful to let them know that I will probably never achieve that level of greatness again, especially training three days a week. I didn't want to train more than that, even though they told me there were teams in town that trained seven days a week. One of my stipulations about getting back into swimming was that I not take it seriously, and that I not get caught up in the severity of training.

But more important to me was the instant camaraderie I made with many members of the SQUID swim team. Patt and David had been together for almost 10 years and were my first official friends. Sensing that I had few friends, they invited me to their home often for dinner and conversation. I was beyond excited to become friends with Patt and David. I admired their relationship and knew I wanted the same thing. In my relationship with Aaron, we did a lot of things together, but we never had the closeness and intimacy that I saw in David and Patt when they made dinner or sat on the couch. Maybe that was because Aaron and I only officially dated for six months, which is hardly enough time to build romantic intimacy and start the foundation of a life together.

David and Patt had an affinity for musicals, which meant we watched a lot of old movie musicals on their big-screen television. David would put on records of Broadway shows and sing along with them. David had a wonderful singing voice. I wondered why he was an engineer for a car-wash company and not trotting the boards on Broadway. It turned out that he had a connection to the famous composer Stephen Sondheim; David's former partner was now Sondheim's partner.

The members of SQUID went out to dinner frequently, and this was my gateway to finding the gay culture outside the bars, since many of the swimmers weren't bar regulars. It was great to sit in a restaurant with a bunch of gay swimmers and just talk about life, love and other assorted topics. None of them had much swimming experience beyond high school and some college, so I couldn't find anyone who could tell me how they managed to carve out a swimming career and be gay.

*****

About a year after starting work at Blockbuster Video in Denver, I was promoted to store manager of a brand-new store in Aurora. I was grateful to get the chance to start a store from scratch, hire my own employees and institute an environment that I felt secure leaving at the end of each day.

My usual morning routine consisted of collecting the previous day's money and depositing it in a bank about a block away. Like clockwork, I headed out the door at 8:55 a.m. to be the first in line when the bank opened at 9 a.m. One day, I nearly collapsed when I got a glimpse of the man who would take my money.

Aaron had just transferred from another bank in town to the one I used every day to deposit money. Both of us were so shocked to see each other we couldn't speak for nearly a minute. It was good that there were no other customers at the small branch, because we froze in our tracks for a long time. I was partially happy to see Aaron again, and he hadn't changed physically since I last saw him 13 months ago. But the anger and resentment I had pushed way back into my subconscious suddenly surfaced when we locked eyes, and I did everything I could to keep him from knowing how upset I was that he nonchalantly dropped me for a career of banking in Denver.

I smiled constantly through our 10 minutes together catching up on each other's lives. Customers intermittently came by to do banking business, and while Aaron was dealing with other customers, I remembered how his smile and machismo turned me on in so many ways when we dated. My hormones were running the show, and I wondered if we could rebuild our relationship. Even though he had abandoned our relationship, part of me wanted reconciliation. I would have settled for one more night of sex as closure.

Trying not to blatantly ask about his love life, I talked about myself and my lack of a boyfriend. In doing so, I figured he would volunteer information about his own dating status. But he didn't, and as I prepared to walk out the door, I secretly hoped for a request for a friendly get-together, but neither of us had the courage to do so. I walked out of the building shaking my head at the curveball fate decided to throw my way. Of all the people from my past to see on a daily basis, why would it have to be Aaron?

I was becoming increasingly disillusioned about working at Blockbuster. I enjoyed the store I ran and the employees I worked with, but with no prospects of journalism work, I began to see my job as a dead end. I had gotten some rejection letters from editors at the Denver Post and Rocky Mountain News earlier that year, so I wasn't sure what other journalism opportunities were out there. But I figured I couldn't commit to a dedicated search while doing a full-time job.

As the holidays approached and the busiest and most profitable time of the year bore down on retail businesses, I submitted my letter of resignation, effective Dec. 21, 1999. I didn't have a job lined up, but I wanted to take the time during the days to find more work than I had found so far in cursory searches. I wanted to use my journalism degree, and at age 25, I knew my ability to get into the business was getting more difficult by the day.

That meant I would have no real reason to see Aaron anymore. In the course of six months of seeing each other three or four days a week, none of us had tried to salvage our relationship. It was enough for me to see him for a couple of minutes every morning, and I sensed Aaron was just fine with that as well. I wasn't sure if our relationship would be much different if we did get back together, even though I wouldn't have to hide Aaron from my friends anymore. I wanted to try out our relationship in this new environment, but it would stink of desperation. For a year I had been searching Denver for someone who could show me what it was like to date in the real world. Once I told Aaron I quit my job, I knew I probably wouldn't see him again. I didn't have any regrets as I walked away from the bank.

I had saved enough money to be able to stay in my apartment for two more months after I quit. I made a plan to find a journalism job before then, but it wasn't easy.

February came, and I had run out of savings. I needed to find some work … fast. I feared that I made a mistake leaving Blockbuster. I had vastly underestimated the job search process. Patt and David were quick to step in and offer their help. They'd allow me to live in the basement of their home as long as I needed to. I'd pay them a very low monthly rent and promise to find some temporary work while looking for a real job. I packed up a U-Haul and moved into the basement, which was a perfect space for me.

I enjoyed living with Patt and David. Since we had lots in common, there was never a dull moment. I learned a lot about relationships by watching Patt and David.

I applied for a job at the downtown movie theater in early February 2000, cleaning the auditoriums after every showing. You really don't want to know what kind of messes we had to clean up after the crowds left each showing. It was a job I really didn't want, but I got to see movies for free and I got a sufficient paycheck.

In late February, the tide turned. I was set to make another attempt to contact the editors of the two daily newspapers when I began to think of David, the man I briefly dated while I lived in Colorado Springs. When I last spoke to him, he was a journalism student in Denver. He probably had some good connections I could use. I had been in Denver for 18 months, but wasn't sure if calling him was a good idea. Swallowing a large wad of pride, I called him. He was naturally surprised to hear from me, but more surprised to know about my situation. He said there were plenty of opportunities available, but I might have approached the editors of the paper in the wrong way. He asked me to give him a couple of days to see what was out there, and he'd call me back.

While David made me feel optimistic, I couldn't shake the feeling that my lack of journalism experience might hurt me severely. I had done some freelance work in Colorado Springs for Splash magazine, which was USA Swimming's monthly publication. I worked as an unpaid intern, doing research and writing a few stories for the magazine. I was also able to write a few movie reviews for a Colorado Springs alternative newspaper, and had a lot of fun doing that. It was then that I was certain I wanted a career as a film critic. I put those articles in my portfolio, knowing full well that they were not up to the standards of a daily newspaper. But what else could I do?

True to his word, David called me with good news. He said that one of the assistant editors at the Denver Rocky Mountain News was one of his former professors, and David managed to convince the editor that I needed an entry-level job that paid well and could get my foot into the newspaper industry.

I called the editor and arranged to visit the newspaper and find out about the job being offered. The city editor and I sat in his office and talked about the job of newsroom clerk, which he assured me was not someone who fetched coffee and made copies. The newsroom clerks acted as the assistants to the staff of editors and reporters in the news department. We wrote briefs and obituaries, answered phones and handled the mail. It seemed like menial work on the surface, and I thought it would be a fairly boring job. But I knew I could probably never get my journalism career started any other way. My writing clips were tepid at best, and since I had just turned 26 years old, I was not a prime candidate for a job as a reporter at the Rocky Mountain News, one of the top 10 papers in the country. I knew it, and was grateful they were willing to give me a chance.

Two weeks after I started working at the movie theater, I quit that job to accept the position as newsroom clerk at the paper. I walked into the newsroom expecting "All the President's Men." Disillusionment set in after the first day. While there were some attractive looking reporters and editors, I didn't see anyone who had the movie star looks of Robert Redford or the punchy delivery of Jason Robards. But I seemed to fit in right away. I bonded quickly with the clerks in the sports and entertainment departments. And it wasn't an extremely heterosexual environment, either. One of the clerks was gay, as well as one of the department's editors, so it felt good to "talk shop" every once in a while outside of SQUID. My co-worker at the front desk was a mousey woman who seemed to be more secretary than journalist wannabe, so we approached our jobs differently but managed to work well together. I accepted the job under the pretense that I could possibly land a job as a full-time reporter after my first year, but that was not a written guarantee. I hadn't done any major journalism work since I graduated from college four years earlier, so I had to catch up to those who had thick portfolios from internships at major newspapers. Since I was only writing free obituaries and briefs, my personality and eagerness were going to be the traits that got me the job.

In June 2000, I moved out of David and Patt's home and rented an apartment in a high-rise building near the state capitol building, and a 30-minute walk from work. The apartment building was located on the edge of the Cheesman Park district, which was unofficially the city's gay mecca. Cheesman Park was where gay men and women gathered to lay out in the sun, play volleyball or other sports and just hang out. On the rim of the park were expensive homes and condos that were heavily populated by gay people.

*****

In July 2000, I was officially into Masters swimming. I had swum two Masters meets and found them thrilling despite my dismal swimming times. I was much slower than I had ever been since high school, and it was disheartening at first. I knew the altitude (Denver sits a mile above sea level) and my lack of rigorous training were big factors, but I wondered if I could ever approach fast times again. I was winning races in Colorado, but I made a promise to never compete outside the state.

One of the swimmers in Colorado tried vigorously to get me to join other Colorado swimmers at the spring Masters nationals. His name was Paul Smith, and after a Google search I discovered he was one of the best Masters swimmers in history. I could never swim freestyle as fast as him, and he was 15 years older than me! How could I possibly manage to keep up with people in my own age group? A little more digging unearthed more information about Masters swimming. Not only was there a regular ranking of the top 10 swimmers in each event in each age group, but there were national and world records! None of the times I swam in my first two Masters meets approached any records, though my swims did put me in the top 10 in a few races. Still, I was apprehensive about showing my face at a national meet. What if people knew me way back when? Certainly they'd be disappointed in my swimming. Paul tried to convince me that no one would really care, and that I would be just fine at nationals. But I knew I would have to train harder to justify tapering and shaving for a national-level meet. I told him to give me a year or two to decide.

Around the same time Paul began pushing me to consider a return to full-on competitive swimming, my teammates at SQUID mentioned two words to me that made me jump out of my skin: Gay Games.

Gay Games is very similar to the procedures and functions of the Olympic Games, where gold, silver and bronze medals are awarded, and pretty much every sport offered at the Olympic Games was offered at Gay Games, with a few additions. Only at a gay competition would ballroom dancing and bodybuilding be the most popular events. To add to the similarities, Gay Games is held every four years in different cities around the world.

I hadn't thought about Gay Games since I saw that article about Bruce Hayes participating in the 1994 event. Now, it was brought up at practically every SQUID workout during announcements. At least 10 people on the team were already making plans to go to the 2002 event in Sydney, Australia.

In the years when Gay Games is not held, an international aquatics meet is held in different locations. In the summer of 2000, it was held in Paris. Many of the SQUID swimmers were preparing for the 2001 meet, which was going to be in Toronto. I was just getting used to the concept of one gay swim team. The thought of going to a meet featuring hundreds of gay men and women was appealing. But no matter how low-key my teammates told me the meet would be, I didn't want to fly to a different country and swim in an international meet with just a few months of training under me. I had just started to reacquaint myself to the idea of training, albeit much reduced from my days in Austin and Colorado Springs. I passed on Toronto. But upon learning that the 2002 Gay Games would be in Sydney, I started planning for the trip Down

Under. Even though I was just returning to work, I managed to save money for Australia. Early estimates put the cost of the entire trip at $1,500. I had $400 in savings. My goal was to have the money to pay for the trip in full by January 2002. I was saving a lot of gas because I walked to work every day. That put almost $100 in the bank each month.

In swimming, I learned a lot about sacrifices. But I didn't have to sacrifice much in saving money for my trip to Sydney. I had never lived a life of great wealth, so as I squirreled away money from my paycheck each month, I never thought much about the things I could be doing with that money instead of dutifully putting it in my savings account. I didn't eat out very much, nor did I buy extravagant items at the grocery store, so I had no problems with eating Ramen noodles or rice every day. I hated shopping, so I had no qualms about waiting until the soles ran out on my shoes to get new ones. Every once in a while I would look at the balance in my savings account and know I was working hard at something worthwhile.

One day in late 2000, while rummaging through Patt and David's magazine collection, I found a copy of The Advocate, which is one of the country's top gay-themed magazines. The issue was all about the 1998 Gay Games, which were held in Amsterdam. Inside, the magazine had small profiles of some of the top athletes who were signed up to compete there. I flipped right to the swimming section, and nearly lost bodily function when I saw the name Dan Veatch.

It was beyond surprising. I hadn't seen Dan since the 1992 Olympic Trials, and the fact that my most recent update on his life was that he had competed in the 1998 Gay Games was shocking to me. My mind instantly went back to those two weeks in Cuba, when we were part of the Pan-American Games team. I knew I had been attracted to Dan on that trip. Now I began to wonder if he might have been attracted to me as well. But would anything have come of it?

I read his profile, which mentioned that he was an Olympian and now living in San Francisco with his partner of two years. I was shocked. Though I had read about Bruce Hayes participating in the 1994 Gay Games, Dan was the first major swimmer I knew personally who was gay. I got the sense that Dan was closeted in 1991, and it made me feel a little better knowing I was not alone in figuring out my life as a gay man nine years earlier.

While my savings account grew, I went online to find out more about the Gay Games, mostly to find out if any other prominent swimmers had competed there. I discovered that Alex Kostich, who was also on the Pan-American team in 1991, swam at the 1998 Gay Games.

A whole new perspective on being a gay swimmer revealed itself when I opened that copy of The Advocate. Suddenly, I began to think of other swimmers who might have been silently gay. Were they quiet about their homosexuality during their swimming careers because it was taboo to be gay? Or was it simply not a big deal, and thus they never made it an issue. In any case, to know that Dan and Alex were able to swim at Gay Games made me realize I wasn't going through this alone. There had been others who had great swimming careers while being gay.

It was great to live in Denver. When Christmas 2000 rolled around, I hardly missed the routine of full-time swimming. I missed my friends from Colorado Springs, though e-mail helped keep in touch with them. Watching the 2000 Olympics was the first time I didn't wish I was racing for a medal instead of sitting on my ass eating junk food. I spent that week cheering for people I knew well and had raced against. Amy Van Dyken and B.J. Bedford had made the Olympic Team and were representing the Resident Team well, but I had heard support was waning, and rumors started floating that the Resident Team was going to be cut. Part of me was very happy I got out when I did. Besides, I was finding the real world a fun place to be.

After that first year at the Rocky Mountain News, we got hit with a sledgehammer: In early spring 2001, our paper and the Denver Post began working under a Joint Operating Agreement, which meant the two papers would have separate newsrooms but share in the profits. This came after many years of what was called "penny wars," in which the newspapers charged a penny a day for home delivery in an attempt to lure people to them. In a way, it helped both papers, but it cut down on the bottom line. Many of us feared it meant the end of the Rocky, and a lot of people quit the paper the first month after the announcement in order to beat the rumors of sudden layoffs. Many others had faith in the paper, or were too advanced in their careers to leave and find some other employment. I stayed because I still enjoyed working there.

By the spring of 2001, I still wasn't ready to accept Paul's invitation to compete at Masters nationals. I wasn't training more than three times a week. I visited the Denver University Masters team occasionally, and while it was great to find a group of guys that could push me harder in workout, it was too intense for me at the time. Since returning to the pool in 1999, workouts were obviously easier to get through than before, and not just because they were shorter. I was able to stop and rest if I wanted and no one yelled at me about it. I needed to rest often because my heart rate still had trouble returning to an aerobic level after a fast swim. It didn't concern me in my last year in college or my two years in Colorado Springs, and I certainly didn't give it more than a minute of concern during the start of my Masters career. I was simply out of shape, and my heart wasn't in the same condition as it was. I knew the best way to do make my heart stronger was to train more, but SQUID was only available three times a week, and I didn't want to defect to the DU Masters team. So I stayed with my training program, which did not improve my swimming in the spring of 2001. I was putting up the same times I swam in 2000, and I began to accept the fact that I was only going to go as fast as 59 seconds in a 100-yard breaststroke. Three years earlier, I was able to swim that race in 56 seconds during the hard training phase of the season.

Life was good — almost. In spring 2000, I was dealing with the repercussions of a life-altering event that was doing more damage than I expected.

I was fortunate to find three great friends and training partners when I joined SQUID (from left): Patt Chaiyaroj, Corey Parker and Keith Pryor.

Riding on a fire truck in the 2001 Denver Gay Pride parade

Chapter Nine

After that first sexual encounter with Devin between my freshman and sophomore years in high school, I was certain about my sexuality. And thanks to late-night cable, I tested out my blooming sexual urges while watching soft-core pornography on Cinemax or HBO. I never found myself wide-eyed and slack-jawed over a woman's breasts. Female full-frontal nudity made me scrunch my face. But the well-toned guys who were having sex with these women had my full attention. Sometimes my mother would wake up in the middle of the night and I'd change the channel to something more appropriate. The creaks in the hallway floor were lifesavers.

If I told my mom that I was attracted to those guys on the TV, I knew she'd throw me out of the house, into the streets or into the care of an aunt or my grandparents. If you remember the moment in the TV show "Desperate Housewives" when the mother drops off her gay son in the middle of nowhere with a wad of money, you have a good idea about what I imagined would happen to me.

She never explicitly told me she was against the homosexual lifestyle (again, we didn't have The Talk), but I could sense her disdain for gay people. After my encounter with Fr. Smith in the yearbook office my senior year of high school, I could tell my mother's thoughts about my being gay were fueled by fear more than concern. My mother is extremely religious and could be viewed as someone who takes the words in the Bible literally. If God said a man shouldn't lie down with his own kind more than 2,000 years ago, that was still true today for her. Never mind that God also allowed a father to kill his son.

My brother moved out when I was 12, and from then on it was just me and Mom. For the most part, everything was wonderful in the house. I was a great student and was doing well in the pool, so I was always in good favor with my mother. But as I got older and preferred to stay at home on the weekends instead of going out with friends – or dating – I felt I was causing a rift that I wasn't sure how to fix. I was certain my hesitancy to date girls or broach the subject with my mother was sending up red flags for her, but she hardly ever pressed for details. I wanted it to stay that way for as long as possible. My brother and Mom had a couple of falling-out spells, and the repercussions lasted for months, or longer. Coming out would cause a serious falling-out, and I was afraid of being out in the big world without my mother. Turning to my father was not an option, since he lived far away and we rarely spoke.

When I got to college, those worries didn't go away. I was on a full scholarship at Texas, so I didn't have to rely on my mother financially. But she was a source of comfort during my freshman year when I felt out of place on the swim team or didn't think I could handle the classes I picked.

While I was preparing for a trip home during Christmas break in 1991, I resolved to come out to my mother. I was almost 18 years old, though four months on my own wasn't long enough to make me feel like an adult. I wanted to be able to explore my sexuality in Austin once the swim season was over in March, and coming out to my family was just the step forward I needed. Once my mother knew, telling the rest of my family would be easy, and maybe telling my teammates wouldn't be so hard, either. The result of all of that would likely lead to a much happier life. But I talked myself out of it that year. Those five days at home were so wonderful. It was the first time my mother and I had seen each other since I left for college. The thought of ruining that Hallmark moment turned me into a coward.

116

I would talk myself out of it for eight more years. Each time, I would summon the courage to make the announcement on the last day of my trip home and make a clean getaway in case all hell broke loose. It was the thought of all hell breaking loose that scared me. I figured keeping a secret from my mother was better than never being able to talk to her again.

It wasn't a good way to live. I was hiding something from one of the closest people – if not the closest person – in my life, and it also happened to be my mother.

I could have told my brother first. I was certain Darryl wouldn't respond negatively. He could have been the test for me. But I felt strongly that my mother needed to be the first to know. The betrayal had to stop. My mother wanted me to give her grandchildren and I didn't want to keep giving her empty reasons why I wasn't continuing the bloodline. Whether or not she had a suspicion I was gay, she needed to know about this part of my life. I didn't need her approval, but I really wanted her blessing.

In 1999, I gave myself a mental slap. I was 25 years old. What was I scared of this time? I was going to St. Louis for Christmas with the family, and after the presents were opened, I was going to spill the news.

I have to thank my best friends, Patt and David, for their encouragement. David told me his coming-out to his mother was worse than he imagined, but it was a necessary thing. He now felt more comfortable in his skin, even though it meant a strained family relationship.

I had nothing to lose. I had quit my job as store manager for Blockbuster Video in Denver because I wanted to start my journalism career. I was siphoning money from my savings while I looked for work and was about a month away from moving into Patt and David's basement.

Hell breaking loose couldn't be much worse.

I waited until the night before I was to go back to Denver. My brother usually comes to the house to say goodbye before I leave, but I called him to make sure he'd be there when I made the announcement. I figured he'd make a good buffer. Or a good shield if things were thrown.

But he called to say he was tied up with work and couldn't make it. My natural instincts told me to wait until next year. But I gave myself another mental slap and walked into my mother's study, where she was

117

playing computer games.

I sat down on her old leather rocking recliner, which was almost as old as I was. My breathing was labored. My heart raced.

"So," I said in an effort to get her attention. "Can we talk for a bit?"

The look she gave me when she turned around made me realize she had been waiting for this conversation for almost 10 years. Maybe she knew that I had been putting this off for almost 10 years and was steeling herself for the fact that I was finally going to make the announcement. If she had been expecting this talk, she didn't look too happy that it was happening.

I swallowed hard. There was no saliva in my mouth.

"Well, I'm not going to prolong this with small talk. Mom, I'm gay."

What I am about to describe probably lasted for 30 minutes, but it felt like the world stood still during The Talk. And though everything went exactly as I expected (though not as I hoped), I still felt tiny jolts with each sentence she uttered.

She asked me how long I had known this. I told her about 10 years for sure. She wanted to know why I didn't tell her before. I told her I was always afraid of this exact moment, of the look she was giving me.

She never blinked. You know that famous moment in the movie "Marathon Man" when Laurence Olivier is pulling out Dustin Hoffman's teeth? I would have submitted to that torture over the agony of staring into my mother's unflinching eyes for unheralded lengths of time.

She never raised her voice. She said something could have been done if I told her earlier. She didn't go into specifics, but I was certain that meant something along the lines of shock therapy or "conversion therapy," which probably incorporated some shock therapy into its program.

Of course, she began to blame herself, as do most parents who believe homosexuality is brought on by wayward parenting. In the most reassuring voice I could muster from my dry mouth, I told her this was not because of anything she did or did not do. I tried to convince her that being gay is a trait in your DNA, not necessarily something that society helps create. It was just the way I am.

She brought up the "s-word," and when she said that homosexuality was a sin, I thought she'd whip out her Bible and lay it on my head. As the conversation wore on, it was clear there would be no sign of understanding coming from her. Given our history, I was sure some statement of love was inevitable.

That statement never came. I still hoped for it after she disowned me by saying "I have a child, but not a son." I still hoped for it when she said she'd mention me only casually when people asked her about me. I still hoped for it when I told her I still loved her, no matter what happened. I still hoped for it when she warned me against telling my grandmother, since the news would kill her, not meaning it as a euphemism. I still hoped for it when she walked into her room, turned off the light and went to sleep.

Somewhere in the middle of all this, my brother called back. I told him I was gay. He said he had always suspected it, but didn't expect to be told then. He asked how Mom reacted. I told him, and he wasn't surprised. He told me he loved me, and I almost cried. It didn't sound forced. It was real love coming from my brother. I thanked him. He told me he'd come to see me at the airport in the morning. I thanked him again. My mother heard my side of the conversation. Certainly, she figured out that Darryl was fine with my sexuality. I told her what Darryl said when I hung up. If she was upset, I think Darryl siding with me made her more angry.

So far, I had told two people in my family. One still loved me, the other – not so much.

The next morning was steeped in awkwardness. My mother had to drive me to the airport. I was surprised she didn't toss me into a cab. We didn't speak to each other until the car drove up to the airport. Fifteen wrenching minutes of silence.

"Do you have anything to say to me?" my mother asked as the car stopped in front of the terminal.

"The same thing I told you last night. That I love you."

What she searching for me to say? "Surprise, Mom! I was only kidding! I'm actually a raging heterosexual! You're on 'Candid Camera!'" Was she expecting an apology? For what?

No response.

"Bye, Mom." I got out of the car, grabbed my bags and walked into the terminal. I forced myself to not look back. I knew she wasn't going to dash out of the car, shower me with kisses and sign up for PFLAG (Parents & Friends of Lesbians and Gays). I knew she was driving away as quickly as possible.

I was an orphan. My father was dead. My mother had disowned me.

I sat at the gate in the airport watching the people go by. I like to watch people at the airport. I always wonder where they came from and where they are going. This time, I wondered if they had any gay relatives, and if so, did they disown them, too?

When my father died, there was some comfort knowing that my mother was still around. But now that I had been abandoned by my only living parent, I felt a sense of disconnect with everyone I watched bustling through the terminal. I had grown used to telling people about my father's death, but what would I say about my mother?

"I'm sorry about your dad," someone might say. "What about your mother?"

"Well, I don't know if I have a mother anymore," I'd probably say sheepishly. "She disowned me when I told her I was gay."

As I thought of ways I'd have to explain this new situation, a familiar figure came into view at the airport. My brother was keeping his promise.

The first thing he did was hug me. For a long time. In an airport full of strangers. I replayed the events of the night for him again, and almost broke down. When I told him what Mom said about Grandma dying if I told her, he laughed. I wished I had been able to laugh when my mother told me that. Darryl said Grandma was a lot stronger than everyone gives her credit for. He was right. She'd raised six kids, buried a son and a husband.

Before he left, he told me my sister-in-law still loves me, and the rest of my family will still love me, which gave me the courage to write some letters to them when I returned to Denver.

Patt and David were the first two friends in Denver to hear my coming-out story. They nodded and shook their heads as if they had gone through the same routine before. To some degree, both of them had, and they were positive I would not be an orphan for long. They were certain my mother wouldn't disown me forever.

I sent handwritten letters to my three aunts, my uncle and a few cousins. Though I was also sure my grandmother would not die if I told her I was gay, I wasn't ready to send her a letter.

I got replies from all my aunts and two of my cousins. Lots of love all around, not to worry about Mom, all that stuff. So far, my mother was the lone wolf in the disowning department. I sensed being the only dissenter only strengthened her resolve. I had a feeling that siding with me cost my aunts and uncle their relationship with my mother. I wondered if they tried to change her mind, or if they also knew that she was quite stubborn when it came to hearing different opinions.

My aunts convinced me to send a letter to my grandmother. I didn't expect a response, but I got one a week later.

"I will always love you," she wrote. "And I will pray for you." I appreciated that, too, because I knew she wouldn't be praying for me in the same way I believed my mother would be praying for me.

A few months after coming out to my family, I got the job at the Rocky Mountain News. Everyone was happy I was no longer unemployed, but communication with the one person who always offered words of encouragement or reassurance wasn't there anymore. I tried to ignore the void created by my coming out, and hearing my gay friends say that parents eventually resume communication with their gay children made me somewhat optimistic. They didn't know my mother's resolve.

I was withdrawing from social interaction in the six months following my trip to St. Louis, and it was my closest friends who gave me a hard nudge out the door again in the summer of 2000. A new bar was opening in downtown Denver, and friends encouraged me to celebrate summer with them. As usual, I distanced myself from the crowd and decided to watch the proceedings from a rooftop patio.

And then I caught sight of someone looking at me. I only noticed the tall and skinny blond man because he was talking to one of my friends, who had waved hi to me. He kept throwing quick glances at me, which meant he was interested. I walked down the steps toward the guy, never taking my eyes off him. If he didn't notice me coming down the stairs, I'd walk in another direction. But he managed to hold a conversation and pull me in like a tractor beam with his green eyes.

I said hello to our mutual friend, who introduced the tall blond as Kent. He had a firm handshake, a deep voice and a smile that had me mesmerized.

I don't remember what we talked about that day, but I managed to get his phone number. Maybe I was desperate, lonely or just plain horny, but I called Kent that night. We talked for hours. Over the next 10 days or so, we would spend many more hours getting acquainted on the phone while he was traveling for business.

Within a couple of weeks, I was in my second relationship. It came at the perfect time. Not only did it keep my mind off my mother, but it gave my life balance. I didn't care that Kent was easily 10 years older than me, but it was obvious that we did have some differences. He wasn't big on TV or movies, and he practically live and breathed college football. Yes, I was dating another sports nut, one who didn't care much about swimming, but was willing to watch the 2000 Summer Olympics on TV with me, as long as I was willing to watch college football with him. He was a diehard Iowa State University alumnus, and every time ISU sports were on TV, the world stopped and we'd watch every minute.

I was quite aware that Kent's financial situation was much better than mine, and as we began to fall in love, I tried not to think about how much more money he made. He owned a great condominium in Denver's Capitol Hill area, and he didn't really blink an eye at spending money on a complete kitchen remodel. We saw each other a lot and fell in love that summer. Though it felt weird to finally be able to do so, I talked to my brother about my boyfriend. Darryl didn't seem to mind much. We talked like two brothers would about relationships, though I tried to water things down to lower the potential shock factor.

Kent and I had been together for six months when it was time for me to return to St. Louis for another Christmas family visit. My mother and I hadn't spoken for that entire year, so I didn't even bother trying to ask my mother if I could sleep in my room. My brother and sister-in-law were more than happy to offer me their futon. We had Christmas dinner at one of my aunt's homes, but I was too nervous to enjoy hanging out with the family. All I kept thinking about was that inevitable awkward moment when my mother would walk through the door.

A polite exchange of hellos was all that passed between us when it actually happened. I think we hugged. If my mother wanted to separate herself from me, I was going to make it easier for her. While she stayed upstairs and chatted with her sisters, I stayed downstairs with my cousins where we played pool and laughed like we were teenagers. And that was it. I went back to Denver saying maybe three words to my mother. No one in my family pressed the matter during my visit, even though the issue was the size of 120 elephants.

In the spring of 2001, I attended my second Colorado state masters meet, where about 300 swimmers from around the state compete during a weekend. I'd made some good friends at the 2000 meet, and some knew of my swimming past. No one made a big event about me swimming for a gay swim team. But I didn't know much about the team's history in Colorado masters, so when some people asked me what the team's initials stood for, I got knots in my stomach when I said "Swimming Queers United in Denver."

"Oh, how cute," most would say with a laugh. And then they'd change the subject.

At the 2001 Colorado state Masters championships, I saw Matt Beck, one of my former Texas roommates, on the deck. My stomach dropped when he glanced at me and waved. I wanted to run away. We hadn't seen each other in five years, and naturally there would be some talk of the team I was swimming for. This was to be my first experience where my past life met my present one. I took a deep breath and gave Matt a hug. He was a Denver native and had returned to run a swim pool in an affluent part of town. Spending many hours in the pool gave him the itch to try a few Masters meets, and he was going to swim against me in a couple of races.

Matt had a heat sheet in his hand. I was sure he had seen my name, noticed the "SQUID" next to my name under the "team" column and had eventually found out what the letters stood for. And probably a few seconds after putting all the pieces together, he began to think about all those secret nights when I snuck away in the house we both lived in six years earlier. The reason behind the absence of a girlfriend was suddenly crystal clear to Matt, if it hadn't been made clear to him before.

But Matt didn't cringe -- or vomit – during our conversation. He asked about the team, and I stayed away from the gay aspect, but wasn't shy about mentioning how great it was to train with them. I knew Matt stayed in touch with a lot of former Texas swimmers, and news of my appearance at masters meet would be a hot topic. Yes, they'd talk about my return to swimming, and how fast I did or did not swim, but eventually the name of my team would be revealed. Would I be ostracized from those alumni reunions we were planning?

Not at all. I continued to get e-mails from teammates as if nothing happened. Maybe Matt didn't spread rumors, or really no one cared when they heard about it. Or maybe they already knew!

I wanted nothing more in the world than to be able to go back to 1993 and give myself the courage to stand up in those team meetings in the Texas locker room and come out to the 30 men in the room. If Matt didn't care that I was a member of a gay swim team in 2001, it's quite likely he wouldn't have cared that I was gay in 1993. I'm not pegging Matt as a homophobe, but I always had the feeling that Matt and many others on the team would have preferred to not know there was a gay man on the team, hence my desire to keep quiet in college.

I have no idea if the chain of events in my life would have changed because of that declaration, but my peace of mind in those final years might have been at a better level. Matt's easygoing nature at the Masters meet showed me he might have been one of the people who would have supported me if I came out. It also showed me that there could have been many people on the Texas team who knew I was gay, but didn't confront me. These two tidbits of information would have been great to know while I sat in those team meetings, agonizing over a simple declarative sentence.

*****

I started to feel a sense of ease after a year of working at the Rocky Mountain News, which I should have read to be a harbinger of change. In March 2001, the editor-in-chief at the paper, John Temple, asked me if I was willing to take my journalism career to the next level. I was shocked that the top guy at the paper was interested in my career path, and that he wanted to take an active role in helping me find the next step.

Unfortunately, that next step would mean moving away from Denver. The News did not have open positions for me that would suit my desires as a journalist, and the paper had too high a pedigree to hire reporters at the bottom of the ladder. Temple suggested a couple of newspapers owned by the same company that owned the News. One was in Corpus Christi, Texas, and the other was in Albuquerque, New Mexico. I didn't know anything about either city. The prospect of Corpus Christi had the most promise. It was close to my friends in Austin, which meant I could drive there to visit often. New Mexico seemed desolate and extremely isolated. On the upside, it was a six-hour drive from Denver.

I visited both cities in May and didn't fall in love with either of them. Corpus Christi was preparing for its hurricane season, and the paper was right on the coastline. I didn't like the thought of worrying about hurricanes for three months each year. And the town didn't sell itself very well. Besides the access to the Gulf of Mexico, I couldn't find any gay culture or any entertainment that appealed to me. I didn't necessarily need a city with "gay culture" similar to Denver, or even Austin, but it would help.

I went to Albuquerque hoping the prospects there were better. I liked the people at The Albuquerque Tribune more, and it seemed nice to live in this desert valley. The weather was pleasant in June and the city didn't seem as desolate as I thought. But the entire time I kept thinking of Kent.

When Temple had suggested that I pursue my career in another state, I told Kent and he didn't seem to fight very hard for me to stay in Denver. He suggested that the move would be great for my career, and that he didn't want to stand in the way of that. I wanted him to fight for me. I wanted to fight for our relationship, but after noticing his lukewarm response to the situation, I decided to pick Albuquerque as my new home. Kent and I could still foster a long-term relationship and see each other a couple of weeks each month. I'd never been in a relationship separated by more than 50 miles before, so I wasn't exactly sure how to handle it. I wanted our relationship to remain monogamous, and told Kent I would hold up that part of the bargain.

Kent and I had been living in his condominium since March 2001 and it may not have been the best idea. I only moved into his condo because the lease on my apartment had ended and the possibility of moving away was so high that getting another lease would have been a bad idea. It was a move of convenience, but at the time I saw it as a big step forward in our relationship.

After about a month, moving in with Kent didn't strengthen our relationship. I don't know what happened to make it take a backslide, and I can't fault either of us for that, but it did happen subconsciously for me. I knew something was wrong but didn't feel the need to face up to it because we were still professing our love for each other. That was enough, right?

I was so focused on making the move to New Mexico that I didn't care to notice any problems in our relationship. I knew the move was going to be hard, and I avoided talking about it. All I knew was that Kent and I would still be together when I moved and once I settled in, we could focus on improving our relationship. I was going to remain faithful, and I trusted that Kent would honor that as well. Plus, there was the chance that after a year in Albuquerque, I would be able to return to the News as a full-time journalist.

It wasn't an easy day, but my last day at work was also my last day as a Colorado resident. I got the typical carrot-cake sendoff at the paper and hugged a lot of the friends I made at the News. I'd already said goodbye to my friends outside of work, with the promise that my frequent weekend visits to Denver would include spending time with them.

Mom and me celebrating New Year's 1997

Touring New York City in May 1999 with my brother's current wife, Ursula; my mother; and my brother. I would come out to my family seven months later.

Chapter Ten

Moving to Denver in 1998 was pretty easy. I was anxious to start life as a normal person. The city had offered so many things to help the transition that I gave very little thought to the life I left behind in Colorado Springs.

Moving to Albuquerque, New Mexico, was a much different situation. In the week before I left Denver to drive 450 miles down Interstate 25, I got seriously cold feet. I was no longer excited about getting a jump start on my professional life. I didn't want to leave behind the friends I'd made. I didn't want to face the difficulties of a long-distance relationship with Kent.

The month before I left, Kent and I were having troubles. A major problem was that I was so focused on this new chapter in my career that I didn't put much effort in making sure Kent knew how much I loved him. That might have been the beginning of the end. A few conversations we had made me realize that our living situation had become one of roommates who happened to sleep in the same bed. We ate together, slept together, watched TV together and I gave him a rent check every month. Somehow in those three months we lived together, we began to subconsciously drift apart. That explained why Kent never fought hard to keep me from leaving Denver.

But I was confident we could rebuild our relationship across such great distances. So I packed up the U-Haul and drove to Albuquerque anyway on July 10, 2001. I didn't make the transition any easier by driving to Denver nearly every weekend. Instead of touring Albuquerque to find aspects of the city that would appeal to me, I preferred to pack up my car for a quick weekend in Denver, hanging out with friends I knew and places I loved.

I was one of two education reporters at The Albuquerque Tribune, and it was a topic that held very little interest for me. Since I didn't have kids and was educated mostly in the private-school system, writing about the troubles of public education didn't get me excited every day. When I interviewed at the Trib, as it was affectionately known, I told them my aspirations to be a film critic. I was given the company line instantly, that they're not looking to put a full-time critic on the staff but they'll be glad to look into it.

One of the high points of the move to Albuquerque was finding a dedicated Masters swim team that I could train with five days a week. It was coached by a former swimmer who had a knack for coaching and gave workouts that were predictable but still interesting. The only downside was that the workouts were at 5:30 a.m.

When 9/11 happened, I was two months into my job and starting to find a groove. I had come home from swimming and had just gotten out of the shower. I turned on the TV and the image of smoke coming out of one of the towers in the World Trade Center had me transfixed. I didn't know what I was seeing, but instantly knew I needed to get to work a little early. As I dressed, I saw the second plane hit. I couldn't move, couldn't breathe, couldn't speak. When the towers fell, I had to turn off the television.

When I got to work, half the newsroom was already buzzing, trying to find local angles to the terrorist attack. From an education standpoint, I had to find out what the school district was doing to keep kids calm, informed and safe. A couple of schools were on the city's military base, and I was to find out if the students there were in lockdown, in case there was to be an attack on the base.

It was a very long day, and from the time I walked into the newsroom to the time I went home 10 hours later, I had not processed the events of the day. All I had the chance to see was the pillar of smoke rising from New York City, President Bush making a statement and images of people crying in the streets of New York.

I got home and called Kent. He said he couldn't find the strength to go to work that day. He was supposed to be in New York City that day in a meeting, in a building very close to the World Trade Center. He kept wondering if he would have been one of the people killed by falling debris that morning as they innocently walked to work. He wondered if this was a call for him to change his life. It sounded a little ominous to me, and I empathized with his emotions. In the end, he was glad to have someone to talk to.

About a month later, Kent drove to New Mexico for a long weekend. We hadn't seen each other since 9/11, and I was anxious to spend three days with him. But from the beginning, it all felt different. Kent's enthusiasm wasn't there. I detected it, but didn't want to make the weekend worse by bringing it up.

The night before he was to return to Denver, we went out to dinner at a fairly expensive restaurant. Kent's mood had lifted somewhat, and the conversation was fun during dinner. The waitress brought the check to me, and Kent paid the bill. We kept talking for a little bit, then I asked him if there was a particular movie he wanted to see. I wasn't sure what prompted it, but his mood suddenly took a downward turn. He asked if we could simply go home and spend the last few hours together there. I agreed, and we went home. Besides sex, I wasn't completely sure what to do that evening to keep him entertained, and I feared the end of his trip was going to end on a bad note. We went to bed silently that night.

I woke up the next morning sad that Kent was about to drive back to Denver. It was a Sunday, and I didn't want to spend the rest of the weekend missing him terribly. We had a light breakfast before he packed up his car. We sat on my futon and hugged. Something seemed very different about the way Kent was hugging me.

He told me he was very upset that he drove all the way down to Albuquerque from Denver to see me, only to be the one to pay for the expensive dinner we had the night before. I began to understand where his emotional downturn had come from.

In no uncertain terms, he wanted to end the relationship. The words shocked me. I told him being 450 miles away is hard on a relationship, but it's no reason to give up on it. Judging by his body language the entire weekend, he had given up on the relationship long ago, and maybe the agenda for the trip to New Mexico was to break up anyway. Even if I had paid for the dinner, we might have still had the same conversation.

Kent didn't want to argue the case. He got up and walked out the door, leaving me there to cry uncontrollably for almost an hour. I couldn't believe that the man I had fallen in love with a year ago was leaving me alone in New Mexico. For those three months I had lived there, the thought of having him in my life was a major source of sustenance. Not having that anymore made the thought of living in New Mexico even worse.

I went to work the next day, but I hardly found any motivation to work or enjoy the camaraderie of my coworkers. I wanted to marry Kent. I wanted to work hard in New Mexico to earn the right to come back to the Rocky Mountain News so Kent and I could officially start our lives together. I knew I had really loved Kent despite our many differences. I understood what love meant.

Now, I didn't know where my life was going to take me.

*****

Things got inexplicably better between Mom and me when I moved to New Mexico. We hadn't had a meaningful conversation since I came out in 1999, but not too long after my breakup with Kent, my mother and I began exchanging e-mails and phone calls. She didn't ask about anything associated with my gay life, and I didn't offer it up. Was my new employment the reason for her correspondence?

Being a single man made it easier to talk about my life to my mother. My gay life had existed solely around Kent, and now I really had nothing else in my gay life to discuss. So work and swimming dominated our conversations, which I was elated to have.

I don't pretend to know what was going on in her head. She never told me why she decided to resume regular communication. I know there are lots of gay men and women out there with worse situations than me. There are teenagers living on the streets because their families wanted nothing to do with a gay child.

One of the things I discussed with my mother was my upcoming trip to Sydney. She had been there before, and she told me lots of places I should visit. I told her I was going for a swim meet, but did not say what type of meet it was.

In February 2002, I had finally earned enough money to make the trip to Sydney for Gay Games. I signed up for the competition, and during the application process, I got knots in my stomach. Who would I meet at

Gay Games? Would there be any swimmers I knew from my past swimming life in the meet?

The psych sheet is a listing of every swimmer in each event, ranked by seed times. Psych sheets are released to let people know who plans to swim in the meet, and in what events. The psych sheet would not be released until early fall, maybe one month before the meet started, so I had to wait the entire summer to find out who I might reconnect with in Sydney.

I made travel plans on my own, and it was a very sad process. Kent and I had originally planned to go to Australia together and compete. He would run a marathon and I would swim. The schedules worked out so we could watch each other compete. The fact that we were no longer together made going to Sydney alone heartbreaking, though a little uplifting. Was there someone I would meet in Sydney that would be the one?

Since moving to New Mexico, I managed to get into pretty good swimming shape. I had been competing for two years, but the only meets I swam in were in Colorado. I had no idea what to expect from an international Masters meet, which got me more motivated to train hard.

The psych sheet for the Gay Games was released in late September. I scrolled straight through to my events, and when I got to the 200 IM, the second event I would swim, I was shocked. I was listed as the top seed in the 25-29 age group. The second seed was Brian Jacobson. Brian and I were on the junior national team, and seeing his name among the competitors in the Gay Games psych sheet immediately took me back to our team trip to Europe in 1990 and Canada in 1991. Brian and I weren't extremely close back then, but I felt an instant connection just from seeing his name among the Gay Games competitors.

After browsing through all my events, and after getting over the surprise that I was ranked first in three out the five events, I looked for more familiar names. And there it was in the 35-39 age group: Dan Veatch. I let out a whoop. He was coming to the meet! I couldn't wait to catch up with him. I hadn't seen him since the 1992 Olympic Trials, so we had 10 years of catching up to do.

This would be the first meet in four years in which I would be fully tapered and shaved. It would also be the first time I was essentially doing it alone. No one else on the team in New Mexico was going to Sydney or preparing for a big meet at the same time. It was difficult planning out the taper. I had always put all my trust in my coaches to handle the tapers, which had worked well for me until 1994. I figured I could start resting for the meet about 10 days from the first day of racing. That meant a lot of easy swimming when everyone else in the water was working hard. I kind of enjoyed seeing everyone else panting after a set while I was in another part of the pool swimming an easy 2,000 yards.

On Oct. 28, I sat in the Albuquerque airport, waiting to board a plane to Los Angeles. Once in LA, I would get on another plane for the 14-hour flight to Sydney. This would be my first time traveling outside the country in 11 years (not counting a day trip to Tijuana in 1997), and I was beyond thrilled thinking about the possibilities. I was pleasantly surprised to meet Laurie and Deborah in the Albuquerque airport. Laurie would be doing the triathlon in Sydney; Deborah would be Laurie's cheerleader. This would be the first time out of the country for both of them.

Because the airline taking me from LA to Sydney was different from the one that I took from Albuquerque, I had to stand in line at the Los Angeles airport to check my bags again. The line was long, and it didn't take long for me to realize that most of the people in the line were also going to Sydney for Gay Games. I found out most of them were basketball players from Long Beach, a city between Los Angeles and San Diego. The line was also filled with runners from Dallas and volleyball players from Los Angeles.

On the plane to Sydney, I sat next to Brian, a water polo player from Los Angeles playing on the San Francisco team. He was writing a journal for The Advocate, and I thought that would have been a great gig to get.

All around me were gay athletes about to embark on two fun weeks in a foreign country. Just like them, I couldn't contain my excitement. I had been told to sleep a lot on the plane, since I would be arriving in Sydney in the early morning. But I think I slept for only four hours in the 15 hours I was on the plane. I couldn't stop thinking about all the possibilities that awaited me Down Under.

Chapter Eleven

We landed at 6 a.m. in Sydney, and nearly the entire plane let out a big cheer when the wheels touched the ground. Those of us who were near a window had been admiring the land below us for about a half hour. The Australian East Coast looked nothing like the American West Coast, even though both are filled with beaches. In Australia, you could see more white sand than in the United States, and the water had a cleaner look to it. The water actually looked blue!

Clearing customs was quite easy, and once through the gates, I searched for David, a local guy who I met through a mutual friend. David agreed to pick me up at the airport and drive me to the apartment I would be staying in while in Sydney. David was quite easy to find. He was very tall and built like a swimmer. Even though we had corresponded only by email up to that point, we hugged in the airport and walked quickly to his car. Though it was so early, it felt like the middle of the day to me, probably because I had already been awake for five hours.

As David drove me through Sydney, I looked around for any familiar landmarks. I didn't want to sound like the typical tourist and ask where the Sydney Opera House and the Harbour Bridge were, but for 30 minutes I kept looking through buildings and trees for just a peek at part of Sydney's skyline. Unfortunately, we were headed inland to register for the competition.

David was certain processing would take an hour, but since it was three days before the Games began, most people had not arrived. I was able to walk right up to a volunteer, take a horrible picture and receive my credentials with no fuss. I also got a travel pass that gave me free rides on all public transportation starting the day before competitions started. That was good news because the pool would be a one-hour round trip by train from my apartment, at the Sydney Olympic pool located outside the city limits.

David had nothing planned for the day, so he didn't mind taking me to many different places. I suggested that I drop off my bags at my apartment before we did any more driving. Finding the apartment was hellish. We drove around the block about six times before finding the building. My room was very small, but I wasn't planning on hosting any parties there. This was simply going to be my base of operations. I figured I would be at the pool for about seven hours every day, plus the one-hour train ride, dinner after the meet and any unplanned sightseeing.

The next item on the list was to take a swim. We drove by a pool that was popular among gay swimmers, but it was indoors and I asked if there were any places to swim outdoors. There wasn't a cloud in the sky and it was late spring in Australia. I wanted to take advantage of the situation. David turned the car around toward Sydney Harbor.

Driving through Hyde Park was thrilling. It felt a lot like Central Park in New York City. As we wound through the park, I saw part of the Sydney Opera House through the trees. The sight literally took my breath away.

The pool we swam in was outdoors and located right on the harbor. It was so close, the water in the pool was actually salt water pumped in from the harbor, chlorinated and filtered to make it suitable for swimming. No one mentioned to me that the water was nearly the same temperature as the harbor water! It couldn't have been warmer than 72 degrees! But with sun beating down on me, it felt comfortable after about 10 minutes.

I swam nice and easy for about an hour, soaking in the Australian sun and every once in a while stopping to gaze out at the harbor. The pool was not in a good place to see the main part of the harbor, where the Opera House and Harbour Bridge are located, but the sights still were beyond remarkable. I was completely convinced I was dreaming. It seemed like just a few hours ago I was sitting in the Albuquerque airport. Now, I was lounging in a pool on an outcropping on Sydney Harbor!

Though David drove me past the supposedly popular gay pool, I got the feeling this pool on the harbor was also a trendy gay spot. Lots of middle-aged men worked on their tans by the pool, and when I got out after my workout, it was obvious that they were checking me out. Not very desirous to play on the fantasies of middle-aged men, I quickly gathered my clothes and got dressed in the locker room.

David purposefully drove the long way back to my apartment so I could see the Opera House and Harbour Bridge in their full glory. Photos cannot begin to prepare you for the magnificence of seeing two of the most popular landmarks in the world.

I had been awake for nearly 12 hours and the excitement of the past six were starting to wear me down. David dropped me off at my apartment and I could think of nothing but a long nap. But just as I finished unpacking, a wave of hunger struck me and I asked the landlady about any restaurants within walking distance. She said a few were about 10 minutes away. I was so tired I decided to just go across the street to the gas station and get a whole chicken. Yes, my first taste of Australian food was a whole barbecued chicken. It tasted exactly like the chicken in the United States. Luckily, it was near lunch time, so I was also getting my body adjusted to the new time zone. As the food settled in my stomach, I flipped through the channels and watched part of a very old episode of "Days of Our Lives" and a local newscast in which a woman protested a restraining order for stalking Ian Thorpe.

I woke up on Halloween morning excited about my first trip out to Sydney Olympic Park. The public transportation system in Sydney is remarkably easy to follow, and though I wasn't happy that I had to walk almost 20 minutes to the train station, I was delighted that I only needed to take two trains out to the Sydney Olympic pool.

It had been two years since the world came to Sydney for the Olympics, and the Olympic Park still looked astounding. Just about every major venue was still intact, the grounds were very clean and lots of tourists still made the trip out to see it.

Upon first seeing the pool, I had to stop and take it all in for about five minutes. The arena looked even grander than it did on television, even though about half the seats had been removed. To know that the fastest swimmers in the world had made history here was mind-blowing. And now the pool was going to be taken over by about 1,000 gay men and women.

I walked along the spectator concourse, where pictures of some of Australia's best swimmers hung. In the pool below, an American team was practicing starts. None of the lights were on, but the sunlight through the skylights lit the entire building quite well. After sitting in the stands for about 10 minutes, I finally decided to get ready for my workout.

The main goal of that day's swim was to get used to the water, the flags and the ceiling (for backstroke). When I dove into the main pool, I was in shock that I was actually swimming in the same lane where such swimmers as Lenny Krayzelburg, Ian Thorpe and others had achieved Olympic greatness not too long ago. I held my breath at the bottom of the nine-foot-deep pool and soaked in the feeling. I had swum in some Olympic pools in my life, but this one took on new meaning. In three days, I would be taking on a much different identity than when I swam in the Berlin Olympic pool or Los Angeles Olympic pool. I would be officially out to the world as a gay swimmer, with no worries about who would find out.

I had two fun days of sightseeing just about every corner of Sydney via train, bus and ferry, but on Nov. 2, the fever of Gay Games was set to reach fever pitch. The opening ceremonies were to be held at a stadium about five minutes from my apartment. The festivities were supposed to start at 8 p.m., but all the athletes were told to arrive at the site at 4 p.m. to get everyone organized for the parade into the venue. We spent three hours sitting in a small cricket stadium next to the larger venue, but it was still pretty fun meeting athletes from other teams, taking lots of pictures and ogling all the pretty men. Surely this was not how the parade of athletes took place at the Olympic Games. Or was it?

After sitting in the cricket stadium for three hours without food, many of us were starting to get ornery. But the mood changed when we began to parade into the stadium at 9:00 (an hour late but on time in the gay world). Disco music blasted from the speakers and I was shocked to see just about every seat in the stadium filled with cheering spectators. Though I was trying to save my legs since I was swimming in the morning, I wasn't going to keep myself from experiencing all the sights and sounds of the event. I began to dance with a go-go dancer on the field and did a little bump and grind with a fellow athlete. Once everyone got to their seats, the official ceremony began with a reenactment of the gay movement in Sydney. It was fairly cheesy, but not totally uninteresting. All I kept thinking was that I hadn't shaved my body yet, and it was almost 10:30.

When the ceremony ended, everyone began walking back to the train stations, but I walked in a different direction as I made the short trip to my apartment, shaved my arms and legs and tried to fall asleep. The memories of that night kept playing in my head, and I could faintly hear the disco music in the stadium about five blocks away.

The train ride to the pool was excruciatingly long the next morning. I was anxious to see how the swimming events at the Gay Games were held. I spoke with a few other athletes on the train, and it took my mind off my nerves for a while, but with practically everyone in Sydney headed to the Olympic Park, the trains took more stops and had longer wait times at each station.

One side of the spectator area in the Sydney Aquatic Center was filled with gay swimmers from all over the world. The meet had started about an hour before I arrived, and many in the crowd were dancing to music during a slow heat. It looked like Mardi Gras. So many colorful team outfits, with many of them sporting the popular rainbow flag colors that are part of gay culture. Before I walked into the pool, my mind was focused on swimming the three events I had that day: the 50 backstroke, the 400 free relay and the 200 IM. I wanted this first day to be great. It was to be my official return to competitive swimming.

The 50 back was first and as I paraded down to the blocks, I got a cheer from my teammates in the stands. It felt real good. Then, as I prepared to swim my heat, I watched the swimmers in the heat before mine. In that heat was Paul Nicholson of Australia, who was 24 years old and therefore not in my age group. But he was swimming remarkably fast, dolphin kicking to 15 meters and posting a 27.64. I got real nervous then. I wasn't sure I could beat that. My goal had been to not only win my age group, but be the fastest overall swimmer in all my events at the meet. I feared I wouldn't be able to fulfill that promise in the first race.

My start was fairly good. My breakout was fantastic. My turnover was superb. But I couldn't beat Paul's time. I went a 27.84, which was a great time. I couldn't tell you if I had ever swum faster than that in my life, since I don't know the last time I swam a 50 backstroke in competition. It felt good to get the one swim under me, and I headed to the warmdown pool with a big grin.

On the way to the warmdown pool, which was only 20 feet from the competition pool, I felt plenty of stares from other swimmers on deck. I didn't know how to handle the circumstances. You don't get this feeling at a USA Swimming meet. Plus, the idea of flirting with men and being flirted with had never registered with me.

And then, out of the corner of my eye, I saw Dan Veatch. I wanted to run over and say hi to him, but warming down was a priority. I figured it was a seven-day meet and we were bound to see each other again. But after swimming only an easy 50, I heard a familiar voice coming from the deck above me.

"Jeff Commings, get your cute butt up here!"

Dan was standing in front of my lane, grinning from ear to ear, looking just as he did in 1991 in Cuba. I jumped out of the pool and gave him a big hug.

We talked for about 10 minutes. Dan didn't give any hint of surprise that I was gay and at the Gay Games. I was still stunned to see him here. And I had to let him know it.

"Gosh, Dan, if I knew then what I know now..." I told him with a sly wink.

Dan laughed. "Well, I didn't really know myself if I was gay back then. But I kind of felt you were, and it was just great to be friends with you."

It was as if those 11 years had never existed. Dan Veatch and I had reconnected. He was at the meet with his husband, who he said had learned to swim in time to compete at the meet. He said he was on the San Francisco Tsunami team that was doing so well, and he said he was on the 400 free relay team that would be swimming in the lane next to us in about an hour. I told him it would be fun to race him.

I didn't get to actually race Dan in the relay. His team was so far in the lead that I never saw him until the end. He flashed that grin again, which helped ease my pain. My team had gotten fourth in the race. The Sydney team, which included David, my tour guide when I arrived in town, just beat us to the wall.

Watching a gay swim meet is not much different from watching any other Masters meet. There are the first-time competitors and the former college swimmers. There are the ones who are there mostly for the social scene and those who, like me, were totally focused on racing. But as I sat in stands waiting to swim the 200 IM, I felt more at ease watching this meet. I can't explain why. Could it be because I was surrounded by "my people?" Could it be that I was finally in Sydney and was feeling the laid-back aura of the Aussies? Or was it because the anticipation and anxiety of swimming in my first major swim meet in four years was finally drifting away?

I hadn't done much training in a 50-meter pool, which will make any race longer than 100 meters painful. You are swimming much more and not relying on the turns for a little bit of rest. I felt so much pain after winning the 200 IM that I had a hard time getting out of the pool. But it was a fun first day, and I was looking forward to a big swim the following day.

The minute I woke up to get ready for the second day of swimming, my thoughts were focused on breaking a world record. I hadn't told anyone I was going for the world record in the 50 breast for my age group, which was a 28.98. I was fearful of the reaction I would get if I didn't break the record. I didn't want to disappoint anyone but myself.

I can tell you that the race went very well, but for some reason, at the 25-meter mark, I had a feeling I wouldn't get the record. And no matter how much harder I swam those last 25 meters, I couldn't shake the feeling that I wouldn't go under 29 seconds. I swam a 29.52, which was the only swim under 30 seconds in the meet. I got a huge ovation, which felt real good, but I was crushed. Since I was 28 years old, I knew I didn't have many opportunities to break that record before moving into the 30-34 age group.

I swam to the side and was congratulated on the deck immediately by four of my teammates. Getting hugs from all of them wasn't new to me. Getting kisses from them – as well as a European kiss on both cheeks by a fellow competitor – was entirely new. After the first kiss that was planted on me, my initial reaction was to recoil in case someone noticed. Of course people noticed! And of course, no one cared. Men were kissing each other at a rate of 10 times per second in this pool. Four friendly kisses from teammates and one from a competitor was not unusual at this meet, but I still felt like the act was busting through barriers. It certainly would have been photo-worthy if done at Olympic Trials or the NCAA championships. I was getting comfortable in my surroundings, but it was clear I still needed some time to adjust to all of this.

I had a day off of swimming, but instead of sightseeing, I decided to go to the pool and watch more swimming. I enjoyed watching all different varieties of swimming ability, and it was great to be able to make some new friends in the process. Though I often thought of Kent and what we'd be doing as a couple if we hadn't broken up, I wondered if there was a chance to meet a handsome swimmer and pursue a relationship. Dating a swimmer would make life easier for me.

But I was extremely shy, and wasn't too sure if there was anyone at the meet I could envision myself with for the rest of my life. While the majority of the single people who came to Sydney for the Games were looking for the quick hookup, I wanted to leave Sydney with more than medals. I saw many male couples holding hands and wearing wedding bands. I wanted that more than anything in the world. What had kept me from getting to that point with Aaron and Kent? I could say it was their faults that I couldn't reach that level of commitment, but you can't ignore the fact that sometimes the chemistry isn't there, as much as you hope it can be. I don't think Aaron was secure enough in his life to know whether he was ready for a major relationship, and given my circumstances of not truly being out among my teammates, the possibility of us taking that next step was not going to happen right away. With Kent, there were so many differences at the start. It took both of us almost a year to realize that those differences, both financial and cultural, were too significant to push aside.

I wasn't sure what kind of man would be able to spend his life with me. Would a swimmer really be the best bet? I looked at all the men sitting around me in the Sydney Aquatic Center and wondered if there was anyone in the building that had the same core values as I did. On the surface, I couldn't find anyone.

*****

When I swam at a Grand Prix meet in 1997, I almost broke the 1:00 barrier in the 100-meter backstroke. I didn't swim backstroke much at swim meets, and I had always put that goal in the back of my mind as something to accomplish in my life.

Call it my climb to the top of Mt. Everest. It took five years, but I finally did it on the fourth day of competition at the 2002 Gay Games.

I swam a 59.87 in the 100 back, and I could describe it as the perfect race. My 50 split was where it wanted to be, and though I got very tired in the last 15 meters, I talked myself into not giving up and getting my hand on the wall. The only sad part was that I had no one to race. Second place was almost seven seconds behind me.

When I saw the time, I went crazy. It was a large weight taken off my shoulders. My teammates were going nuts in the stands, and I waved to them. It felt like I was in the Olympics. The rest of the crowd applauded the swim, and I felt a wave of emotion come over me. Not only did I swim a lifetime best time at the age of 28, but to get that kind of reception was unexpected.

Paul Nicholson, the guy who swam faster than me in the 50 back three days earlier, was swimming in the heat after me. He was standing at the edge of the pool when I finished, and as I exited the pool, I gave him a little nod of encouragement. I wouldn't have been upset if he beat me again, but I was sure he was going to post a time very close to mine, and made me wish we had been able to race in the same heat.

Paul swam an equally perfect race. His 50 split was a little slower than mine, but he came home like a rocket. His time: 59.91. I did a tiny fist pump when I saw the time, then walked over to his lane to congratulate him.

My final day of swimming at the Gay Games consisted of only 50 meters of breaststroke in the medley relay. I was more nervous about this event than any other I had swum that week. I had convinced the three others on my relay team that we were capable of winning the event, and I really wanted it to happen for Mark, Patt and Corey. None of them had won a medal at Gay Games, which only hands out gold, silver and bronze medals in each age group. Add that to our fourth-place finishes in two relays, and we had nothing to lose. But that didn't mean we were all business.

We sat in the marshalling area wearing bathing caps with plastic flowers on them, similar to the ones you see on elderly ladies at the rec pool. We were the hit of the marshalling room. Behind us sat the team from San Francisco Tsunami, which had won every relay in our age group, thanks in large part to Dan Veatch's contributions. Dan wasn't on this relay, but I had watched a couple of the swimmers about to race us earlier in the meet and I knew they'd be very fast.

As we walked out to the blocks, I got into the zone. All I was thinking about was making sure I got a fast start and worked hard to beat the Tsunami breaststroker, who I was certain would enter the water well ahead of me. I stared down my lane as I removed my clothes and put on my goggles. I could see that medal waiting for us at the end of the race. It was only a matter of time before we …

"Excuse me, could you do me a favor and zip me up?"

I was jolted out of my focus by these words from a handsome blond in a full bodysuit. He was the freestyler on the Tsunami team, and was asking me for help in closing the zipper on the back of his Speedo bodysuit. Even though I saw him as my potential roadblock to a relay gold (he was one of the fastest freestylers in the meet, while our freestyler was just above average), I wasn't going to say no. I zipped up his suit and was just about to re-enter my focus zone.

"Thanks. I'm Geoff, by the way."

"Really?" I was genuinely shocked. "That's my name, too!"

We shook hands and smiled at each other. Though the backstrokers were just about to enter the pool to swim their leg, I couldn't help but notice the blue-green eyes looking back at me, and the smile that had me momentarily hypnotized.

He said he lived in San Francisco; I told him that I lived in New Mexico despite swimming for a Colorado team. He told me he lived in Fort Collins for many years before moving to San Francisco. He said he grew up in central Illinois; I told him I grew up in St. Louis.

By this time, the horn had sounded and the backstrokers had started the race. As much as Geoff wanted to continue the conversation, I had to cut him off with the promise to pick it up after the race. Was he trying to rattle my cage and throw me off guard before my race? Or was he genuinely having a conversation/flirting with me? Either possibility was likely at Gay Games. I stopped thinking about it right away. Mark's backstroke had put us well behind the pack, and I had a lot of catching up to do.

I dove in with one singular goal: catch the Tsunami breaststroker. Without looking, I could sense that I had caught him after 25 meters. Now, I needed to put myself about two seconds ahead to give Patt a cushion for his fly leg and hopefully allow Corey to dive in ahead of Geoff. I touched the wall and looked to my right. The breaststroker from the Sydney team touched at the same time as me, but the Tsunami swimmer was indeed about two seconds behind. I quickly swam to the side of the pool to watch Patt complete his leg of the race. I was getting nervous. All I had hoped for was a bronze medal, but could we actually win this? Patt was still ahead when he touched the wall, though the margin was greatly reduced. I was certain we could win. Corey came up swimming hard. He was kicking hard. He didn't take a breath for 20 meters – and then I saw it. When he turned his head toward me to breathe, I could see that his goggles had flipped off and were now under his nose. This wasn't good. Unless you're Michael Phelps swimming for gold in the Olympics, it's hard to maintain concentration and continue to swim fast when you can't see anything. Corey still put up a good fight, but Geoff took advantage of the situation and sailed past Corey for the win. The Sydney team touched second, and we finished third by a comfortable margin.

I wasn't upset that we lost the gold medal. I was thrilled that I had a part in getting Mark, Patt and Corey their only medals of the meet. We all got together after the race and hugged. You would have thought we won the race.

I was so caught up in the emotion of winning the medal – and being done with swimming in my first Gay Games – that I forgot to find Geoff in the warmdown pool. I didn't see him the rest of the day.

It was time to party at last. I overheard a lot of the swimmers each morning talking about parties they went to every night, yet I went back to my apartment every night and slept. I was ready for the release.

I attended a party that was a long ferry ride away at a small condo not too far from the ocean. You couldn't get to downtown Sydney from this part of town unless you had a car or a ferry pass. I could smell the salty ocean air on the patio of the condo and met some wonderful people from many parts of the United States. There was even a male couple from the Netherlands who looked like magazine models. They were in Sydney mostly for the parties, though they had made it through a few rounds in the tennis competition.

I went to the final day of swimming the next morning to watch the 1500 freestyle. I watched a couple of people that I knew swim fairly well. I also saw Geoff, the Tsunami freestyler whose bodysuit I had zipped the day before, swim the fastest time of the event. As I watched him gracefully swim up and down the pool, I wondered about his marital status. Surely, good-looking people such as him were taken, and I didn't give it another thought about the possibility of hanging out with him. The last time I saw him in Sydney was when he climbed out of the pool after swimming the mile.

The Aquatic Center had become quite crowded by the time the mile had finished. We couldn't get the spectator seating to fill to half capacity during the meet, but it was standing room only for the meet's final event: the Pink Flamingo.

The Pink Flamingo is a tradition at the annual championships held by the International Gay and Lesbian Aquatics federation, and it's continued in the years of the Gay Games. It's essentially a synchronized swimming event with male participants. The sparkling costumes and set pieces are probably more extravagant given that gay men had a hand in creating them. As I watched my first Pink Flamingo competition, I was awed by the spectacle of it all, and how much the crowd loved every moment.

I spent my final three days in Sydney as a tourist. Many of my friends had left the day after swimming was completed, but I knew all along I wanted to make the most out of my time in Australia. I wasn't sure when I'd make it back to this great country, so I made sure to take in as much of the sights of Sydney as I could.

Before they returned to the States, my friends David and Patt joined me on a climb of the Sydney Harbour Bridge. It's an exhilarating experience that cannot be put into words. Nothing could explain the view of Sydney Harbour, the sight of the Pacific Ocean in the distance, the Sydney Opera House below or the landscape of the city of Sydney. All I could do in the 10 minutes we had at the top was to stand there and soak it all in.

Then, we took a bus tour out to the Blue Mountains, which included a trip to a tropical rain forest and a visit to a wildlife park, where I petted my first kangaroo.

I didn't mind spending my final two days in Sydney alone. I spent the first two days alone, and was enjoying every minute of it. Had Kent been there, or if I had another mate to spend the time with, I would have enjoyed it just as much. But I was relishing the time to not worry about being on another person's schedule or having any plans at all. Besides visiting the wonderful "Star Wars" exhibit, my only goal at the end of my trip was to wander the streets and waterways of Sydney to see what I could experience. I spent about 30 minutes eating fish and chips on a pedestrian bridge on a sunny day in November in Sydney, Australia. That half hour was one of the most perfect moments in my life.

The plane ride from Sydney to Los Angeles offered me a final chance at breaking out of my shell and being a little more outgoing. I had been exchanging coy glances with a guy on the other side of the plane for about 11 hours, and only when we were making the approach to Los Angeles did I swallow my nerves and walk up to him.

"Hi, my name is Jeff."

"Hey, I'm Mark."

"Hey, Mark. I kind of noticed we had a couple of moments during the trip, and I just wanted to introduce myself. It's about 13 hours late, but I figured it's better than never."

We talked for about 15 more minutes. He was a hockey player from Boston whose team had won the gold medal. He had watched the Pink Flamingo event at the pool and made a comment that he would have watched the actual swimming if he had known people like me were swimming.

Nothing came of that conversation with Mark, except that I realized there's no harm in simply introducing yourself to someone for pleasant conversation. As I boarded the plane for Albuquerque, I realized that Mark was my last contact with the exciting gay world out there. I was headed back to Albuquerque, where gay life begins and ends in lifeless dance clubs and the occasional drag theater show. But knowing that didn't deter from knowing that I had just experienced two of the most thrilling weeks of my life. I was now out there as a gay swimmer, and I was truly ready for it.

You can't help but get excited in the opening ceremonies of the Gay Games. We danced/paraded around the stadium floor.

Petting a kangaroo at the Australia wildlife preserve

Chapter Twelve

When I returned to Albuquerque after two weeks in Sydney, I was on such a high. I wanted everyone to see pictures of my trip to Australia, and I showed them to just about anyone who was within reach. Showing photos extended my emotions about Australia. As glad as I was to be back in the United States, I couldn't stop thinking of the things I would do if or when I went back.

My great swims in Sydney gave me confidence that there was a great future for me in Masters swimming. I was glad that my first meet shaved and tapered turned out to be a success more than a failure. Out of the five individual events I swam, I got a lifetime best in the 100 back and came within three seconds of my lifetime best time in the 100 breast. With the severely reduced amount of training I had done since 1998, I was happy to do so well in the pool. I wasn't thinking about the fact that my times were slower than I swam when I was 15 years old. I was beginning to have fun again.

In January 2003, after the results of the Gay Games had spread throughout the Internet, I was pushed harder to attend Masters nationals. I had resisted so many times because I didn't want to swim at that level again. But one of the things that stuck with me after Gay

Games was the rush I felt just before stepping onto the blocks before a big race and the elation of seeing a faster time than I expected on the scoreboard. I wanted to have that feeling again.

The 2003 short course Masters nationals was to be held on the campus of Arizona State University, just one state over from where I lived. That made it convenient. I remembered the pool well from my days swimming there in college dual meets, so I knew the pool was fast. For the first time since joining Masters, I allowed myself to set goals. Many of those goals were set after looking at the national records for the 25-29 age group. They all looked very fast, and the names attached to them were a Who's Who of great swimmers: Greg Rhodenbaugh, David Lundberg and Andy Gill. The record for the 100 breast was 56.12, which seemed approachable. I knew if I wanted to break the record, I would have to work harder in the pool and commit myself to more dryland exercises. Being one who doesn't wake up in the morning thrilled at the prospect of what each new workout can bring, I wasn't excited at the thought of doing more work. The workouts in Albuquerque were heavily geared for the distance swimmers, and that group made up more than 90 percent of the team. I could identify very few people who could say they felt comfortable doing sprint sets. On the so-called "sprint days," the rest interval was too short to put much quality into each fast swim, so I was always swimming at 90 to 95 percent effort, instead of the all-out race pace that sprinters often do in the majority of workouts.

On the plus side, my endurance level increased. Swimming sets of 200s would help me finish the final 15 meters of my sprint races, and keep my strokes strong in the 200 IM. I made a vow to never do the 200 breast again, and though I was sure I could win my age group in the event at nationals, I didn't want to go through the agony of a 200 breaststroke again. No matter how the race turns out, the intense pain at the end of a 200 breaststroke is always there. Your lungs burn, your legs feel like lead and you can hardly lift your arms. Now that I was totally in control of my swimming life, I imposed a strict ban on that event.

Training for sprint events among a group of distance swimmers took a lot of work. After talking to my coach, Bobbie Goldie, I began to manipulate many of the workouts to suit my training style. Instead of swimming ten 100-yard repeats on two minutes -- with every other swim fast -- I would swim every third or fourth 100 fast. Having more time to recover between sets meant I was able to swim each 100 as if I were swimming in a race. Though I was starting from in the water, I still treated the first 25 aggressively, the second 25 equally strong, then attack the third 25 and put everything into the final 15 meters. Each fast swim left me exhausted and spent, but having the extra recovery time helped me to physically and mentally prepare for the next swim.

I got chided by my teammates for slacking off. Instead of doing the set as given, they saw me as doing the set half-assed. Since many of the people in my training group came from a competitive swimming background, I knew they were really joking with me, and I was able to let the insults slide off. I was the only swimmer on the team going to nationals.

The 10 days of taper were just as excruciating. As much as I didn't know what I was doing in preparation for Gay Games, I was more nervous about tapering for nationals. I prepared for Gay Games with a lot less care than I was getting ready for Tempe. I wanted this taper to work well. I needed to be physically ready to swim fast in all six of my events. My competition would definitely be ready. I took those 10 days of taper cautiously. If I felt like I was too tired, I would postpone my fast swims to another day. I slept more than usual and stayed off my feet at work, which isn't easy. How do you explain to your boss that you can't cover a press conference because you can't stand for two hours? How do you find a way to do your work and still take care of your body? This is the essence of being a Masters swimmer. How do we juggle the important responsibilities of work and home with the demands of being a competitive swimmer? I knew I couldn't conduct my taper for Tempe in the same way I had done many years ago. I couldn't sleep all day and spend the rest of the time watching movies and eating. I had to make a living, and every time I had to walk to an interview or stood in the back of a room during a board meeting, I wondered if my taper was ruined.

Tempe was a seven-hour drive from Albuquerque. Every mile got me more excited about what I would find in Tempe. There were old friends to get reacquainted with and new friends to make. There were new frontiers to explore in my swimming.

I arrived in Tempe on Thursday afternoon. After checking into my hotel, I went to the pool for a brief swim. The first day of the meet is traditionally set aside for the distance events, and both courses were full of people swimming the 1650-yard freestyle. I didn't see many people on the deck, but seeing people of all ages walk around in full-body swimsuits made me realize this wasn't just a normal swim meet. Even the lower seeds in each event were taking the meet seriously. The butterflies were back in my belly as I swam an easy 1,000 yards in the warmup pool.

My first day of the meet would be a relatively easy one. I only had the 100 back and a couple of relays to swim. And I wasn't scheduled to do the 100 back until about 1 p.m., which meant I could sleep in and take my time getting ready in the morning.

The Mona Plummer Aquatic Center is a vast outdoor facility. It contains three separate pools: a 50-meter pool, a 25-yard pool and a diving well. On the first full day of competition at the 2003 short course Masters nationals, the entire deck was filled with swimmers basking in the sun. The 50-meter pool had been divided into two 25-yard competition courses.

I was so stunned at the sight of more than 1,000 swimmers on the deck. Age-group meets don't have this many swimmers.

Two hours after I arrived at the facility, I stood at the edge of one of the competition pools ready to swim in my heat of the 100 back. I was nervous about the race for many reasons. I hadn't swum backstroke outdoors in many years, so I was worried about the glare of the sun, which could keep me from swimming straight and cause me to run into the lane lines. And Eddie Reese, my college coach, was at the meet swimming a couple of races and socializing with old friends. I told him I was swimming backstroke at the meet and he said he would watch. More than anything, I wanted to show him that I was indeed a backstroker, despite my inflexible ankles.

The race went better than I thought. Because I was swimming at nearly high noon, the sun shone brightly in my eyes. But I managed to avoid the lane lines, and I won the race with a 50.98. I could say it was a lifetime best time because the fastest swim I could remember was in the 52-second range, and that was unshaved. I was proud of my swim, mostly because I had beaten swimmers who were probably longtime backstrokers. Neil Peiffer, the swimmer who was the top seed, finished second by a little more than a tenth of a second.

As I warmed down, I felt a large wave of confidence wash over me. My first event at a swim meet is often not very good, but with a very good 100 back, I was very anxious to see how the rest of the weekend would turn out.

I watched nearly 200 men and women suffer through the heats of the

200 breaststroke, and even though Olympians Roque Santos, Ron Karnaugh and Richard Schroeder were making it look easy, I was confident that I made the right decision to never swim the event again.

The only relays I had swum in Masters were of the same-sex variety. I had never participated in a mixed relay, which consisted of two men and two women. The SQUID team was 98 percent men, so getting two women at a swim meet to do even one relay would have been an amazing accomplishment. So it was with great trepidation that I prepared to swim my first mixed medley relay.

I looked across the lanes and saw some of the people I had raced in the 100 back, and a few others that looked impossible to beat. Even the women looked like they would be able to swim faster than me. We were starting off with a female backstroker, Katie Luellen. I didn't know much about her, except that she wasn't a backstroker. As the backstrokers entered the water, I counted all the men who had jumped in the pool with Katie. I noticed three men who would very likely give their teams a big lead. I knew I could catch any of the women who might dive in ahead of me on the breaststroke leg, but what about the guys?

When the horn went off, I tried not to think about who was stepping up for the other teams to swim breaststroke. I just stared down my lane as Katie flipped and swam back to me. I climbed on the block and timed my takeoff to her finish. The first 25 felt rushed but strong, and when I turned at the 25-yard mark, I could see that only one person was ahead of me three lanes over, and it was a male swimmer. Not knowing how fast he was, I did everything I could to reach the finish before him. I touched the wall and looked at the scoreboard. The split for my lane was the second-fastest out of all eight lanes.

Rob Nasser was our butterflier, and he was slowly working on getting a lead for our female freestyler, Cecelia Gadd-Siegel. Cecelia dove in just a hair ahead of the female freestyler for Arizona Masters, and when she surfaced, I knew she was going to win. All the men who dove in after her were too far behind to catch her. We were going to win the relay!

Though I was confident of this with 25 yards to go, the female swimmer for Arizona Masters was not giving up easily, and a male swimmer from another team was making a big move off the turn. I cheered so loud for Cecelia that I'm sure the people outside the facility heard me over the other cheers and whistles. When she touched, I could tell she finished first, but I needed to see the scoreboard to make it official. I had won my first national relay!

The elation would be short lived. About 30 minutes later, I stepped up to swim on the men's 200 free relay. There was no way we were going to win this. Swimming for The Olympic Team was 1996 Olympian Brad Schumacher, and many people had told me that team would be chasing the national record. The other three guys on my relay were not as fast as me, and I knew I could only muster a 22-second swim, especially so close to my swim on the mixed relay 30 minutes earlier.

I swam first and tried my hardest, but there was no way we could catch teams that averaged 21 seconds per leg. We finished sixth in the heat and seventh in the age group, which was an accomplishment.

At the end of the first day, I wondered why I had been hesitant to sit out Masters nationals. The atmosphere is very loose. A few people swam slower than they expected, but it was all forgotten at the end of the session, when teams went out for extravagant dinners that were events in themselves. If not for the early start of the next day's session, I'm sure that dinner with the Colorado Masters team would have gone on through until dawn.

The next day I swam two of my two favorite events: 100 breast and 200 IM. After the thrill of winning the 100 back the day before, I was ready to swim the 100 breast. I had trained hard with the goal of breaking the national age group record in the event, but as I climbed the blocks, all I wanted to do was win. I had two strong competitors on either side of me: Christian Claytor and Ben Christoffel. The pain in the final 10 yards was excruciating, but I had swum this race so many times, I knew that I would get to the wall if I simply held my technique together. I touched the wall and the scoreboard was right in front of me. Next to my lane, I saw it: 55.99.

I couldn't believe what I saw. I heard the announcer declare that the time was a new national record. I heard the crowd cheer. I heard Christian say "Congratulations." But I still could not believe the time. In all the visualizations I had done in the weeks leading up to the meet, I had never imagined that I would go under 56 seconds. I didn't think it was possible. At 29 years old, I had stopped comparing my times to those from college and even high school. It was pointless to think I could swim as fast or faster than I did when I was in peak shape. My body was on the downslope of athletic prowess.

But seeing "55.99" made me ecstatic. It was the first Masters national record I had broken. As I walked toward the warmdown pool, I began to fully digest the meaning of the situation. No one in Masters swimming in my age group had ever swum faster.

The 200 IM was going to be the icing on the cake. When I'm feeling good, the race is always fun for me, because my best stroke comes at the crucial part of the race, when muscles start to tire. Also, the non-breaststrokers in the race fall apart after swimming so hard on the butterfly and backstroke legs.

The first time I looked across the lanes to see my competition was after the backstroke leg. I saw that three other swimmers were even with or ahead of me. I got a boost of energy from that and sprinted the breaststroke leg. After those 50 yards, the race was solely between myself and Neil Peiffer. He was three lanes over, but I could see him clearly. It's possible I sprinted too hard on the breaststroke, because I struggled on the freestyle leg. At the turn heading into the final 25 yards, I saw Neil turn even with me. I pushed off the wall and tried to find another gear, but everything was gone. It felt like an eternity, but I finished that final 25 and looked at the clock. Neil had beaten me by almost a second, and I swam a time that was three seconds off my lifetime best, which I had swum eight years ago. I swam fast because I had fun, because the competition gave me a lift at a crucial moment and because I'm always up for a fight to the finish, even if my muscles turn to steel.

The only events left for me to swim in Tempe were the 50 breast and 50 back. These events were on opposite ends of the spectrum for me. I felt confident I could win the 50 breast, but I wasn't sure I could even manage a top five finish in the 50 back. Backstroke since the early 1990s had become an underwater stroke, especially in short-course pools. Given my lack of ability to do underwater dolphin kicks, I knew I had to outswim everyone in the heat.

I won the 50 breast, but I felt I could have gone faster. It's always been difficult for me to swim 50s. Even though I am a sprinter, my body isn't ready to swim at top speed until 25 or 30 yards, which is too late to start swimming fast in a 50. I was happy that I won, but I was sure that I could swim faster than 25.80.

About two hours later, I placed second in the 50 back, a major surprise for me. The race had started around 5 p.m., when the sun was angled just enough to blind us on the second 25 yards. I was happy I had placed so high in both of my backstroke events. Either my age group had a dearth of great backstrokers, or I had made drastic improvements to the point that I could compete with the top backstrokers in Masters swimming.

Masters swimmers are a very jovial lot. Once the intense swimming is over, everyone lets loose for the post-meet party. The Colorado team gathered for a final dinner at a Mexican restaurant in Phoenix, and there was hardly any talk of swimming. Again, I wondered why it took me so long to decide to attend a Masters nationals. It was the most exciting meet I had ever attended, and I was sad to see it end. Because I lived in New Mexico, I had not seen many of my swimming friends from Colorado for a few months, and knew that returning to New Mexico meant more isolation from the swimming world. But on the drive back to Albuquerque, I was already mapping out my training schedule for my next major meet: the International Gay and Lesbian Aquatics championships in San Francisco. The meet was scheduled for mid-August at Stanford University. A friend of mine from Albuquerque, Matt Fisher, decided to train for the event, and we would travel together to save some money.

The day I registered for the event was probably one of the most nerve-wracking days of my life. After filling out the entry form, I noticed that the person who was handling all the entries was Geoff Glaser. This was the guy who asked me to zip up his suit in Sydney about six months earlier. I hadn't thought much about him since that day in Australia, but seeing his name made me think of those beautiful eyes and how I wish I had continued our conversation after his team beat us in the medley relay.

As I put the envelope with my entry form and check in the mail, I wondered if Geoff would recognize my name. The image of him sorting through the entries and stopping for a brief moment at my name gave me goosebumps. I had only spent a total of two minutes talking to this guy. Why was he making me smile from 800 miles away?

Chapter Thirteen

Just about every gay man dreams of visiting San Francisco. We call the city "the motherland." For us, it's a trip somewhat similar to Islamists making the trek to Mecca, and I finally got to go there in August 2003.

I was traveling with Matt Fisher, a friend from Albuquerque who I met at Gay Games. Neither of us had been to San Francisco, so we planned to arrive three days before the meet and see the sights.

On the night of our arrival, we discovered that the room we'd reserved wasn't ready, so we waited in the hotel lobby for more than an hour, where we gossiped about the other gay men and women checking into the hotel. Not long after we settled into the lobby sofas, a man sat down next to us and started a conversation. His name was Al, and he lived in Massachusetts and was swimming in the meet. Al was a very nice person, a very gentle soul. He was an officer in the Coast Guard and was very soft-spoken. I surmised he was in his early 40s and he looked every bit the military type. His hair was close-cropped and he wore his Coast Guard ring proudly. I can't recall everything Matt, Al and I talked about that night, but I do remember becoming attracted to Al. His demeanor had a very positive effect on me, and when the desk clerk said our room was ready, I made a promise to Al that we'd reconnect over the course of the weekend.

We began our first day of touring San Francisco in earnest. After finding a place to swim early in the morning, we took our rental car and headed straight for the Castro. Rounding the corner onto Castro Avenue, I saw the large rainbow flag at the end of the street summoning me like a beacon. I was in the land of my people.

Eating breakfast in a quaint restaurant, Matt and I saw many gay men traversing the street from all walks of life. What caught my eye the most were the couples holding hands while walking. Even in Denver, which is a very liberal city, I rarely saw that. I never saw two men kissing in public in Albuquerque, but here was a couple kissing in the restaurant in between sips of coffee. Maybe it was the feeling of *c'est la vie* or the notion that no one really cares what anyone else is doing, but I instantly wanted to live in San Francisco. If not for the high price of real estate and the danger of a major earthquake putting the entire state at the bottom of the ocean, I just might have packed up and moved there. Ever since leaving Colorado Springs, this was the kind of town I wanted to make my home. Maybe I just wanted to be in the exact opposite environment I experienced during my two years in Colorado Springs, and San Francisco certainly fit that bill.

After sightseeing in the Castro, we headed for downtown San Francisco. A great deal of our tour was from the rental car, but we did a fair amount of walking, which might not have been good for our tapers. We were enjoying the city so much we forgot that we shouldn't be walking to the top of Lombard Street, the most crooked street in the world. Or that we didn't have to walk through a street fair not far from our hotel. Or that it wasn't necessary to walk the ¼ mile to verify that the water of San Francisco Bay is indeed frigid and watch a flock of seals resting on a pier. It was a fun day that made me forget that I needed to prepare for a big meet ahead of me.

The night before the meet, the organizers held a party at the city's gay and lesbian center, which was in the heart of the Castro District. I recognized a lot of faces at the opening party. Many of them I had met in Sydney. I was shocked to see Mark Tewskbury there, who had come to the meet to get people interested in attending the Gay Games in Montreal in 2006. Shortly after Mark won the gold medal in the 100 backstroke at the 1992 Olympics, he had come out as a gay man and was suddenly thrown into the spotlight. He'd taken advantage of the situation quite well and was one of the more popular Canadian sport celebrities.

I created a challenge for myself at the party. I made a goal to be very outgoing and meet at least six new people. Happily, I accomplished that task and felt good about myself for getting out of my comfort zone for one night. I had a blast at the party, and as we went back to the hotel, I noticed that the serious swimmers had started to put on their game faces.

Unlike the heat sheets at nationals three months earlier, I did not recognize any names in my age group in any of my events. Brian Jacobson, who attended the Sydney Gay Games and was a teammate of mine on a couple of USA Swimming national teams, was not entered in the meet. I did see Dan Veatch's name in a few events, and was excited to see him again. But most of all, I made a point to find Geoff Glaser, who was signed up to swim the 800 free on the first day.

My training had changed slightly in the three months since I came back from Tempe nationals. I focused heavily on sprinting, which meant I was going to be in a lot of trouble in the 200 IM. Training for that event requires a swimmer to not only work on all four strokes, but train for each as if he or she were training for the 200-yard or 200-meter equivalent of each stroke, in addition to doing a lot of 200 IMs. I decided that my focus for the meet would be the sprint breaststrokes, in which I had a chance to break the world records in the 50-meter and 100-meter distances. I thought there was an outside shot of me setting a new world record in the 100 IM, as my time from Tempe converted to a shade under the record. But again, I hadn't done much IM training.

The 200 IM was the first event, and it hurt like hell. I could barely push off the final wall on the freestyle leg, and my kick was almost nonexistent. I felt like a Mack truck had landed on my lungs, and I fought for every breath after the race. Walking to the warmdown pool was a chore, but I still felt good about the race because I had won. No amount of pain and suffering after a race can overshadow the feeling of getting your hand on the wall before everyone else.

Despite the win, my first day of the IGLA championships was sort of a letdown. The excitement I felt in Sydney was not matched at Stanford. For whatever reason, the meet seemed to be running at a much lower key than Gay Games. It didn't have a championship feel to it. The swimming seemed to be an afterthought for most people. I noticed more than half the people there spent a good part of the day not watching any races. The Avery Aquatic Center at Stanford University had become a giant singles club, with swimsuits and sunglasses substituting for tight shirts and watered-down drinks. Perhaps the memories of

Tempe nationals were too fresh in my mind, and I expected a similar meet. This was, after all, the annual world championships for IGLA.

I did get to see Dan Veatch, who was feeling a little sick and said he might not swim the rest of the weekend. I did not see Geoff Glaser that first day, because I arrived at the pool after the 800 free had finished. I assumed he had left the pool not long after his swim.

The second day had more promise. After swimming 100 meters of freestyle in the 400 free relay, I was ready to chase the world record in the 100 breast. The conditions were fantastic. It was a very sunny day, but not hot at all. In the mid-afternoon, the temperature hadn't climbed higher than 90 degrees, which kept me from getting dehydrated. The pool we were swimming in was 10 feet deep and had been renovated recently. USA Swimming was holding its national championships there the following summer.

The time to beat was 1:02.87. I stood behind the blocks thinking about what it will feel like to own a Masters world record. While it wasn't a world record in the sense that it was the fastest swim ever done by anyone, it was considered the fastest swim done in a Masters competition in that age group. And Masters swimming had been around for about 30 years, with Olympians and NCAA champions making similar record attempts. I had never owned a record that would be chased by people around the world. The most prominent records I owned were the two national age group records in the 100 breast and my high school state record. It was a great honor to have those records, but a Masters world record would be different. The world Masters community would be chasing me.

That knowledge gave me a little boost when I stepped up to race. Even though I was swimming in a short course meters pool – a course relatively unfamiliar to me – the logistics of the race hadn't changed. I was still swimming four lengths of the pool and I would swim the race as if I were in a short course yards pool. The only difference would be that I would take one or two extra strokes each length.

The first 50 meters went by like a blur. I don't remember much of it, except I heard my teammates yelling for me at the turning end of the pool. When I made the turn at 50 meters, I saw Audy Octavian at my feet in the lane next to me. I didn't expect him to be so close, and it lit a fire in me. I turned on an extra gear and sprinted hard on the third 25. Turning for the final 25 meters, I willed myself to find an extra burst of energy for the sprint home. I found it for maybe three strokes, then my body began to go into oxygen debt. This was nothing new to me.

The final 10 meters of a 100-meter race always hurt if you're swimming the race correctly. But I had worked endlessly that summer on finishing my races well, and I used that to get my hand on the wall. Barely a second after touching, I whipped my head around to the opposite end of the pool, where the scoreboard displayed the times. *Please let it be faster than 1:02.87*, I begged the scoreboard. The scoreboard answered with a 1:02.83. I had beaten the world record by a mere four-hundredths of a second. I was more relieved than excited. One minor screw-up in the race and I would have been hanging my head in defeat. That's how close I came to not breaking the record.

After about 10 seconds, the realization hit me: I now have a world record! The time on the scoreboard was the fastest anyone in my age group had ever swum the race in history. I let loose with a few cheers and slapped the water with joy!

I climbed out of the pool, and two of my friends were there to give me big hugs. One of them was Al, the guy who had spent more than an hour with Matt and me in the hotel lobby. I told him I had just broken my first Masters world record, and he gave me another hug. It almost felt as good as breaking the record.

Another friend, Jason Klugman, knew something great had happened when he saw my celebration in the water. I verified the world record to him, and he sprinted to the announcer to make sure everyone knew. David and Patt came by to give me more hugs. David had recorded the race, and was there to document my reaction. I was stunned. I knew what I had just done, but I hadn't fully processed all of it. I walked to the warmdown pool just as the announcer told the crowd that I had broken the record. I stood next to the warmdown pool as some of my SQUID teammates came by to congratulate me. It's a cliché to say that everything felt different after breaking my first world record, but that is exactly how I saw the world. How does one live after breaking a Masters world record? I had seen a couple of world records happen in front of me by Jenny Thompson, Tom Dolan and many others, and I knew their lives had to be remarkably different after touching the wall. They were now the fastest on the planet in their event!

About five minutes into my warmdown, I saw Geoff Glaser in the lane next to me. His presence took me completely by surprise. I hadn't seen him all week, and suddenly he was two feet from me. He looked just as good then as he did 10 months earlier in Sydney. He had a dazzling smile, wonderful eyes and was very well-spoken. He was about to swim the 400 free, and I was starting to feel the lactic acid permeate my muscles, so we didn't talk long. Again, I proposed a time away from the pool to have a decent conversation.

I watched Geoff annihilate the field in the 400 free and break a meet record held by Olympian Bruce Hayes. He made it look effortless. I didn't know anything about Geoff besides the fact that he lived in San Francisco and was a fast freestyler, but I was optimistic that I'd know everything about him before I returned home.

I never truly came out of the haze of breaking the world record that day. I found myself reliving the race repeatedly. In the same week, Michael Phelps was setting multiple world records at the world championships in Barcelona, making his case as the most outstanding athlete that ever lived. Was my singular accomplishment as good as what Phelps was doing in Spain? Definitely not. But in my little world, it meant everything to me.

*****

The final day of the 2003 IGLA championships was going to be the most fun of all. The only two individual events I had to swim were the 100 IM and 50 breast. I always have fun swimming these events. The 100 IM is an all-out sprint from start to finish. It was the chief reason I returned to swimming. Unlike the 200 IM, you don't have time to build up the effort within each stroke. You have to push off each wall with the intent of sprinting your guts out, then do a turn and sprint another stroke. The 50 breast is very similar. It's a mad dash, and I always feel like I have it under control more than a 50 freestyle, which always feels like arms and legs flailing from one wall to the other.

The world record in the 100 IM was 56.67. The holder of that record was Atilla Czene, the 200 IM champion in the 1996 Olympic Games. I had no expectations that I would come close to a record held by an Olympic gold medalist. I had swum in a couple of short course meters meets unshaved and had come within two seconds of the record. But I still didn't allow myself to think that record could be mine. I stood behind the block prepared to swim as fast as I could, and the time would be secondary.

I have mixed feelings about butterfly being the first stroke in the individual medley. It's my worst stroke, so it's great to get it out of the way. But I have to try harder in that stroke, which makes me more tired for the rest of the race than most others I swim against. In this 100 IM, the butterfly felt fantastic for the first time in quite a while. I didn't have time to think much about it. About 12 seconds after I started, I was swimming backstroke. Just swim straight, I said, and spin those arms hard. Sprinting breaststroke was obviously an easy thing to do, but by now I had expended so much energy that I was starting to worry that I would crash and burn on the freestyle leg. I have a tendency to seriously deteriorate on freestyle, but I only had 25 meters to swim, and I felt like something amazing was happening. Everything had felt great up to this point. Unfortunately, I had no competition in the water to give me the boost I needed for the finish, so I had to dig deep and find the gear that would produce the freestyle leg I needed.

I touched the wall and was utterly spent. It was the hardest 100 IM I had ever swum – and the fastest one as well. I had broke Atilla Czene's world record by .04 seconds. I was stunned. If I was exploding with emotion after setting the world record in the 100 breast, I was on the verge of going ballistic with this one. To know that I just swam faster than an Olympic champion, in an event that is not my best, was too much to take. I climbed out of the pool and was in such shock that I couldn't move for a couple of minutes. I bent over and rested my hands on my knees while the thought of swimming faster than a world record for the second time sunk in.

Two hours after that swim, I still couldn't comprehend how I put up that time in the 100 IM. Perhaps lowering my expectations was the key to the race, or the fact that I enjoy swimming it so much. But I had one more race to swim, and it was the 50 breast. The world record was 29.30, and I was very confident I could swim faster than that. I swam 28.60, and knew I could have put up a faster time. I spun my wheels too much and panicked on the last 25 meters. Even a 50 has some element of control to it. But it was the third world record I had beaten in two days, and the fact that I was a world record holder was indescribable.

Though the swimming races had come to an end, the meet still had one more event: the Pink Flamingo. The Denver team had put together a routine, and I was anxious to see it and the others in the competition. I packed up my bag and walked over to the diving well, where the routines would be performed. Halfway there, I saw Todd Oakes and Geoff Glaser also walking to the stadium pool. Two of the most handsome men in the facility together! Like Geoff, Todd swam for the

San Francisco team and was a fast swimmer. Todd had swum at Stanford in the 1980s and was a talented sprinter. Todd, Geoff and I talked about our swims, and I was very modest about my world record swims. I've never been the type of person to be boastful about my accomplishments, even when people say I have the right to do so. Vanity is not one of my strongest suits.

Geoff remembered that I lived in Albuquerque and asked if I liked living there. I told him it was the equivalent of living in a wasteland. I told him something was wrong with a city if I looked forward to driving away from it most weekends to see friends in Denver.

The conversation couldn't have been more pleasant. I noticed that Geoff was hanging onto every word I said, and I was doing the same with him. This was the third conversation we'd had, and I was finding myself more attracted to him each time.

Geoff asked me if I was going to the after-party that night. I said I was, but he said he wasn't sure if he wanted to go. I tried to convince Geoff that we could learn a lot more about each other through more conversation, and he said he would seriously consider it. I gave both of them a hug and went to find my teammates in the stands as the Pink Flamingo competition started.

After watching a dozen routines filled with glitter, costumes, heavy makeup and plenty of showtunes, Matt and I drove back to San Francisco to prepare for the evening's festivities, which were to be held at a nightclub not far from our hotel. It was so close, it only took us 20 minutes to walk there.

The entire night was mildly entertaining. I kept thinking about Geoff. I wanted to see him walk through the door. I smiled at the thought of him entering, our eyes meeting and getting another hug from him. I felt a great connection with Geoff, and I hoped to learn more about him that night to see if my attraction was genuine, or if was spurred on purely by hormones.

Geoff never showed up to the party that night. I wanted to leave after the second hour, but something told me I should wait until the end, in case he had a last-minute change of heart. Apparently, he never did, and I wasn't sure if I'd ever see him again. Since we'd only seen each other at gay-related swim meets, I could only wonder if our next meeting would be at the 2004 IGLA meet in Fort Lauderdale, Florida.

I left San Francisco with the feeling that the four days I spent there was the start of something wonderful. I was sure my swimming had taken its largest step forward since I began swimming Masters. In three months I had swum times I didn't think were possible given the drastic lifestyle changes I had made in the past two years. How was it possible that I was able to come within two seconds of my best time in the 100 breast swimming only 3,500 yards per workout?

I could only attribute it to the strong training base I had built in my younger years, and my older body was now able to make a withdrawal from that. Plus, I was now having more fun in the sport than I was in the mid-1990s, when my swimming had reached a plateau and I was spending much of my days wondering if I should come out to my teammates instead of focusing on my swimming. Being publicly out and making a larger investment in my swimming was a major plus in my life.

Now that my swimming had been resurrected, all I needed to do was find a job that satisfied me and a man that wanted to marry me.

Just a month after returning from San Francisco, I received a large envelope from FINA, the international governing body for aquatic sports. Inside were three certificates verifying the world record times I had swum at the IGLA meet. I couldn't stop admiring the certificates. I got them framed so I could have a daily reminder of what I had done that summer. Unfortunately, that joy was short-lived.

That November, when FINA released the updated list of Masters world records, I realized that I only held one world record. FINA updates its list of Masters world records only twice a year because so many are broken, so it's hard to know if someone has swum faster than the published world record. That fall, I discovered that Canada's Russell Patrick had swum faster than the published world records in the 50 and 100 breaststrokes in a meet earlier in the year. I was crushed. I had believed that I was the fastest swimmer in history in my age group, only to discover that someone else had gone faster. The bright side was that my time in 100 IM stood as the world record. I had to laugh at the fact that my first official world record – Masters or otherwise – was in what I would say is my third or fourth best event.

I didn't want to falsely display the certificates which named me as a world record holder in the breaststroke events, so I took them off the wall and put them in a scrapbook. At the very least, it was a lasting record of a great weekend in San Francisco.

Me and Dan Veatch at the 2003 IGLA championships

Chapter Fourteen

I had been dreading the arrival of Feb. 11, 2004, for about a year. With each passing day, I became more depressed about turning 30. This wasn't the kind of depression that is used as a punchline by comedians in jokes about aging. This was a very noticeable, very real depression that took over my life.

By the time the calendar turned to 2004, I had almost completely withdrawn from social interaction. I had less interest in swimming, even after my summer of fast swims. My depression began when I looked at the life plan I set out for myself, suddenly realizing that many of the things I expected and hoped to achieve by my 30th year had not happened.

By the time I hit 30, I wanted to be a homeowner, but instead I was renting an apartment below a guy who blasted episodes of "Star Trek Generations" at 2 a.m. I wanted to be a film critic, not a journalist who had been given empty promises for three years that my dream job would, in fact, be mine in a very short time.

But most of all, I wanted to be married. Yes, married in the going-to-the-chapel-and-we're-gonna-get-married sense of the word. At the time, the only places that would happen were in the Netherlands and Belgium. No one was willing to touch the notion of full-on marriage rights for gays and lesbians in the United States. In lieu of packing up and moving to Holland, a committed and loving relationship would have been just fine.

All of these things were supposed to happen by the time I turned 27. I don't recall why I picked that age. Maybe it seemed like that perfect time when I was saying goodbye to my free-living young-adult years and ready to usher in the real-adult years with a wonderful job, a home of my own and a husband.

To this day, I wonder why I desperately wanted to be married. Being raised by a single mother should have created the mindset that living alone was just fine. Maybe my constant (and unsuccessful) urges for my mother to remarry caused me to believe that every person deserved companionship.

It wasn't for lack of trying that my life plan was slowly slipping away. I worked hard at the newspapers in Denver and Albuquerque, trying to prove my worth, to pay my dues. I got plenty of compliments from my bosses, but I always heard the same line: Newspapers didn't need full-time film critics anymore, especially when they could take movie reviews off the wire for free from The Associated Press.

Because I was never willing to call Albuquerque my home, I wasn't willing to go house hunting there. I wasn't ready to buy a home anyway; my savings account was anemic after returning from my two-week trip to Australia, and I barely had enough for that "rainy day."

The idea of me owning a home in Albuquerque was just as likely as finding a good husband there. The only likely husband prospect was a handsome guy who I saw regularly at the gym. In my fantasy world where everything worked out with no fuss, this man turned out to be the gentle soul with the great body and bedroom eyes I had been looking for. Despite my attraction to him – and despite the fact that I noticed him sneaking a few glances my way – I never talked to the guy. I wasn't the type to pick up people at the gym, and I didn't want to participate in such an endeavor.

Swimming was the only thing in my life that gave me any pleasure. I found it difficult to will my mind and body to take pleasure in the little things. Seeing that the big picture was blank and desolate discouraged me.

I didn't allow myself to believe that I was clinically depressed. I didn't even want to bring it up to my doctor. When I thought of depression, I thought of people who were suicidal. I certainly had no desire to kill myself. I only wanted to spend entire days in bed.

When I came home from a particularly rough day at work or just wasn't feeling emotionally in a good place, I could always count on a viewing of my favorite movie to instantly lift my spirits. After watching *Ferris Bueller's Day Off*, my mood would lift considerably. But as 2003 ended and 2004 surged ahead, I found myself still in a funk after watching Ferris and his pals cavort around Chicago. This was a major clue that something was wrong. One of the funniest movies ever made was failing to make me laugh. I didn't want to turn 30 thinking about depression, so I pushed all the thoughts to the back of my mind and surged ahead through my days.

I did have few bright spots leading up to my 30th birthday. In the fall of 2003, I had become an assistant coach for Kirtland Aquatic Club, which was a small but prospering age-group swim team. Some of the parents had discovered that I lived in Albuquerque and had been trying for a year to get me on the coaching staff. I continually turned them down because I didn't think I would make a good coach. But I said yes eventually because I needed the money, only to find that the young kids I coached, ranging from 8 to 11 years old, were fun to be with every day. They enjoyed swimming, and I enjoyed teaching them about the sport. Occasionally I got to work with the older kids, and sometimes got to train with them.

Another spirit lifter on the road to my birthday was the idea of swimming in a new age group. I knew spring nationals in Indianapolis in late April wasn't going to be a cakewalk, but I took on the task of attempting to swim as fast as I did the year before at nationals. That would be a major feat, since many of the times I swam were inconceivable to me.

I knew that three months of serious training wouldn't get me to the goals I made for myself, and I knew deep down that I wasn't fully invested in this swimming season (another effect of the so-called depression). But I had set some major swimming goals, and all but one of them would take place at Masters nationals that April in Indianapolis.

The other goal would be attempted at a meet in Boston one week after nationals, where I would attempt to break a world record in the short-course meters 50 breaststroke. Now that I was 30, I could take a shot at what I thought was a very easy world record, which was held by my friend Dean Putterman, a standout breaststroker in Masters who had set the record about 10 years earlier. Knowing that FINA only published the latest records in May and November, I was certain the gods weren't smiling on me; surely someone had been swimming fast since the last list of records was published on Nov. 1. But I didn't think much about that as April rolled around and I prepared for two big swim meets.

Al, the Coast Guard officer who I had met in San Francisco last summer, invited me to spend the week with him at his home in Cape Cod, then spend the weekend in Boston and swim in a meet hosted by the Boston gay swim team. It was an offer I couldn't refuse. I wasn't expecting anything other than an extension of our friendship, and the trip would be a nice way to take my mind off my life in New Mexico.

I celebrated my birthday alone, but I wasn't upset about that. I didn't want people to make a big to-do about turning 30, and I made very little fuss about it when I got phone calls from friends or well-wishers at work.

I forced myself to believe that I wasn't clinically depressed now that I was entering my 31st year of life, and as such I wasn't aware of the telltale signs in the pool. I was never a peppy person during the 5:30 a.m. workouts, but in the six months after the IGLA meet in August 2003, I was barely going through the motions in workout. Swimming fast was a chore, and I found myself unable to recover as quickly as I used to. I could hardly get my heart rate down to a manageable rhythm, and my breathing was always labored at the end of most sets. I attributed it all to forcing myself to work hard when my body refused to do so.

When I visited my doctor in February for my annual birthday checkup, the furrow in his brow began to worry me. He didn't like the way my blood pressure readings had skyrocketed in the past year. The blood pressure reading from the nurse read 120/110, which he said was very unhealthy – and surprising, given my diet and exercise. He took another reading, and it was nearly the same. We talked for about a half hour about my lifestyle. I had told him I was gay, but he knew I practiced safe sex (the safest kind in fact – unforced abstinence!) and I always took steps to eat well. Certainly I didn't need to exercise more. He suggested a stress test, but I was worried that many people had died recently while performing that test. Because I ate well and was in above average physical shape, he wanted to see if the high blood pressure was genetic, and if my current life had exacerbated the condition. I broke down and told him I had days where I was so tired I could hardly concentrate, that

I wanted to spend entire days in bed and not see the sunlight. He didn't want to call it depression. He wanted to see if a change in blood pressure could have a positive effect on my moods and tiredness.

When he recommended that I start taking pills for my blood pressure, I got very nervous. I had just turned 30 years old; no one that young should get the news that they will be on medication for the rest of their lives. Plus, I was scared that I would forget to take the pill each day. What would happen then?

Despite my fears, I agreed to start the medication. I took two pills every day. One pill was called Lisinopril and the other was hydrochlorothiazide (HCTZ). The latter is a diuretic, which meant that I was going to the bathroom three times more than normal for the first month I was on the medication. Because the pill worked hard to force all the water out of my system – and thereby thinning the blood – I got frequent headaches. Some days the headaches were of migraine strength, and it made the days worse.

I wanted to get off the pills and try something different, but I agreed to give it three months, the normal time period for the body to adjust to new medication. As the winter of 2004 turned into spring, I did notice that workouts were getting more manageable, but not to a degree that I felt like the pills were having a major positive effect.

Out of curiosity, I checked the World Anti-Doping Agency's list of prohibited drugs to find out if Lisinopril and HCTZ were there. Masters swimming doesn't monitor drug use at all, so swimmers can get away with taking anything without legal repercussion. But I wanted to know if I was getting any unfair advantage anyway.

I wasn't surprised to find HCTZ on the list. Diuretics have long been a staple among drug cheats, but I was happy to know that if I found myself swimming a major FINA meet where there was drug testing, I could show proof that the medicine was being used to treat high blood pressure. Plus, I was only taking 10 mg a day. The cheaters were taking four times that much.

Within a month of taking the pills, I began to feel lighter in the water. My recovery rate after hard sets had improved so much that it only took about a minute for my heartbeat to return to normal instead of the usual two or three minutes. My body was working overtime to cleanse itself and thin my blood, so I was still tired every day. But I knew I was on the road to wellness.

Less than a month after my birthday, Kirtland Aquatic Club won its first state championship. The victory came as a small shock to us; beating the state's bigger teams was a huge boost for such a young team. I was able to contribute to the win not just as a coach, but as a swimmer. After much prodding, I agreed to swim in the meet, though I didn't shave and taper as many of the older kids had done. I won four events at the meet and helped the team to victory in a couple of relays.

Between the physical turnaround with the pills and the state championship, I began to sense the clouds parting on the malaise I had placed on myself. It had seemed that turning 30 wasn't as bad as I predicted. The final month of preparation for the spring nationals was one of the best training sessions I'd ever had, but I knew I hadn't built a strong base to swim as fast as I had the year before. First and foremost were my goals to win. I had four more years in the age group to set records.

The previous year in Tempe, I had intense competition in all six of my individual races. At my first nationals in the 30-34 age group, I found myself swimming alone in four out of the six events. In the 100 back and 200 IM, I was racing an old friend, Andreas Roestenberg. Andreas and I were roommates at Texas during my sophomore year. Andreas had transferred from junior college to swim at Texas, and he had a great future ahead of him as a distance swimmer. When I saw him at 2003 nationals, he was co-owner of a company that catered mostly to triathletes. They also made competition suits for pool swimmers, and he let me try some of them. That was my first formal introduction to racing in a suit that wasn't a brief. In a couple of the relays in Tempe, I wore the suit Andreas gave me, and it felt awkward to swim with material covering my entire upper leg, all the way down to my knees. Those suits are called "jammers," and I had refused to wear them in a time when they were the norm because I enjoyed the feel of water rushing past my skin as I swam. Wearing jammers, or the full bodysuits, you hardly feel the water on the covered part of you, and it can be uncomfortable.

As a favor to Andreas, I wore the jammers he gave me the year before in our two races together in Indianapolis. I beat him in the 100 back and 200 IM, swimming times that were slower than the previous year, but not by much. I scored a new national record in the 100 breast to go with the one I set in the 25-29 age group last year, but I was confident I could go faster.

I left Indianapolis a little disenchanted with swimming in the 30-34 age group. I watched some of the races in the younger age groups, as well as the older ones, and they all seemed to have swimmers that I would have enjoyed racing. The rules in Masters swimming only let you compete in your age group for national and international competitions, so I was swimming against the clock. It is said that the clock is your fiercest competitor, but that would only be true if the clock were swimming in the lane next to me. I saw a hotly contested race in the 100 IM in the 25-29 age group and wished I had been a part of it. Gary Hall Jr., the multi-Olympic medalist, had brought several teammates from the Race Club to the meet and were putting on a show. Gary was one of the competitors in that 100 IM race, and though we had swum together at Texas, we never raced.

The Monday after nationals ended, I hopped on a plane to Boston. Essentially, this was not a vacation. I had to maintain my taper for one very important swim that would take place in five days. Because Al would be working during the week, I made plans to visit downtown Boston alone for one day only. The other four days before the meet would be spent mostly relaxing.

The gay swim team in the Boston area is called Liquid Assets New England Swimming, or LANES. They were some of the nicest people I met, and also the most accommodating. When I told them I was tapering to swim in their meet, they were willing to let me essentially do my own thing when I showed up for their workouts. Most Masters teams don't allow guests to do that. I wasn't sure how to maintain my taper for another week. In the five days between nationals and the LANES meet, I swam two hard workouts and three easy workouts. I knew I still had some speed and it was all I needed. I wasn't swimming more than 100 meters in one race, and the event I was concentrating on was only 50 meters. In most cases, a sprint race can be salvaged if the taper is wasted, but I didn't want to leave anything to chance. It was a great feeling to get that world record from last summer, and I wanted to enjoy that sensation in a new age group.

I arrived at the campus of Northeastern University and wasn't too thrilled with the pool. The starting end was about nine feet deep, but the turn end was only four feet deep. Not a good depth for breaststrokers. It reminded me of the pool in Columbia, Missouri, where I swam in my high school state championships. I remembered how well I swam in that pool, so why not here?

As a way to prepare for the 50 breast, I signed up for the 100 free, which was about an hour before the 50 breast. I could have signed up for the 100 breast, but swimming the 100 free was a good excuse to swim a different event, and I was afraid the 100 breast might take too much out of me if there was not enough time between races.

Stepping onto the blocks for the 50 breast, I quickly glanced over to the side of the pool, where Al was cheering loudly for me. He was the only person I had told about my record attempt, and I asked him to keep it a secret – unless I broke the record. I knew no one in the heat would challenge me, and what I typically do in those situations is create a lot of self-talk. There's a voice in my head that's reminding me of the key points in each race, and pushing me to swim harder, faster and stronger at the end of the race. When I dove into the water, that voice told me to not glide too long before the underwater pull. Then, it got me on top of the water and churning away to the 25-meter turn. I pushed off the wall and remembered to bend my elbows slightly to avoid scraping the bottom of the pool. I surfaced off the turn and the voice in my head said, "Go! Go! Go! Get those arms moving faster! Come on! Almost there!"

When I touched the wall, I immediately looked to the scoreboard on my right. It took me less than a second to recognize that the 28.50 on the scoreboard was a new world record. No one in the stands knew what was going on, and since they could not see the scoreboard, they probably didn't know why this guy was celebrating enthusiastically.

"Ladies and gentlemen, Jeff Commings has just set a new Masters world record!" I heard the announcement and everyone started applauding. I couldn't take my eyes off the scoreboard. I had just broken Dean's record by six tenths of a second. The record was indeed a soft one, but more than that, I had swum a tenth faster than my swim at the far superior pool during the IGLA meet last year.

Then came the hard part. Masters swimmers who set world records at meets that aren't nationals or world championships usually have to make sure the meet director and referee submit the proper forms to make sure FINA ratifies the record. After my warmdown, I talked to the meet referee, who assured me all the paperwork and certification would be done by meet's end. One of things that needed to be done after the meet was over was to make sure the pool measured 25 meters. One tenth of a meter short or long, and the swim would be deemed null and void. I watched the officials measure the pool with my heart racing in my throat. The starting end was on a bulkhead and it was quite possible the pool staff hadn't placed the bulkhead at the right point. I wanted to trust that the pool was the right length. Why wouldn't it be?

After measuring the length in every lane of the pool, the referee looked up to me in the stands and gave me a thumbs up. The pool was the perfect length.

That was the last thought I gave to the world record submission process. The referee said he had gone through it before, and said he'd make sure everything would be sent to the right people.

I was ready to celebrate. As I exited the locker room and walked onto the deck, I was met by a fairly burly guy.

"I just wanted you to know that Massachusetts made it legal for us to get married, and I know you and I are going to get married."

Certainly this stranger was handsome, but I wasn't turned on by his directness. All I could say was "OK." I walked away and didn't think twice about it.

Because it was Saturday night, it was only customary to head to the gay bars. Again, I was in a very celebratory mood and I was in a new town. I was feeling a little bit more outgoing than usual. A group of us took the subway to a few popular Boston bars, and while I was glad to see that the men there were all quite fetching, I wasn't very excited about the atmosphere. The third bar was more of a dance club, and by this time it was after midnight. I wasn't really looking for sex or anything beyond a place to hang out with friends.

After about 15 minutes of dancing, I suddenly felt someone grinding behind me. In a different place, I might have jumped away and moved to another part of the dance floor. But I got into the grinding for a little bit before turning around to find the guy who proposed marriage to me a few hours earlier.

"Hi!" the strange man yelled above the music. "Remember me?"

"How could I forget?"

That made him feel good, and he continued dancing very close to me. He had his shirt off, and I could tell he worked out regularly. I wasn't ready to accept his marriage proposal based on his looks, but the offer had become a little more interesting.

After a few minutes of dancing with him, I was ready to leave. I had danced pretty much all the sweat out of me in the course of our three-hour bar tour. I was tired, and I think it was about time for the bar to close. I wanted to find Al and head back to the hotel for a good night's sleep before we drove back to his home in the country. But the man who wanted to marry me – who I now knew as Peter – wasn't ready to say goodnight. It took very little convincing for me to get in his car and go to his home not far away.

In the drive to Peter's house I tried to wonder what it was about me that convinced him that I was the perfect choice for him as a husband, and if I should consider his proposal strongly. During the drive to his home, I learned he taught math in elementary school, played on a gay rugby team and was 32 years old. He was doing his best to show that I should think strongly about accepting his marriage proposal.

The sex was very good, but I was not sure I could uproot my life and move to Boston. I knew I had nothing keeping me in Albuquerque, but the thought of moving to the other side of the country for a man I had known for less than 12 hours wasn't appealing. The next morning, I tried to convince him that we needed to know each other a lot better before any long-term commitment could be made. As flattered and honored as I was that there was a man who felt I was the one after only one day, I knew I couldn't act brashly.

As a way to get to the next step as quickly as possible, Peter handed me a cell phone that we could use to communicate as often as possible. I had never been thrilled with the idea of a cell phone, but if he wanted to give me a cell phone free of charge, I wasn't going to argue. I told him we would talk every day, and I meant it. At the moment, this was the only option out of my life in Albuquerque, and as much as I wanted to jump into it headfirst, I wanted to make sure this guy was authentic. The bloom was certain to fall off the rose within a couple of weeks.

On the drive back to the country, Al told me to be very wary of Peter. He didn't know him very well, but he knew him well enough to know that I shouldn't be so quick to rush into a relationship with him.

That advice played continuously in my head as I boarded the plane to Albuquerque.

Chapter Fifteen

The month of May started very well for me. Three months after turning 30, I felt like my life was starting to take the path I had expected it to take two or three years earlier. I was still battling with some bouts of depression, but they had become a little more manageable after my trips to Indianapolis and Boston.

I had just gone to Boston to spend a week with a good friend and came away from the trip with a new world record and a potential life mate. The world record was expected; the hunky man begging me to marry him was not.

I couldn't stop telling all my friends about the circumstances behind meeting Peter, the rugby player and occasional swimmer who wanted very much to marry me. It felt like a slightly surreal fairy tale. My friends warned me against such a major long-distance relationship, but I told them that if all this worked out, we'd be sharing a life in the same city soon.

Peter and I talked on the phone every day. We spent lots of time learning about each other. I liked the fact that he was very athletic. The fact that he was a rugby player was not lost on me. It added a large degree of masculinity to him. His job as a teacher was a bigger bonus. It was not a high-paying job, but he felt fulfilled in his career choice, a goal I had not yet achieved. I admired Peter greatly, but after two weeks of our relationship, I still wasn't certain this was the man to marry.

A couple of weeks after my first visit to Boston, I returned to see film composer John Williams conduct a concert at the Boston Symphony Hall. This was to be the first time I was going to see my idol in person, and as a way to thank him for hosting me for a week, I had invited Al to join me when I bought the tickets in February. I told Peter I was coming to Boston for the concert and he was very excited. Al was willing to give up his ticket so my new boyfriend, Peter, could go, but I was adamant that Al go with me. I stayed with Peter in Boston that weekend, and most of it revolved around sex. Not much of it was spent really getting to know each other.

I watched Peter at a rugby practice, and I thought about his potential as my husband. Among all the players on the field, he was definitely the handsomest man out there. But why wasn't I still feeling that connection I felt when I first saw Kent at that bar four years ago? Back then, I wanted to know everything about Kent, and after a week I felt like I had spent a lifetime with him. With Peter, I still had a long way to go, but I was willing to take the time.

In the days before Memorial Day weekend, I noticed that Peter and I were not talking as long on the phone. Usually, I was the one ending conversations early, but suddenly he was the one who said he had things to do. I didn't think much of it at the time. Every day we talked about the logistics of me moving in with him and starting a new life in Boston. Every day I felt touched by his sentiments, and by the time he packed up for a long holiday trip to Vermont, I was growing more sure that Peter was true to his word.

Memorial Day weekend was very long. Peter and I did not talk the entire time. He had taken a drive to Vermont with friends and warned that cell phone coverage might be erratic. I understood and was willing to wait until his return Monday to restart our daily talks. But on Monday evening, I wasn't able to reach Peter. I left nearly a dozen voicemails that night, asking him to call.

I still hadn't talked to him by Wednesday morning, and now I was worried. What had happened in Vermont?

On Thursday morning, I could not concentrate at swim practice. Where had Peter gone? Was he dead on the side of a road? Did he meet

176

a better candidate for marriage in Vermont? Too many questions clouded my head during the early-morning swim that day.

I got the answer when I arrived at work at 9 a.m.

Opening my AOL email account, I saw Peter's email address among the list of senders, and immediately my spirits rose. The subject line was pretty simple – "hey" – and I opened it, wanting to know that everything was fine.

In just a couple of short paragraphs, Peter wrote that he talked with his best friends during the weekend trip, and he came to the conclusion that we might not be compatible as a couple. He asked me to mail back his cell phone. The End.

I stared at the email for at least thirty minutes. I was too stunned to move. I felt my blood turn to ice from the cold shoulder Peter had given me. I could not believe that he broke up with me over an email. I couldn't believe the suddenness of it. He was practically ready to reserve the U-Haul six days ago; now, he was acting as if I was a leper. It was significantly more devastating than the breakup with Kent, in which he immediately got in his car and drove back to Denver, leaving me in shambles.

Since I was sitting at my desk at *The Albuquerque Tribune*, smack dab in the middle of the newsroom, I tried hard to maintain my composure. It wasn't easy.

I got up and took a long walk. I was mad, but curiosity was the reigning emotion. I was very curious why he felt afraid to call me to talk about his feelings. Sending the e-mail felt cowardly, and I refused to respond to it. I was tempted to throw the cell phone against a wall and mail back the pieces.

I don't know why I was so torn up over the breakup. Peter and I hadn't connected on a real emotional level, and in many ways I had had my doubts about the nature of our relationship. But he had made a vow to marry me, and to go from that promise to a sudden cutting of the cord in less than three weeks was the most devastating part. Why did I let myself get duped? What transpired over the holiday weekend?

For the third time in seven years, I had the rug yanked out from under me. I know there are men and women out there who have this happen monthly, or maybe weekly, in the dating world. Three strikes, and I wanted to be out of the game.

Over the weekend, I told many of my friends what had happened. Many of them had warned me against Peter, including Al, and they tried hard not to take an "I told you so" attitude. But I commend them for convincing me to not give up on love. Part of the dating game, they reminded me, was about trial and error.

It took a couple of weeks for the fog to clear. One of the first faces I saw in my mind was Geoff Glaser, the gorgeous blond man I met in Sydney in 2002 and again the following year in San Francisco. We lived almost 1,000 miles apart, but he seemed like such a nice man.

That wasn't the first time I thought of Geoff that spring. Just a month earlier, Dean Putterman had asked me if I planned to attend the 2006 Gay Games in Montreal. I told him since it was close to the 2006 Masters world championships (which I was definitely attending), I might pass on another Gay Games experience. He tried to convince me that we could put together a group of fast gay men and set some world records under Team Homo. The idea kept me interested, and among the people I thought to join us on the team was Geoff.

As I climbed out of my breakup funk, I figured Gay Games would be the way into a conversation with Geoff. I'd recruit him for Team Homo at the 2006 Gay Games.

I did a Google search on Geoff Glaser and obviously, his swimming accomplishments were at the top of the list. I scoured the results to find a phone number or email for him. I knew I could be setting myself up for another heartbreak if I discovered he was happily in a relationship, but I was under the impression he was single both times I met him.

One thing I did find was a Web page of pictures during one of San Francisco's Gay Pride Parades, and a picture of someone named Fr. Geoff Glaser standing with a group of men. The picture wasn't high quality, but the man wearing clericals looked very much like the Geoff Glaser I saw in San Francisco. Was Geoff a priest? Clearly not a Catholic priest, since he was so publicly gay. Maybe he was an Episcopal priest. They are allowed to marry, have money and live regular lives. The problem was that I didn't know any Episcopal priests to help me verify if one could be openly gay.

In the two times I'd spoken with Geoff, I got no sense he was a priest. I spent years around priests, and none of them were like Geoff. I took the plunge and sent an e-mail to Todd Oakes, who was our mutual friend. I asked Todd for Geoff's e-mail, which he gave me. I wrote to Geoff using a casual tone, asking him about his swimming plans for 2006 and whether he had plans to attend the Gay Games. Whether or not Geoff was interested was not the point; this was a first contact between us, and his response would judge how I would move forward. I prepared myself for a response saying he was attending Gay Games – with his partner.

On May 28, 2004, I received a long response from Geoff, and the words contained in it gave me hope.

More than once, I read such phrases as "I was really happy for you," "It was nice to get your e-mail" and "I enjoyed reading it." But most of all, the declaration "You're adorable!" gave me the courage to continue the communication.

Over the next two weeks, Geoff and I either sent an e-mail or talked on the phone every day. On June 1, he left San Francisco to spend a month in Fort Collins, Colorado, with his parents and train at altitude for a Masters meet in July. I was curious how someone could take an entire month off work to train, but wasn't sure if I wanted to know. I thought he could either be a teacher on summer break or unemployed. The unemployed angle didn't seem right to me, so I outright asked him about his job in an e-mail. In his reply, he said he was an Episcopal priest. That meant the photo I saw of a Geoff Glaser in clericals was actually him. He said he rarely tells people about being a priest because so many of them are immediately turned off. I wasn't turned off by it; I was actually more intrigued about him. I looked forward to learning more about being an openly gay man in the priesthood, among other things.

A few days into June, Geoff invited me to visit him for a weekend in Fort Collins. I knew it would be a long drive. It took seven hours to drive to Denver, and Fort Collins was easily another hour's drive north, but I didn't want to pass up the opportunity to make up for the missed time together in Sydney or San Francisco.

I couldn't drive fast enough to Fort Collins on June 18. I was excited to explore the possibilities with Geoff over the next three days. Because he had invited me to spend the weekend with him at his parents' home, I assumed his parents knew he was gay and were OK with him bringing a gay man to stay at their home. But what would we do if the possibility of sex entered the conversation? I'd feel weird having sex in my mother's home, even if she were 100 percent fine with my sexuality; Geoff and his family couldn't be that open.

A snowstorm just a few miles outside of Fort Collins slowed things down, but I managed to arrive at the house in less than eight hours. It felt like much less.

Geoff opened the door and greeted me with a wonderful smile and a much-needed hug. It was one of those hugs that had "friendship" written all over it but suggested that he was hopeful for more. It was our first hug, at least in my memory, and I liked what I felt. Not necessarily the physical part, but as I was holding him, something immediately felt right.

His parents were in the living room watching television. Madeleine and Walter Glaser welcomed me into my home right away and didn't flinch when they saw I was black. That was my biggest concern. Had Geoff mentioned that to them beforehand? I never felt an ounce of judgment or hesitation from Geoff's parents.

Geoff had made plans for us to swim with the local age-group team, but before that he took me on a tour of Fort Collins, which wasn't much of a town. We ate at a pizza parlor and talked endlessly. Though we had talked constantly through email, this was the first true conversation we had face-to-face since we saw each other in San Francisco. Naturally, swimming took up a large chunk of the conversation. I loved hearing his hearty laugh and seeing his eyes light up when he talked about things that interested him. I also opened up about my experiences in college, including my adventures coming out to two of my teammates. Very few people in this world knew that, and I felt no qualms about telling Geoff. After spending just a couple of hours with him, I felt free to reveal everything to him.

We arrived at the pool for workout a little early, and we were the only ones in the locker room. We both dressed in the same aisle, and as he took his shirt off, I tried my hardest to not stare at his washboard abs and very tan torso. Absolute beauty. As I dressed into my swimsuit, I noticed that he also tried to look elsewhere.

During the workout, Geoff had noticed many problems with my freestyle, specifically that I was having a problem balancing my body when I turned to breathe. I took his advice to heart. He was an accomplished English Channel swimmer and was a world-ranked Masters swimmer. After the workout, Geoff and I stayed at the pool and he taught me new drills that eventually fixed my freestyle and helped me work towards getting rid of my insufferable scissors kick. I still use his drills.

I don't recall much of the conversation that took place during dinner at a Mexican restaurant. I do remember that I was getting nervous about returning to his parents' home. When we got to the house, we went downstairs to watch "The Omen." Not the most romantically-inclined movie, I know.

Geoff and I sat on opposite ends of the couch for the entire movie. Neither of us knew how to broach the subject of initimacy. We had really only had one day together. Was it presumptuous to think sex was included in the visit? The one thing I knew was that after only eight hours together, I knew I wanted to pursue the chance of a romantic relationship. I didn't need to have sex with him to know that much.

The movie ended around 11 p.m., and I knew the conversation had to happen. We needed to know if I would be going upstairs to sleep in the guest bedroom, or if I would stay in the downstairs bedroom with him. The words that got Geoff's head resting in my lap escape me, but I remember the big smile he gave when he knew there was a very good chance we would be having sex in his parents' basement.

After watching 15 minutes more of television, we went into the bedroom and laid in bed together, just staring into each other's eyes. After about a minute, we had our first kiss. It was frightening and exhilarating at the same time.

Geoff and I made plans to spend Saturday in Denver. We would hang out at Elitch Gardens, an amusement park owned by Six Flags, then eat a great dinner and spend the night in a nice hotel before returning to Fort Collins the next morning.

It was mid-June in Colorado, so I wasn't surprised that the temperature only topped out at 70 degrees that day. But it didn't hamper my mood. Geoff and I were enjoying the day at the amusement park, and I was glad to spend time talking to him while waiting in lines.

We planned to leave the park around 5 p.m., and one of our last rides was the Sea Dragon, a makeshift pirate ship that swings back and forth. Geoff and I sat on one end of the ship, having an entire row to ourselves. As we waited for the attendant to check that all restraints were secure, I looked at Geoff and without thinking, grabbed his hand and squeezed it hard, not out of anticipation of the thrills the ride would provide, but out of happiness that I might have found the man I wanted to live with forever. The gesture wasn't planned; in fact, the sudden grab of his hand shocked me a little. The look of pure joy on his face made me feel happier that I made the gesture. Could I possibly be falling in love with Geoff already? I didn't want to make the same mistake I made with Peter and fall head over heels without knowing for sure that there was a real future, but everything in my heart told me I could afford to take the risk. I had wanted to feel this way since I was in my early 20s, so the desire had been building up in me for a decade.

Geoff continued to woo me that evening by getting a room in the Westin hotel in downtown Denver and romanced me more with a great dinner at Wolfgang Puck's restaurant not too far from the hotel. That night, we went to the hotel roof to enjoy the hot tub there. As we walked from our room to the elevator, Geoff took my hand and held it as we waited for the elevator and as we rode the elevator up to the roof. We had both made fairly serious romantic gestures in the span of about four hours. This was getting serious quickly, and I liked it.

The next morning we drove back to Fort Collins. I planned to get in my car and drive back to Albuquerque no later than 2 p.m. At 4 p.m., I was lying in bed with Geoff, trying to convince myself – and him – that my departure was not the end of our communication. The hardest part was not knowing when we would be able to physically be together again. The act of walking to my car, closing the door and driving away remains on the list of the most difficult things I had to do in my life. About six times between Fort Collins and Castle Rock (about 100 miles apart) I entertained the notion of turning around for one more night with Geoff. I'd call work and make up something. Being apart from Geoff physically hurt. In all my relationships – well, all three of them – it never physically ached to be apart from the man I was dating.

I wanted to call Geoff the instant I got home around midnight, but knowing he was asleep, I settled for a quick e-mail.

We would talk by phone or e-mail nearly every day. It was never an obligation to call or write to each other. Some days, it felt like a subconscious desire. I always wanted to just say hello or talk about things.

The best thing I learned about Geoff was his swimming background. I could talk about workouts or meets or anything pertaining to swimming and he would just get it right away. No need to explain what a taper is or who Michael Phelps is or why they swim so far underwater. And since his passion for sports essentially began and ended with swimming, we both never felt the need to feign understanding of the other person's sport fanaticism.

The first week after my visit to Colorado, Geoff invited me to go to Hawaii with him during Labor Day weekend. I didn't care if it would break my bank account; I wanted to know what it was like to travel with him and spend time at one of his favorite places in the world. He also made plans to visit Albuquerque in August, which would be the first time we'd see each other since Colorado.

Geoff was a hopeless romantic in his e-mails, but like me, he was afraid to be sentimental when we talked on the phone. Geoff had openly said he didn't like talking to me on the phone because hearing my voice made him miss me more. We'd have plenty of awkward silences in places where it seemed natural to say things like "I miss you." Despite our hesitancies at vocal affection, we officially became boyfriends on July 17, meaning, among other things, we pledged to be monogamous. That would be hard to monitor in different cities, of course, but I had no reason to worry about Geoff as much as he had no reason to worry about me.

But the "L" word was still lacking from either of us. Saying it meant there was no going back. If we weren't sure about being with each other, getting out before the first declaration of love would involve much less heartache.

The week after Geoff and I made our relationship official, I got permission from my bosses to start a blog at the newspaper called "Love Across the Miles," which would detail the rollercoaster ride Geoff and I took in our long-distance relationship. I was surprised a newspaper in a fairly conservative town would allow me to write about a gay relationship, but I got support from many of my co-workers, many of whom I'm sure didn't know I was gay before they read the blog.

Through the blog, I was able to give advice to others – gay or straight – who were dealing with long-term relationships. I got a few comments on the e-mails, mostly from gay couples. I even got one from a woman in Australia dating a woman in Los Angeles. After reading that, being 800 miles from Geoff didn't seem like a big hardship.

Our relationship became more secure after our Labor Day weekend trip to Hawaii, our first trip together. We didn't want to kill each other at the end of the vacation, which is always a great sign for two people still feeling out a relationship.

Geoff was coming to Albuquerque to stay with me during the week between Christmas and New Year's Day. On Christmas Day, Geoff handed me a medium-sized box for my present. I didn't know how to respond when I saw the box under the wrapping paper. Geoff had given me Christmas lights as a gift? Geoff was grinning from ear to ear; I was giving him my best "I love it!" expression. He urged me to open the box and see what was inside. I didn't want to open the box and string out a bunch of Christmas lights, but I did as he asked.

There were no Christmas lights in the box. It was mostly full of paper to make the box feel full. In the middle of the balls of paper was a much smaller box. I pulled out the box and instantly recognized it as a ring box. I could feel my breath quickening. Inside the box was a solid gold wedding band. Lodged inside one of the creases was a small piece of paper with a simple statement: MARRY ME.

Within one second of reading the words of paper, I turned to Geoff and said yes. We hadn't talked at length about marriage, which didn't mean we hadn't thought about the topic, and which made the proposal that much more surprising. Geoff took the ring out of the box and put it on the fourth finger on my left hand, the finger rarely used by gay men's wedding rings. That act made me love Geoff even more. Without prompting, he put it on the finger that I wanted to wear the ring on, not the finger that society dictated.

It took many weeks to get used to wearing the ring on my finger. I am not a fan of wearing jewelry. Even watches. When I got my high school class ring, I was almost required to wear it every day during my senior year. When I got my first ring in college commemorating our team's conference championship, I quickly stowed it away. I think I wore it twice.

I felt a little uneasy wearing what was advertised as a wedding band. It was actually an engagement ring, but there are no engagement rings for men. I had it reduced by one size so I could wear it while swimming and not worry about it falling off. I showed it off to friends as if it were a ring of engagement. Many of my friends were more in love with the story of the proposal than the ring itself. Surprisingly, no one questioned why I wore the ring on my left hand.

The year 2005 came faster than I expected. Now that we were engaged, Geoff and I had serious discussions about where we would live. He understood why I didn't want to move to San Francisco (earthquakes, high housing prices), and he said he was ready to move to a new town. I did plenty of job searches for newspapers looking for journalists with my skills. Sadly, no one in Ohio, Missouri, Texas, Tennessee, Illinois or Colorado wanted an aspiring film and/or TV critic. And even worse, Geoff couldn't find a church willing to hire him.

I wanted to get out of Albuquerque badly and start my life with Geoff. Plan B was to apply for work at Blockbuster Video in the city we decide to move to, using the time to look for reasonable work in that city.

Odd Man Out

In February, Geoff asked me about the possibility of living in Tucson, Arizona. I remembered the city well from my college days when we would visit Tucson to swim against the University of Arizona. I remembered being in love with the fact that they swam outdoors all year and didn't have to worry much about the cold in the winter. Very few cities on the separate lists we made of possible homes meshed, but Tucson did. The weather was admirable and there was bound to be a great Masters team to go along with the great college team. Geoff's parents also lived about 20 miles south in Green Valley, a retirement community. I made the drive from Albuquerque to Tucson for a weekend of house hunting with Geoff.

I arrived at his parents' home to find that Geoff and his mother were not there. Geoff's dad let it spill that Geoff had found a house he liked and might be signing papers to buy a house at that moment. I tried to hide my surprise, worry and fear.

The next day, Geoff and I traveled all over Tucson to look at possible places to live. We were certain we wanted to move into a new home to avoid the extra cost of renovating, which neither of us knew how to do and didn't have the time to learn. Many of the homes we saw were very nice but most of them were too far from grocery stores, movie theaters and other essential places. I didn't want to be more than 10 minutes from a major highway. One house was easily 20 minutes from a major road.

At the end of the day, I was getting tired and Geoff was getting more excited. We drove into a neighborhood in southern Tucson that was built on the foot of a large hill. We stopped at a home that was still being built. All I saw was a wooden skeleton.

"What do you think of this house?" Geoff asked.

I took another long look. "I suppose it's OK, but I can't really tell at this point," I responded.

"But do you think you could live in this house?"

"Yeah, I guess."

"Good, because this is our new home. I bought it yesterday."

I couldn't speak. Geoff was grinning to ear to ear, and I could never be mad at him when he flashes his irresistible smile. But it suddenly dawned on me that I had a quick decision to make.

Geoff took my hand. "I signed the papers for this house while you were driving here. They were going to keep raising the price of the house and I wanted to grab it while the price was good."

I took another look at the house and stared for about a minute. Turning back to Geoff I said, "I guess we're moving to Tucson."

The house wouldn't be ready until July, so Geoff and I had time to work out our plans to move to Tucson. After much deliberating, we agreed that Geoff should stay in San Francisco for a few months at his present job because it paid well and none of the Episcopal churches in Arizona had openings for full-time priests. I applied for work at the Arizona Daily Star, which is Tucson's largest newspaper. Despite telling them of my desire to be a film or TV critic, I was told the only open spot was in education reporting. I didn't want to go back to education reporting. It was uninteresting in Albuquerque, and probably wouldn't be more enjoyable in Tucson. So it was with a heavy heart that I accepted the job.

There are many things people do for love. That was definitely one of them.

Chapter Sixteen

Swimming remained high on my list of priorities as my relationship with Geoff got stronger, but it was no longer the top priority. I wanted Geoff and me to succeed not only to prove to myself that I belonged in long-term, committed relationships, but because I really loved him and couldn't imagine a better person to spend my days with on this Earth.

In July 2004, just one month after the relationship began, I had one of the best meets of my life. I returned to Austin, Texas, to compete in a USA Swimming meet. I was also coaching one of Kirtland Aquatic Club's top swimmers, a female breaststroker who had lots of talent and promise. I hadn't rested much for the meet, but I was excited by the possibilities of racing younger folks and to see how well I was training in preparation for the season-ending meet in October: the International Gay and Lesbian Aquatic Championships in Fort Lauderdale.

Two of my most memorable races were the 100-meter back and the 200-meter IM. In the prelims of the 100 back, I swam a lifetime best of 59.21. That evening in finals, I swam a 59.25, and I wasn't discouraged by the slower time because it was still the second-fastest time I'd ever swum in the event – and I hadn't rested much or shaved! The next day, I swam a 2:15.9 in the 200 IM, my fastest Masters time ever. I was beginning to feel very optimistic about the swims I would have in Fort

Lauderdale. Plus, I had done very little training in a long-course pool, which can affect your endurance at the end of races of 100 meters or more. I was optimistic that I was going to have a wonderful time in Florida.

But when October rolled around, I had difficulty getting my body excited about the meet. Whatever the reason was, my 100 back time in Fort Lauderdale was slower than I had swum in July in Texas. My times were the slowest I had done shaved in Masters, and it discouraged me. I thought back on the training I had done to prepare for the meet, and I couldn't find anything that I had done wrong, except maybe I had tapered too much. I was discouraged about the times I swam and needed a mental break from competition, which can be intense even in Masters swimming.

Upon leaving the meet in Florida, I didn't want to quit swimming, but I was sure I had begun to do what I feared most: I was preparing too intensely for competition. I didn't realize until I got to Florida that I was falling into the same trap from my days in elite swimming. This was becoming a job again, and the pressures of it began to take away the enjoyment I had rediscovered for the sport in 2002. No major meets were on the horizon, so it was a perfect time to step away from the pool to recharge and re-energize my body and mind. I wanted to be ready for the 2006 FINA Masters world championships, which is the highest level of competition in Masters swimming.

I did not swim at all for the last two months of 2004. I returned in 2005 with a new drive that I wanted to last all the way to worlds in August 2006. I wanted that meet to be the best of my swimming career, and I figured a year away from competition would be the best way to feed my hunger for racing. Absence, as they say, makes the heart grow fonder. I wanted to be so fired up for racing in the summer of 2006 that I would explode during that week in Palo Alto.

While I was refocusing my energy in the pool in the first half of 2005, I was also anxious for Geoff and I to celebrate our first anniversary. None of my previous relationships had ever made it to that milestone. I suppose Kent and I officially did make it past one year, but by the time 12 months had rolled around, I suspect Kent had already begun to check out.

Geoff had been with another man for almost eight years, so it might not have been as big a deal for him to celebrate one year together. I anticipated waking up on our eighth anniversary, when both of us could commemorate our longest relationship ever.

The day of our anniversary – June 18, 2005 – was pretty much normal, except that I knew I had achieved something special in my life. After believing I had actively doomed my previous relationships to fail, I had finally found someone who made the difficult parts of serious dating easy. Both of us actively wanted to our relationship to succeed, and we both did things to ensure its survival. Most of them were little things, such as physical contact and constant reminders of our love.

The time away from competition allowed me to focus on moving to Tucson. I was happy to leave Albuquerque, but I genuinely missed my co-workers at The Tribune. Even though I felt slighted by my bosses as I tried to advance my career, I enjoyed coming to work most days. Now, I was about to start working at a much bigger newspaper, and to make things scarier, I would be doing it alone.

Though Geoff had moved his furniture to Tucson in June, he was staying San Francisco from July 2005 to July 2006 because he hadn't found work in Arizona. I was very lonely in the home we shared. To help me cope with the new surroundings, Geoff brought his cat to stay with me. We bonded quickly, but it didn't make me miss Geoff less. He came to visit often, but only for four-day weekends that didn't last long enough. I tried to push away the feelings of loneliness by working hard at the newspaper. I wanted to put in the time "in the mines," doing the work I didn't really want to do and proving I was worthy to be considered for the work I wanted to do. My constant hints about my desire to be a film or TV critic went unnoticed, though, after my first year at the paper. I tried not to be devastated, and set out to prove that maybe one more year of hard work with little complaint would be enough. I began to feel like the editors at the Albuquerque paper were living in the bodies of the editors at the Tucson paper. I was being fed very familiar lines for more than a year.

My training for world championships hit its apex in May 2006. I started doing double workouts for the first time in eight years, and I could feel the positive and negative effects. Because the Masters team in Tucson leans heavily toward distance freestyle training, I swam five of the eight workouts each week by myself, devising sprint-oriented workouts that lasted a little more than an hour. I used the University of Arizona's Power Towers to help gain strength in many of my strokes, swam lots of race pace sets (such as 3x100 breaststroke on a five-minute interval in a 50-meter pool) and swam through the boredom that comes with swimming alone. I told myself that my competitors were not getting out of the pool halfway through workout because they were bored, and if I got out, I might as well concede the race to them. Nine times out of 10, it worked. But there were days when the "garbage yardage" workouts — those times in the pool where you're swimming back and forth with little to no purpose to the sets — got the best of me and I would stop in the middle of a set and enjoy a longer shower in the locker room.

In July 2006, Geoff officially moved to Tucson, marking a new chapter for us. In the two years we had been together, all we knew was how to live in separate states with occasional visits that lasted a few days. Now, we would be sleeping in the same bed every night, eating meals together regularly and coming home each day with the knowledge that we'd see each other. There is no greater feeling after 24 months apart than the one that accompanies the walk through the door every day and seeing your significant other sitting on the couch, a smile on his face and a kiss waiting on his lips. In those first two years of our relationship, I looked forward to seeing his face at the end of the day so much that the sight of him when I arrived home from work gave me goosebumps.

On August 2, 2006, Geoff and I loaded up his red Volvo and drove to the San Francisco Bay area to swim in the Masters world championships. The car couldn't get us there fast enough. I had waited so long for this meet that flying to Palo Alto in a supersonic plane wouldn't have been fast enough. With the exception of one meet in January, I hadn't competed in 23 months, and I was ready to break loose. The only downfall to not racing much before worlds was that I was unsure how fast I would swim. I also was unsure about my competition. Many of them came from other countries, and I had never seen some of the names at the top of the rankings in many of my events. I got the kind of good nerves that put little tickles in your stomach and get you so antsy you can hardly sit still. I noticed that my former roommate and teammate at Texas, Josh Davis, was swimming in the meet, and we would get to race together in the 200 IM on the meet's third day. I knew that even if Josh's training had been greatly reduced, he would have no problem beating me. But I remembered the times we'd race each other in college, and I always got a kick out of making up some ground on the breaststroke leg. At the very least, I wanted to outsplit Josh by two seconds on the breaststroke leg. If he won by five seconds, I'd be OK with it as long as I won the breaststroke.

Goeff swam the 800 freestyle about two hours after we arrived at the campus. He swam amazingly well, winning the bronze medal for his age group, and I was thrilled to film his race and know that was the man I loved. This was what I wanted to experience in college and my postgraduate years. Geoff had hoped to swim faster, but I was ecstatic for him in ways that defy explanation.

My first event of the meet was the 100 breast. The tension and excitement of the meet was getting to me when I walked onto the pool deck that morning. I wouldn't be swimming until mid-afternoon, but I was there early to watch Geoff swim the 100 freestyle and cheer for other friends and teammates.

I was so nervous about the 100 breast that I had forgotten to eat throughout the day. The race was to begin at 3:30 p.m. The last time I put anything in my stomach was about 9 a.m. I hadn't felt any hunger pangs, mostly because I kept drinking water to calm my nerves. As I sat in the marshaling area waiting to parade to the blocks for my heat, I felt slightly woozy. The adrenaline was pumping full blast, and I had no fuel to keep my body running at that level. It was too late to do anything about it, except get fearful that my body might not be able to perform as it should.

I stood behind the blocks shaking out my arms and legs. The attempt to get my heart rate up was not working. My body wanted to go into shutdown mode. The swimmer in the lane next to me was from Germany and had entered a seed time that indicated he could be a serious challenge.

The start of the race was fine. I felt like I had overcome my physical disabilities and was pushing hard towards the 50-meter turn. That was the adrenaline propelling me the length of the pool.

As I approached the wall to make the turn, I could feel the energy slipping away. Usually, that doesn't happen until at least the 75-meter mark. I made the turn at 50 meters in the lead, but I could tell I was about to crash hard.

At 75 meters, my body began to go numb. I had no stored energy to help combat the lactic acid buildup in my muscles, and I felt a pain so severe that I thought my muscles would go into atrophy. If not for the adrenaline – and years of experience – that was keeping me moving forward, my body might have locked up. And to make matters worse, I could sense the German in the lane next to me making a surge. I would be swimming the final 25 meters on willpower alone.

The wall drew closer, and I engaged in serious self talk: "Dammit, get to the wall! You can't lose this! Come on! Just a few more strokes!"

I felt like a catfish flopping on dry land as I made the final few strokes to the wall. I felt I had lost the race when I touched. In the second between touching the wall and looking at the scoreboard, I relegated myself to the fact that I would get second place. Not so bad when you think of the number of swimmers in the world in my age group, being second is pretty darn good. (This is likely the sentence heard in the heads of many silver medalists, many years after receiving their medals.)

The scoreboard had to be lying. Did it really have a "1" next to my lane? I took off my goggles and heard people cheering and clapping. There was a "1" next to my lane number – and next to the German's lane number as well. I closed my eyes and thanked the Lord for the tie. Knowing my history of losing close races, the result could have been worse. Technically, I won the race. Sharing it with another person was definitely not disheartening, nor was the fact that the time – 1:06.24 – was horrendously slow. I had expected to go at least a second faster. My 50 split was about eight tenths slower than I wanted, and I know my last 50 was subpar.

Hours later, after I warmed down and stuffed my face with food, I vowed to be more conscious of myself during the meet. The hours in the day had slipped by so quietly that I had not noticed that I missed lunch, nor did I realize that I hadn't even snacked throughout the day. That is a cardinal sin at any competition.

I didn't race the second day of the meet, and used it to prepare for what I expected to be a monster day. On the third day of the meet, I would swim the 200 IM followed by the 50 breast about two hours later. Not only was I looking forward to racing Josh Davis in the 200 IM, but I wanted revenge in the 50 breast. I wanted to show people that I was better than my 100 breast swim. I also wanted to take a shot at the world record of 29.17. At the IGLA meet in October 2004, Brian Jacobson had swum faster than that record, but it was not made official because the proper paperwork hadn't been submitted. I swam next to Brian during that race, and was certain that the record was indeed in range.

With no expectations in the 200 IM other than to have fun, I dove into the water swimming butterfly with a slight smile on my face. Very rarely do I smile – or feel blissful – when swimming butterfly. After the backstroke leg, I saw Josh about three body lengths ahead of me. I was sure I couldn't make up that difference in 50 meters, but I put all of my energy into trying to bridge the gap. To my surprise, I did catch Josh, but paid a big price on the freestyle leg. Every muscle hurt, and Josh – a finalist in the 200 freestyle at two Olympics – sailed ahead of me as if I were going backward. I swam a 2:13.49, my fastest time in Masters.

I took the positive energy from the 200 IM and bottled it up for the 50 breast later that day. I visualized what it would be like to swim the race in 29 seconds. If I had a great start, all I had to do was focus on getting to the wall and I would win the race. The record was firmly planted in the front of my mind, but I knew I had to focus on winning the race first. Records don't matter if you finish second.

The start was not perfect. I dove too deep, which meant I wasted too much time working on getting back to the surface and lost maybe a little bit of forward motion. But I got into the rhythm of the stroke quickly, which is essential in any race lasting 50 meters. I was fully into the stroke by the halfway point and could feel every muscle in my body working in harmony. My new German competitor, the one who I tied in the 100 breast, was two lanes over, so I could not sense his presence in the pool very well. All I could sense was that he was not going to make many mistakes and wanted the win just as much as I did. I zeroed in on the wall and made a final lunge for the touchpad.

The sun was directly behind the scoreboard, making the times difficult to see at first. I squinted hard to find my lane and see the time displayed next to it. I saw the "1" next to my lane first, and a beat later, saw the time. A world record! I had beaten the record, and in an instant, all the hard work, mental preparation and focus on sprint training, on this event, had paid off. I couldn't believe the "29.01" displayed next to my lane number. I squinted at it in the sunlight's glare for a minute, wanting to make sure the clock wasn't playing a prank. It was my first world record in a long course pool, and the Masters records set in 50-meter pools are generally more difficult to achieve. So, to have my name etched in the list of long-course world records was mind-boggling. Yes, I had worked hard for that moment, but once the moment arrived, I wasn't fully prepared for what it truly meant.

I was congratulated by many when I exited the pool, but I only wanted to see Geoff, who had filmed the race from the spectator area on the other side of the pool. I walked back to the starting end of the pool and collected my clothes. Running toward me was Geoff, and we hugged for a long time. This was the type of moment I had dreamed of back in college. I wanted to celebrate winning a conference championship with my boyfriend. I wanted to be consoled by my partner after my disastrous swims at both Olympic Trials. I wanted to do all these things in front of hundreds of people without worrying about their reactions, just as Geoff and I were doing on the deck of Stanford University's Avery Aquatic Center.

I was able to have some fun the day after setting my world record. The entire day was devoted to relays, and I swam on a team that was made of swimmers from different states, recruited to make attempts at world records. While I was certain I could help the team, called Team TYR, set a world record in the medley relay, I was confused when they asked me to swim on a freestyle relay. I didn't want to let the team down, so I swam my heart out and we managed to get second place in the men's 200 free relay. It got me excited about our medley relay.

I had always assumed that I would swim the breaststroke leg on this 200 medley relay, so I was a little worried when they asked me to do the backstroke. Yes, I was a good backstroker, but was it enough to make a run at the world record? The others on my team were quite good in their own right, and I felt that if I could put together a good backstroke leg, I could at least put us in contention for a win.

To my surprise, I touched first after my 50 meters of backstroke. In the lead we stayed, and almost got the world record. We settled for a national record, which was still an amazing feat in itself. The only letdown was that our Team TYR teammates in an older age group swam faster than us.

The next day was the 100 backstroke, and I always put low expectations on myself in this race. My only goal was to swim under the one-minute mark, a feat I accomplished three times in the past four years. If I was able to swim under that barrier once more, I felt I could win the race.

Swimming backstroke outdoors is akin to swimming in an obstacle course. With your eyes unable to divert themselves from the glare of the sun, and without any markers above you to keep you swimming in a straight line, it is understandable when swimmers find themselves scraping the lane lines. By the time I reached the 50-meter turn in the 100 backstroke race, my left arm was lightly grazing the lane rope. It was enough to break my concentration for just a moment. The best thing to do is not try to return to the center of the lane, but get far enough away from the lane rope to reduce the risk of banging your hand against the rope and losing precious momentum.

One of the great things about the backstroke flip turn is the ability to turn over onto your stomach. Not because it allows you to use one arm to do a freestyle-type pull, but because while turning onto your stomach, you can look to one side and quickly see your competitors. I made the turn and saw three swimmers even with me. I freaked out.

The final 50 meters was an all-out sprint. Similar to the final 15 meters in the 100 breast, the final strokes in the 100 back were done on pure adrenaline. The famous saying goes: "I left it all in the pool." The final stroke was definitely the last stroke I was able to give to the race. Luckily, it was enough to achieve two goals. I won the race, and I swam it in less than a minute for the fourth time. I was happier with the time than the win.

Essentially, the meet was over for me. If I had low expectations for the 100 back, I had nearly none for the 50 back. I only signed up for it to complete the five-event limit for the meet. I got fourth in the race, mainly because I scraped the lane rope badly, had a poor start and, again, expected nothing. And I walked away from the race not upset by not getting a medal.

Geoff still had two races to swim. He won a silver medal in the 400 free and also competed in the 3,000-meter open-water swim in the San Francisco Bay. He wasn't happy with either swim, but he has always been the type of person that always expected perfection from himself, and wasn't happy if he didn't achieve it. I couldn't have been more proud of him. It was a joy to have him there the entire week. The meet might have turned out differently for me if I didn't have a support system to get me through the highs and lows of the competition.

Back in the real world after world championships, I found myself dealing with the same symptoms of depression I felt while living in Albuquerque. I was very happy living with Geoff, but I was starting to realize that my journalism career had once again reached a dead end. I started to wish I hadn't agreed to move to Tucson. I was afraid what the returning depression symptoms would do to my relationship with Geoff. I had already noticed my decreasing desire to be intimate with him, and that was troubling me severely.

I visited my doctor to talk about the problems. He prescribed anti-depressants, which did not improve the situation. The pills further lowered my sex drive and had other side effects I didn't want to deal with daily. After a month I stopped taking the pills and tried to find more positive aspects in my life to lift my mood. Besides my relationship with Geoff, swimming was the one thing going right in my life, and I poured energy into that.

I relished the hunger for competition I felt after world championships, but I was careful not to let it overwhelm me. I set two short course meters world records at a meet the November after worlds. I was on a roll, so instead of taking the break from the pool that I had planned, I surged forward to short course nationals in 2007, where I reset my 100 breast national record and finally got the 50 breast national record I had been chasing for four years. The record had stood since 1991 and was held by the great David Lundberg. I will admit that the addition of dolphin kicks to the breaststroke underwater pull gave me a slight advantage, but the hours of hard work and focus I put into the pool and in the weight room (and even in the yoga studio for a few months) can't be denied.

Just for kicks, I shaved and tapered for an age-group meet in Tucson just two weeks after short course nationals in 2007. I desperately wanted to take a break and was not keen on training hard that summer. Plus, the men's team from the University of Arizona would be swimming unshaved at the meet, which meant I had a chance to race some of the best swimmers in the world. Yes, it was a little bit skewed to my advantage, but without the benefit of a shave and taper, I would have not stood much of a chance against them.

For the fifth time in my life, I broke the one-minute barrier in the 100 backstroke. It was completely unexpected and that made it more thrilling to see the time. I was in a heat racing such swimmers as Simon Burnett (British Olympic finalist in the 200 free) and Albert Subirats (Venezuelan Olympian in the 100 fly). I didn't beat them, but it was a thrill to share the pool with them. I also swam my fastest Masters time in the 100 breast: 1:05.10. It was only five-tenths of a second slower than the Olympic Trials qualifying time, and though I hadn't put any thought into swimming at Trials, some suggested that I put in more training time to make the cut. I knew exactly what would be required of me to make the cut, and I didn't have the time or the desire to put that much energy into swimming. I had just completed another series of doubles before my series of fast swims at short course nationals and the meet in Tucson, and I had sacrificed quite a bit to make that happen. Masters swimmers already sacrifice too much for this sport; I wasn't sure if I had anything left to give to it.

Chapter Seventeen

By the fall of 2007, my life had officially settled into some semblance of the one I wanted 10 years earlier. Geoff and I loved our home and our life in Tucson. We had started a swim school that had become very successful since it started in January, and though Geoff was working 13-hour days, he enjoyed teaching lessons to kids and adults. It also helped that it was a very lucrative business in Tucson. I was teaching some lessons on the weekends to those who wanted lessons for strokes other than freestyle. Given that Tucson is a haven for triathletes, I had very few students on my schedule.

Working at the newspaper grew increasingly frustrating as 2007 wore on. Geoff noticed that my mood changed on Sunday nights as my mind prepared for another week of fairly unfulfilling work. I spoke with the editor of the entertainment section about the possibility of working in her department. Instead of trying to find a proper fit for me, the editors moved me to another office in the company to essentially do the same work. To make matters worse, the new office was further from home and gave me assignments just as dull as those at the previous bureau. To placate me, they allowed me to be one of the writers on the TV blog, but they praised the other writer's work much more than mine. I felt

197

the events in Albuquerque repeating all over again. I didn't want to be placated any longer by my bosses, but I was at a loss for options. I wasn't certain our swim school could sustain two full-time instructors, and I didn't think it was a daily routine I wanted. I made a visit to the other daily newspaper in town, but their offers were just as stale, and they were in danger of shoring up operations in the wake of budget cuts.

So it was in October 2007 that I decided to discard my dream of being a film critic. It was quite clear no one in the industry was willing to give me a chance to prove myself. I was growing increasingly frustrated with the newspaper business.

In early October, I made a call to Swimming World Magazine to inquire about any job possibilities. Since the office was in Phoenix, it wouldn't be too far-fetched to make an offer for a telecommuting job or something that would allow me to continue living in Tucson. It would be impossible for Geoff and I to uproot, and I didn't want to sell our home in the middle of the housing slowdown.

My conversations with Brent Rutemiller, the company's CEO, were promising, but he did not have any job offers at the moment. This was my third attempt to work at the magazine since I graduated from college, yet knowing that the magazine's office was so close gave me some hope.

Brent and I continued to talk every other week as October rolled into November. I began to write freelance feature stories for the website. I interviewed Jim Montgomery, the first man to swim the 100-meter freestyle under 50 seconds. I wrote a fun story about platform diving. I thought I would make a great writer for the magazine I grew up reading fervently. But the company did not have a large budget for full-time staff writers, and I tried to broaden my horizons.

With the possibility of a job at Swimming World Magazine looming closer each week, Geoff and I began to have more serious conversations about how our lives would change if I accepted a job in Phoenix. Geoff had supported my decision to make contact with Brent Rutemiller, but I could sense he gave me the support with the feeling that, like all other job searches I had been making in the past three months, this too would turn up empty and I would fall back onto working at Blockbuster Video until something better came along.

In the middle of all this talk of changing jobs, Geoff and I traveled to St. Louis for his first meeting with members of my family. This would also be the first time I would see my nephews, who my brother and sister-in-law had adopted that spring. I was brimming with excitement to return home. I hadn't been to St. Louis since 2004. We planned to go there in 2006, but a heavy blizzard prevented us from making the tip.

I was intensely nervous about bringing Geoff to St. Louis. My brother and sister-in-law were beyond excited to finally meet him. My grandmother planned to make us a great lunch. Two of my aunts and my uncle were going to meet us at a restaurant for dinner.

I knew in my heart that my mother was not going to welcome Geoff into her home with open arms. As much as I wanted to believe that there was hope for moving past her feelings about me as a gay man, I couldn't help but remember back to 2004 when she subtly criticized Geoff for whisking me away from Albuquerque to our new life in Tucson. That moment ended the reconciliation we had started. It seemed that buying a home for your loved one was not acceptable to my mother.

Despite all this, I called my mother about a week before we were to arrive. The tone of my mother's voice upon hearing mine was not one of elation. Very nonplussed would be an accurate way to describe it. I told her about the upcoming trip and said that Geoff and I would like to stop by for a visit.

Slight pause. "You know I don't feel comfortable about this," my mother said.

"What do you mean?" I asked, though I knew exactly what she meant.

"I just don't ... feel comfortable. Can't you just come by and we'll visit?"

I almost wanted to hang up. I was incensed. "Mom, I'm not going to just leave Geoff out in the car or sitting at the hotel while we sit and have a conversation. We're a package deal. It's either both of us or neither of us."

Another pause.

"I'm sorry to hear that," my mother said. No remorse in her voice.

"I'm sorry, too." I was driving home from work, and tried hard not to cry. "Well, I guess I'll be talking to you later."

I hated my mother. I hated myself for hating my mother. It left a sour feeling in the pit of my stomach. I wanted to call her back and find out what was really bothering her. Her vague reply about not being comfortable still bounces around in my brain.

I knew it was wrong to turn Geoff into a bargaining pawn in whatever the situation was between my mother and me, but the situation had severely changed the moment Geoff proposed to me. I flashed back to the day my brother told me he had married Ursula. It was a happy moment and I was glad to hear the news. A few months later, I had seen my mother and Ursula interacting and instantly knew my mother didn't approve of her. Did my mother ever tell Darryl that, because she did not like his wife, that only he could visit her home? I seriously doubt it.

Why did my mother not want Geoff in her home? Was it because he was having sex with her son? Was it because he was also gay? Had she started to accept my homosexuality, but wasn't going to accept a total stranger's? There were so many questions after I hung up the phone. That night, when I told Geoff of the conversation with my mother, he said he would have been happy to wait in the car, that he didn't mind being invisible to my mother. And that was the point. Geoff is my spouse as much as Ursula is Darryl's spouse – at least in the spiritual and non-governmental concept of marriage – and he is never invisible in my life.

The visit to St. Louis was very eye-opening. I loved every minute I spent with my nephews, who instantly bonded with me and were always at my side. I got a little choked up when, just 30 minutes after meeting me, the oldest ran to me from across the room and hugged me without prompting. I knew immediately that I would love being their uncle. I look forward to watching them grow up and want to be the type of uncle that lavishes so much affection on them – even when they feel they are too old for that kind of crap – that I get chided by their parents for spoiling them.

And my grandmother, the one who my mother said would die if she found out I was gay, couldn't stop smiling when she opened the door and saw Geoff for the first time. I was not shocked by my grandmother's actions, nor was I surprised that in all her letters to me following the visit, she always took time to inquire about Geoff.

My aunts and uncle met us at a restaurant, and we all had a wonderful time. When Geoff excused himself to go to the restroom, I got unanimous approval of him.

But with every family member, the big elephant in the room was my estrangement from my mother. Everyone knew it and yet no one wanted to talk about it. My brother and I talked about it when I made another visit home the following February to accept my induction into the Ozark Swimming Hall of Fame. I asked him what he would do if my mother said she didn't want Ursula in her home. Though he didn't fully understand why my mother and I haven't talked in so long, he began to see my side of the story.

We returned to Tucson after our first visit to St. Louis excited that we were welcome back for many more visits. We almost considered buying tickets to come back for Christmas, but decided against it. In hindsight, it was a good decision.

On Dec. 6, 2007, I was driving home from work, disillusioned as usual. My cellphone rang, and the number that showed in the display was the number for the main office. On the phone was the executive editor of the Arizona Daily Star, essentially the second-in-command. I had spoken maybe 10 words to Bobbie Jo Buel since I started working at the Arizona Daily Star, and her request to meet her at the main office the next day at 10:20 a.m. surprised me.

I immediately called Geoff, who was in Florida visiting the manager of a swim school. I told him they weren't firing me. If they were going to fire me, I would have been summoned to the office that day. Maybe they were going to discuss a new career path? Or talk about my domestic partner benefits? A few financial cuts had been made at the paper in the previous weeks, and in a company filled with journalists, we all had tons of questions. Every top editor assured his or her staff the day before that jobs wouldn't be lost. So I thought they would try to say that Geoff's domestic partner benefits would have to be cut. With my boss' assurance that I had a job, I walked into the office of the human resource manager the next morning with no fears.

Within one minute of entering the office, I was informed that my position at the newspaper was being eliminated, and I was being offered a not-very-generous severance package. It sounded very rehearsed and impersonal to a person who had not heard the spiel before and was still processing sentences uttered to me five minutes ago. When asked for my comments, I had nothing to say. I did wonder in that instant who else had been let go, and if they lashed out in a *Network*-style rampage. Part of me wanted to go off like Peter Finch did in that classic film.

I was told to surrender my work badge and my work cellphone. I could go to the office the next day and retrieve my personal belongings, but I told them it was best if I did it that day.

The 20-minute drive from the main office to the bureau office on the northern end of Tucson was agonizing. I was also given the option of telling my now-former coworkers about my layoff, or I could just grab my stuff and leave quietly. I wasn't sure what I would do until I walked in the door, where eight pairs of eyes immediately saw me walk through the door and the conversations in the office stopped instantly. Apparently, the word had already begun to spread through online instant messaging about the layoffs, and though no one officially had heard any names of people let go, the speculation started quickly. When I walked into the office, I realized I was the only one who had been unaccounted for. Everyone else was there and huddled in the middle of the office.

"Is it true?" one of them asked.

"Yep, it's true." I said. In that moment, it was official: I was unemployed.

I tried not to cry as I looked at my friends and co-workers. A couple of them were nearing retirement age and said they didn't understand why I was picked. There were tears and hugs, and when I couldn't hold in my tears any longer, I packed up my gear and went to my car, where I sobbed heavily. It made things worse that Geoff was on the other side of the country and hadn't picked up the phone when I called to tell him.

I went home and my cat sensed that something was amiss. Not because I was home in the middle of the day, but because I emitted a very negative aura. She rubbed herself against me and never left my side the entire day. I was very grateful that Geoff's parents offered to drive up from Green Valley and spend some time with me.

Naturally, I wanted to call my mother. Everyone wants to talk to a parent when something like this happens. I decided to not make the call. No good could come of it.

I woke up the next day feeling numb. Though I had wanted to leave the Arizona Daily Star at some point, I wanted to do it on my terms. I hadn't planned on making an exit until at least March or April. The severance package gave me one month's pay with benefits, which gave me time to grieve, but it also stunk considering that I was let go in the middle of the holiday season. Not considering the money, the layoff was now going to put a major damper on any holiday spirit I tried to muster.

For two weeks I did nothing but swim and sleep. Geoff allowed me the time to mourn the job loss, but we couldn't function forever as a one-income family, and I couldn't expect Geoff to take care of all the bills.

A few days before Christmas, I made a call to Brent at Swimming World. I vowed to not mention the layoff unless he brought it up, which he did about five minutes into the phone call inquiring about any job possibilities.

When he told me he was working on an Internet news show devoted to swimming, he said there might be a job there for me, but he wasn't sure what it would be and if it would be full-time. He wondered what I would do at my current job if there was work for me at the magazine. At that point, I was forced to tell him I was laid off. He said he'd put this job creation quest into high gear and get back to me the first week of 2008.

True to his word, Brent offered me a job not soon after the calendar flipped over to 2008. I would be the associate producer of "The Morning Swim Show," which meant I was responsible for coming up with the content of a 10-minute news show that would stream on the magazine's website five days a week. I worried that my print journalism training wouldn't translate to what was essentially broadcast journalism, but Brent's confidence in me gave me the courage to say yes. On Jan. 13, 2008, I began work at Swimming World, and Geoff and I took a plunge into another aspect of a long-term relationship. For the first few months, I lived in the studio apartment next to the office during the week and drove to Tucson for the weekends. I was able to keep training by swimming with Brophy Masters at a pool just around the corner from work.

The commute was hard on me for a long time. After a long week of work, it was difficult to get in a car and make a two-hour drive through Friday night traffic. But it was always worth it when I saw Geoff. Work always kept him in Tucson, though he did come to visit me in Phoenix for a couple of weekends. In April we bought a new home in Phoenix. We also worked out a plan where I would still drive to Tucson on the weekends, but Geoff would drive to Phoenix after preaching at a small church every Sunday and then return to Tucson on Tuesday morning. That meant we were only apart on Wednesdays and Thursdays. We still live on this schedule.

Though the new job certainly had challenges, I welcomed them all immediately. Covering aquatic sports every day was infinitely more enjoyable than covering a school board meeting or an art museum opening. Since I knew many of the coaches and athletes, it was easy to establish contacts in the sport and get some of the top people on our show.

I continued to train very well in 2008 as I made the adjustment to a new city and new job. The masters coach at Brophy, Mark Rankin, is easily the best Masters coach in the country. Even at 6 a.m. there is always an enthusiasm in his voice as he describes sets or calls out times after fast swims. His enjoyment of his job spills over into the pool.

But I wasn't preparing well for the 2008 spring nationals, which were held in Austin. I was excited to be visiting my friend Arthur, who I hadn't seen in about four years, but I had the sense that I wasn't going to swim very fast at the meet. The stress of a new job, new home and re-arranged life can quietly take its toll.

I managed to win all six of my events, but I was only pleased with my 50 breast when I swam faster than my national record. It was my final short course yards race in the 30-34 age group, and I desperately wanted David Lundberg's national record in the 100 IM. I didn't get that record.

In December, Geoff and I traveled to Long Beach, California, for a short course meters meet there that is generally regarded as the fastest short course meters meet in the country. My times in the 50 and 100 breast, as well as the 100 and 200 IM, were the best times I had ever done in Masters. I owe a portion of it to the high-tech suit I wore, which was given to me by Roque Santos, a former competitor of mine who was also a Masters swimmer. The high-tech suits were made of polyurethane, which many believed unfairly increased buoyancy. I wasn't the biggest fan of the suits and felt they might have hindered my performances a little because I wasn't used to have material cover my body from the neck down. A lot of my success at that meet had to do with the new training I was getting with Mark Rankin, plus the fact that I wanted my final meet in the 30-34 age group to be one of my best.

*****

It took five years, but when 2009 began, Geoff and I finally felt settled in our lives. We are in careers we feel will be long-lasting and we couldn't be happier together. In June we celebrated our fifth anniversary, marking the occasion with a viewing of *The Omen* (the movie we saw in his parents' basement in Fort Collins).

In January 2009, we took a trip to South Africa, a place I had wanted to visit since my two years in Colorado Springs swimming for Jonty Skinner, who was from there. What I saw was eye-opening, and it also made me more aware of the fact that I was in an interracial relationship. Wherever Geoff and I went, heads turned when they noticed us together. Many years after apartheid was abolished, blacks and whites still were not fully integrated. Geoff and I saw very few South African black people in the same vicinity as South African whites.

The experience made me happy to live in a country that at least allowed Geoff and I to sit at the same table at a restaurant or simply exist together without much condemnation. Naturally, there is still rampant homophobia in the United States, but Geoff and I mention often that we would not have survived if we lived in the 1960s.

I try not to think of my mother. It hurts too much to do so. When thoughts of her come to mind, I remember things like our trip to New York City in 1995, when she surprised me with tickets to see *The Lion King* on Broadway with my brother, sister-in-law and a family friend. The five of us had a wonderful time in New York City. My mother and I both deeply loved the movie version, and I remember seeing her constant smile when we talked about all the great moments we saw onstage that night. If she had known I was gay at the time, which I believe she suspected, she didn't act as if it bothered her. We were a mother and son enjoying a wonderful evening in the Big Apple.

Every year, when the Oscar nominations are announced, I am filled with excitement and sadness. I am always anxious to hear the names of Oscar nominees, but one part of that day is sorely lacking. For many years, my mother and I would talk on the phone that morning to discuss our picks and laugh at each other for the nominees we missed. In the 11 years since I came out, I can still physically feel that void each year on Nominations Day.

The relationship I have with my mother now isn't really a relationship. How can it be when there is no communication? I have tried extremely hard to not hate my mother, but that's not easy when she turns her back on the man I love and looks on me as an abomination. Ten years before I came out to her, she was crying tears of joy when I made my first senior national standard. There couldn't have been a happier parent in the building that night. Now, I can't imagine any expression but a scowl on her face when thoughts of me surface.

We both arrived at this point in our lives willingly. We made conscious choices to sever the connection. But it doesn't make it right. I don't like the fact that neither of us sends each other birthday cards. In 2009, we did not get a Christmas card from my mother, though we thought it would be the honorable thing to send one to her. I want to give up on trying to reach out to her, but the thought of that paralyzes me.

In February 2010, I received an e-card from my mother on my birthday. I didn't know how to react to the sentence "Life's a gift ... and so are you" as it appeared on my computer screen. I watched it three times. I still don't know how to react to it.

I count my blessings every day for Geoff's parents. They have welcomed me as another son, and they did so from the first moment I met them. *That* is unconditional love.

I am 36 years old. I love my life. I own a home (actually, two of them!), I have a loving husband and a job that makes me feel fulfilled at the end of the day. I no longer have symptoms of depression. It's been at least five years since I've felt the urge to pop in the DVD of *Ferris Bueller's Day Off* to lift my mood. From 2000 to 2006, it was not unusual for me to watch *Ferris Bueller* two to three times a month.

Geoff and I have run into many roadblocks as we try to work out a wedding date. Those plans were yanked away when Proposition 8 was voted into effect. The vote outlawed gay marriage in the California, where we planned to hold the wedding, and once again made me feel like a second-class citizen. Watching several states on the East Coast of the United States – as well as Iowa, of all places – approve gay marriage gave me some hope that it would be accepted all over the country.

I was in a deep funk about the marriage ban for many days in 2008, despite the presidential victory by Barack Obama. Geoff offered some light when he told me that the rector at the church he used to work at in San Francisco would happily marry us when we were ready.

I hope to see my mother at the wedding. The last time we spoke was in 2007, when she refused to allow Geoff into her home. I often wonder if that will be our final conversation. When it is time for Geoff and me to send out wedding invitations, we will mail one to my mother. I wonder what she will do with it. Will she use the card to start a bonfire? Or will she immediately make plans to attend?

Just as I am hopeful that my mother will return to my life, I am hopeful that the bigots who make laws will also reconsider their homophobia and allow gays the same marriage rights as heterosexuals. I have to believe they will – just as much as I believe I will answer the phone and hear my mother on the other end with positive words emanating from her.

Only then will I have everything I ever wanted. Maybe then I will no longer feel like the odd man out.

Geoff and me, 2008

Acknowledgments

Odd Man Out started as a "what if" idea back in 2000. I sat in front of a computer and started writing, just to see if it was an easy venture. The bulk of chapters four through seven came out of that first year. Kent Hopkins was the originator of the idea for this book, and though I thought his motives were not in the right place, I will be forever grateful to him for planting the seed.

Every word in this book came from my head — except for the title. I knew *Odd Man Out* was the best title for this book the minute Mike Munson suggested it, and I never seriously considered any other option.

To the members of the Commings, Rembert and Glaser families who gave me their blessings and support to write this book: Thanks from the depths of my soul.

I didn't make writing this book a serious venture until 2005. Geoff Glaser was my muse, my guiding hand and my foundation then — and he continues to amaze me with his undying love and devotion, not just to me but to the life we have built in the past six years.